This book has to be dedicated to all those to whom worked and lived in the Old Town of Hastings during the years from 1850, through to the dreaded redevelopment, and the opening of the new road through the Bourne in 1963.

All rights are reserved. No part of this publication may be reproduced, stored in a retrieval system or transmitted in any form or by any means, electronic, mechanical, photocopying recording or otherwise - without the prior permission in writing from the author, via the publisher.

E&OE

ISBN 978-0-9569366-1-5

Published by: Richard Pollard
Printed by: Berforts Group Ltd (Stevenage) 01438 312777
Copyright © R. Pollard 2013
Email: richpenbooks@aol.com

Acknowledgements

Hastings Council for the reproduction of the Towns Crest.
Hastings Public Library for the use of copyright photographs.
Hastings Museum for the copyright use of photographs.
Mr John Hodges for the use of pictures in his own collection.
Mr Denis Collins for special permission to use whole or part of transcribed notes on the Old Town clearance scheme.
Mr & Mrs Parsons for their personal memories of the Bourne.
All the Leslie Badham pictures contained within this book were donated from the late Ron Fellows collection before his untimely departure from this world.

Many of the pictures shown within this publication are from old newspapers and linen plans of the time, consequently, some were feint and required digital enhancement to be reproduced for your pleasure. Some might not be as good as others, but please don't let this spoil your reading enjoyment.

Photos within this publication come from those listed above, and my own private collection.

Every effort has been made to trace all copyright owners.

Bibliography.

Extracts from the newspapers and written reports of the time.
Sidney Little, Looking back to the future publication by this author.

Extracts taken from the full report written for the
General Board of Health by Mr Edward Cresy (1850),
into the sanitation of inhabitants of the Town of
Hastings & St Leonards.

All pictures in this book are copyrighted © R. Pollard 2013

Other books by the same author:

Hastings, Looking back to the Future. A Tribute to Sidney Little.
Borough & Water Engineer 1926 - 1950
ISBN 978-0-9569366-0-8 Priced @ £14.99

IV

Content information.

This publication does carry some reports (some in part, and others in full) from the Housing and Improvement Committees of the time, in respect of the insanitation conditions and the overcrowding of properties within the Old Town of Hastings, and how the Council's of the time toiled with various ideas to set about in dealing with these massive problems with little to no money!

Although, some reports are in their own words, as spoken in Council, some are compiled by the author in his own words, but there are no biased reports added from the author on anyone's side. Some names have purposely been removed to protect their anonymity, as their names weren't really relevant to the text.

These reports mostly cover to what properties were listed as by the Health Inspectors, as only fit for demolition. It also contains pitiful amounts offered to the tenants in poor compensation packages to be paid to those that were told that their houses were unfit to live in, and they were more or less forced to move to other parts of the town away from the Old Town, many into areas which were not acceptable to them.

Some reports may appear to replicate the facts, but, they are different in other ways, these were at that time very important to how the Council was to set about the problems ever since the dreaded Cresy report of 1850, basically to when all the problems arose.

You will read to how some of these reports contradict each other from month to month, year to year. It's all good reading, believe me; but not to those seriously effected by them then!

The clearing of certain properties deemed not fit for human habitation within the Bourne were originally spoken about after the big Cresy report of 1850, it reappeared in 1873, again in 1894, then laid dormant till 1923. It was reinvented again in 1924, 1925, 1927, then into 1931, 1933, 1935, 1937, 1945, and finally into the 1950s and early 1960s......Quite a lot of talking, but little action till the very end, (over 110 years) by then, spasmodic demolition had taken place all within the Old Town over a very long period of time, causing heart ache to every one that lived there, mainly because the Council couldn't make a decision, or have the ready money to carry out such a scheme, loans were not always possible due to the fact they had to be paid back! And finally, many folk refused to be moved.

All the adverts that we have included are genuine, and from the era's between the early 1920s through to the mid 1950s. These are there for your entertainment, remembering to what we bought, and to how we used to live.

Please also note....

That all measurements, and likewise money quotations within the text of this book are of the imperial nature, it would make peculiar reading if these were transferred into metric from the period of the time to modern day.

V

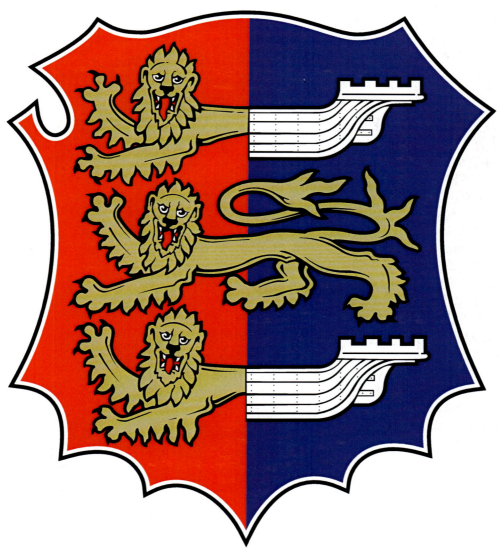

The Borough of

Hastings & St Leonards

VI

Mr. Philip Palmer
Borough Engineer 1888 - 1924

Mr. George Wittaker
Borough Engineer 1924 - 1925
(no photo)

Mr. Sidney Little
Borough Engineer 1925 - 1960

VII

Index to contents.

Page	Year	
1		Where it all started and The very early days.
7		Hastings Old Town.
15	1850	The big report of 1850 and the after effects.
37	1894	Keeping Hastings to the front.
53	1924	First steps towards a full scheme.
59	1925	Clearing the Old Town & Traffic problems.
		Fifty steel houses, & Houses at Halton & Broomgrove.
81	1926	Slum clearance scandal, Land at Hardwicke Road &
		Old Town property, Rents for steel houses.
88	1927	Purchase price of Council houses.
91	1928	Big trouble with Hollington houses, and Old Town
		Improvement scheme.
95	1929	Proposed new thoroughfare, Councillors call for full
		investigation.
		£96,000 referred to Finance Committee.
		Looking 10 years ahead.
115	1930	Widening of the Croft and Chief Constable's report
125	1931	Ratepayers meeting -Replanning the Old Town
		Old Town Improvement - Criticism to Johnson plan
147	1932	Hastings of the future - First steps
149	1934	£100,000 Slum clearance scheme
		Where are all the dispossessed people going to?
		Final notice to clear slums from Hastings Old Town.
175	1935	Borough Engineers alternative to Bourne highway.
		The storm brews for the Bembrook Farm Estate.
		Chief Constable and Traffic.
		24 votes to 4 - Borough Engineers alternative adopted.
		Torfield Road scheme adopted.
		An independent persons view as to the Bourne scheme.

VIII

Index to contents continued.....

Page	Year	
209	1936	Old Towner's move out! Plans Old Town rebuilding. Site to be acquired for 300 houses at Ore.
217	1937	More buildings proposed for demolition. Road through the Bourne. When will work start? Compulsory orders sent out!
233	1938	Old Town redevelopment plan. Owner offered £15 compensation, Judge's comments.
241	1939	Housing question in the Old Town.
243	1941	Demolition of Old Town House (4 Winding Street).
245	1944	Ministry ban demolition of steel houses.
249	1946	Old Town Scheme stopped! Problems linger on.
257	1961	1,000 'Unfit' houses, £180,000 new housing scheme. Inquiry into Bourne Road Clearance plan.
262	1962	Inspector's recommendations & decision on Bourne road site purchase.
264	1963	Committee's 'NO' to The Bourne

Conclusion

265	Memories of the Past from an Old Town resident.
271	The Final word

Where it all started!

Hastings, since very early times had been a major port for ship building along with a thriving fishing industry too. It had been for decades now a beach based fleet, whereby, the entire fishing fleet are drawn up onto the beach from the sea, this was unique for a fleet of fishing boats to be drawn up from the sea and moored on dry land so to speak. But Hastings at that point, nor now even had any such facilities to moor up a boat in a protected wet harbour. Hastings is virtually the only port left in England to have such rituals as these, and we can never see this changing.

The Old Town in earlier days was the centre point of Hastings, where the town nested between the two hills. This was a very close knit community, as all the fishermen and boat builders lived and worked out of the Old Town.

Many an industry thrived here in the valley, there were numerous fish smokers and curers. The small boys from the fishermen would load up small hand carts with fish and walk the Old Town selling door to door, they even ventured into the lower parts of what is now Clive Vale too.

There were many warehouses and shops scattered all over the area, all trading in one form or another. The area was also adorned with quite a few public houses, today you need only a few fingers to count as to what is left! Yes, the Old Town was crammed full.

Hastings can boast of being one if the not the best and largest shore based fishing fleets anywhere to be found in the country. Nearly all the fishermen lived within the Old Town, and again Hasting must have had the only town to have Twittens, Alleys, and passage ways at that time.

Hastings Old Town was destroyed in words alone many years ago, when schemes were first spoken as far back as 1850 in the Cresy report as regards houses unfit for human habitation.

An Idea put forward to widening the road network within the Old Town came about in 1894, when, Mr. H. Palmer the then Borough Engineer devised what would have been a most ridiculous plan if put into action, this would have seen the complete destruction of the High Street as we know it now today, details of his scheme are listed further on.

Even going back to this early date, people were concerned about the amount of traffic using All Saints Street, High Street and the Croft, be it mainly horse and carts that used the Old Town every single day.

There had always been strong opposition to anything in the way of alterations to the Old Town. For a start All Saints Street was adorned with shop after shop, as was Courthouse Street, this is not to mention the High Street nor the lower parts of the Croft Road. When you consider to how much trade and businesses were carried out in the vicinity of the Old Town compared with that of today, there is certainly no comparison whatsoever.

The very early days

The late Borough Engineer Mr. Sidney Little from what has been said by many was to take the full blame for the destruction of the Bourne and indeed the Old Town in general. Mr. Little was not to be blamed for the total destruction of the Old Town as we see it today, although many people will have seen that he was the man that brought down the final axe! He simple had to follow orders and complete what others before him had started and left! When you read Sidney Little's history you will find that he was actually against the full redevelopment of the Old Town and came up with several different ideas that would have saved the area more or less completely.

Yes, there were a few dwellings that would by today's standards have had to be pulled down for health reasons alone. When you look back there were many interlaced twittens and passageways tied up in the heart of this community, in fact the Old Town was a warren of alleys and twittens.

Sanitation was probably the biggest issue at that time whereby, many families had to share the same ablutions, or not one at all!

Obviously there was little fresh running water, that was until it rained! Then there was quite a lot. Dampness was a major issue in many abode, because there was little to protect you or the dwelling from the driving winds and rains, consequently, the rain constantly absorbed into the structure and made the rooms smell damp, let alone looking at the walls, which were wet nearly all the time. Many properties were rented, and the landlords if they could be found, were very reluctant to carry out any repairs no matter how minor they were. Those that were owned by the tenants couldn't afford major repairs.

Not all were equipped with electricity when offered at the time cables were being laid in the area during the early 1900s. Gas was still the main form of lighting, although candles were used a lot as well. Heating, was normally confined to just one room, an open fire in a grate fuelled by whatever was at hand at the time, sawn up drift wood from the beach, tree parts found on the hills or sometimes from the wilderness at the top end of the Bourne; coal was used but proved quite an expensive form of fuel, thereby, was rarely used on a commercial basis in the home. A scullery equipped with no more than an area to prepare food on a wooden board, a china sink (if you were lucky) most had a tin pan. A single tap supplying cold water, and a place to boil up a kettle on an old gas ring, or perhaps on the open fire, very basic to say the least, but these houses were loved by many and loathed by a few.

Many families were born and brought up in these houses over the years, despite the fact that many ailments were lurking about due to the damp and insanitation conditions, yes, of course there were deaths in the infant group, but the older folk suffered the most with severe chest infections like bronchitis and pneumonia, as then, there were cures as we have in today's society.

Not many complaints were diagnosed properly, and if they were, a simple medication was prescribed, people just couldn't afford to buy potions, so had to try and fight off these ailments by themselves. Some relied on herbal medicines from flowers and plant roots boiled and taken internally! But the expertise did not exist in what different herbs would cure, and some took what they thought would be good to take for a certain illness, where upon it was for the worse! But that's another story.

There were many a property to where you could open your window and talk directly with your neighbour next door doing the very same as you, you were only a matter of just a few feet apart. Fire was the biggest risk, as if there was a serious fire outbreak within the community, a very large part of the Old Town would have been destroyed for ever, in fact much bigger than the destruction that was created by mankind today. As records stand today, the Old Town suffered very little in fact from fire disasters, despite that many lit their homes by candle power alone. There were very few reported incidents where candles had been knocked over and the net curtains caught light, (mostly the candle went out,) also to where the open fires in the living room spat burning embers from the wet logs causing holes to be burnt in the rugs that lay on the floor, very few had spark guards as these were not commonly used.

Communal drying grounds were provided, as virtually none of the properties had a garden to speak of, all there was in many cases were just a back yard where everybody used to communicate with their properties. Natural light was quite a rare thing for many, as the properties were so close together this starved light from entering many rooms, another reason as to why dampness never dried out and illnesses became so apparent. It was spoken about the poor sanitation conditions suffered by many too. People spoke of rats in their houses too. In a few cases a privy, of which consisted of a bucket in a shed covered by a board with a hole in it was shared by as many as ten families, and when full who emptied it and where? The Bourne stream by now had been stopped further up the valley to form reservoirs at Clive Vale, and the stream, of which did run freely at one time had now been reduced to a trickle, but this, being the only form of water running out to sea was where many buckets were emptied. The water Bailiff occasionally sounded a horn when the sluices were about to be opened to allow fresh water to flow once again through the Bourne stream to clear all the foul smelling debris that was building up.

The decision had basically been decided upon years previously to clear some of the derelict and run down properties from the Old Town. Plans were drawn up as far back as 1894, when the then Borough Engineer Mr. H. Palmer came up with a plan to completely demolish the left hand side of the High Street from top to bottom, (this is the high pavement side as we look at it today) to widen the roads for the foreseeable future of traffic. Even then, the High Street became blocked on many occasions by carts stopping to either deliver goods or moving items from houses etc., this blocked the free passage for others to pass, something had to be done!

The plans as shown in this book were rather ruthless to say the least, virtually nothing was to be spared. All the properties would have been wiped away and the banking that would have been left was to be cut back quite severely and reshaped to those properties that remained in the Croft; their gardens would now be the front line of the High Street. Fortunately, this plan never came to fruition. As you will see on the plan and read further on, All Saints Street was not to be left out of the massive demolition order either.

Other schemes were drawn up and shelved several times but nothing of consequence ever came of them until the 1920s. This is when the axe was once again thrown full force at the Old Town.

We have to step back in time to a date that stuck in everybody's mind, that of 1850, when the original ideas were set out to thin the highly populated areas of the Bourne, when a Government Health Inspectorate in the form of Mr. Edward Cresy was asked to survey the Town as a whole, but with special emphasis placed on the Old Town.

The council at that time in question knew that something had to be done to try and alleviate the highly congested areas, especially those within the Old Town part of Hastings. The council had little money at that time and loans were scarce to obtain because there was little chance of repaying the capital lent in the time period set out. There was precious little work for people and the income in rents and rates was quite low compared to other seaside towns on the equivalent standards to Hastings. Unfortunately, at that time Hastings didn't own a great deal of property in its own right, most was owned by people from outside the town and rented out privately, so this was one area to which the council couldn't collect money.

The report was fully justified in many ways, but how the council thought they were to implement the findings was yet another story as you will read.

You might have already guessed that his report would not be a soft hearted one, of course not, it was a full damming report, stating that most of the properties were unfit for human habitation, due to severe dampness, little to no drainage at all, and sanitation not even fit for an animal.

The report was about 60 pages long, and this is just what the Council had not only been expecting but wanted! This was the report of all reports, and from a Government Inspector too, the axe was to fall big time now, or was it? The report was a full to the point report with not even a rusty nail left out, the biggest commodity was the poor state of the drainage, and in many cases none at all, this is to where most diseases were magnified.

The report as you will read further on told of many cases to where property was totally unfit for human habitation as was only fit to be pulled down.

This all of course would have cost many thousands of pounds, money to which the council didn't have; and on the other side of the coin — where do you now place all these people that would have no homes?

Other schemes right up to the early 1920s were suggested, but the same dilemma popped up every time, money and where to put these people.

1924 was when the first eviction notices went out to clear some of the densely populated areas in the heart of the Bourne and All Saints Street, demolition was slow to start with and by 1927 it got faster and wide open spaces began to appear everywhere. Nothing was completed by numbers as they say, demolition was spasmodic to say the least, one here and one there, the whole area was looking more like a bomb site than a carefully planned demolition site.

What happened next was a surprise to all, the demolition stopped for a time, nothing now followed until 1929 when the new Borough Engineer Mr. Little had to resume where it had been left by the previous Engineer Mr. Whitaker who, took this job over from Mr. Palmer when he retired. But due to Mr. Whitakers early departure from office left it for the next engineer to take hold where he had left it. As I had mentioned earlier, Mr Little was given the task (ordered as you might have it) to carry on where others had left the area in one hell of a mess. People didn't know the earlier engineers as much as the present one Mr. Little, this is to why he consequently received much of the bad press and comments that were by now freely passing around, when it bore fair and square on Mr. H. Palmer who threw the first blow to the Old Town.

Mr. Little, knew that there was much disapproval from the people of the Old Town as to why the wreckers carried out so much unnecessary demolition to their community. He tried to make good by coming up with several different schemes that would put a stop to any further demolition to their properties, he wanted the community, believe it or not, to stay within the area and rebuild the community spirit that once shone across Hastings Old Town.

Mr Little offered before the Council several schemes that would add delaying tactics to the already unpopular schemes, whereby he was hoping that these would alleviate any further demolition, but the Council were hard and fast in their minds to proceed with scheme as before, and told Mr. Little in no uncertain terms that the scheme would be completed as planned, and this was now to take top priority over more or less everything else he was doing at that time.

What the past had in store! Was this to be the worst plan of all?

Since the early days, even dating back to 1894, plans had been drawn up for a complete modernisation of the 'Old Town' even then!

The plans, (of which you can see further on) showed part demolition of the 'High Street' and All Saints Street on a big scale. An ambitious scheme that was thought up primarily for the intention of keeping the heart of the 'Bourne' as it was, but 'High Street' especially on the high pavement side would not have been with us as we now know it today, nor the side backing onto the

Bourne of All Saints Street had Mr. Palmer got his way!

The scheme called for the complete demolition of all the properties in the High Street on the high pavement side, basically from the bottom end beyond George Street through to more or less the top end of the 'High Street'.

Even the Old Town Hall wasn't to be saved! the clearance would have been up into the 'Croft', with those backing onto properties on the 'High Street' losing virtually all their gardens. The area according to the plans would have seen the higher level sloped down and cut back dramatically to meet the road as it is today but the carriageway would have been much wider.

All Saints Street from the top end down to the junction of Rock-a-Nore Road would have seen virtually all the properties backing onto the Bourne being demolished, this would of course taken away most of the alleys and twittens that entwined the properties between the Bourne and All Saints Street.

I suppose in a way no one had ever thought of demolishing in whole or part of the community residing within the heart of the 'Bourne', as the road network would not have been quite so devastatingly severe as it was originally planned in this scheme.

Although we have no exact costing of this very ambitious scheme, it would have taken Hastings Council into many thousands of pounds, and noting from more modern times (the 1930s) the compensation paid to all those that were about to be made homeless would have been extremely little if at all!

At that time in the late 1800s, the community in the 'Bourne' was a well endowed population, with many businesses thriving, not only in the 'High Street' but 'All Saints Street' and the 'Bourne' as a whole. The area boasted of many tradesmen operating from the Old Town. There were a wide variety of shops and a Brewery within the heart of the 'Bourne', an Ice House and the local Fishermen that lived and fished from the beach fleet on the stade selling their wares in the area, there were several fish curers and smokers within the community; even ship builders had a good trade going for them on the beach.

I do suppose that this may have been looked at, at some point, but knowing what the Council may have had to contend with gave it a wide berth and chose the simpler method of just clearing the 'High Street' along with All Saints Street. We all thank our lucky stars that this particular scheme never left the ground, as this would have caused more heart ache than what the Bourne clearance did.

Had this plan ever come to fruition, it would have given road widths on both accounts as 22 feet, whereby, traffic from the seafront would have proceeded up the High Street and down All Saints Street. This would have allowed for vehicles to park on one side for deliveries etc, whilst allowing the through traffic to pass unhindered on both streets. Plans to demolish parts of the Old Town came into operation firstly in 1894 with a break till 1924, then 1927, again in 1933,35,37 and 1939, final destruction took place in the early 1960s.

HASTINGS OLD TOWN

Hastings, looking back to the turn of the century, was a well-noted seaside resort for the cure to most health problems. Doctors in and around London would prescribe rest and sea air for those suffering from chest complaints of all types, rather than prescribe some ill fated herbal medicine that would cost the earth, most of which people could not afford, and a very good chance that it would not have had any long lasting effect on you anyway.

Of all the seaside towns to choose from, Hastings was singled out as one, if not the best for fresh sea air qualities, boarding and lodging places of high repute all beyond those neighbouring towns of Bexhill, Eastbourne and Brighton. The Old Town had its own problems in the way of health; The area was laced with a maze of pathways, alleys and twittens. The small houses, mainly terraced were crammed into a small area between the two hills with the Bourne Stream running through the middle of the community, straddling either side of the Bourne Walk.

The Bourne Stream was used for every purpose you could imagine!

Everybody used the stream for washing their clothes, dogs used the water for frolicking about in, small children would play daily in and around the waters edge. The stream became heavily polluted, all types of rubbish and effluent were regularly tipped into the stream daily from the entire neighbourhood, it now ran as black mud, and smelt, the odour was quite pungent and could be smelt all over the Old Town at certain times. For many, this was their only source of water not only to cook and wash by, but in some instances to drink as well!

The Hastings Water Company sealed off the flow of water to the Bourne Stream as early as 1835, thus reducing the flow to just a trickle when the reservoirs in Clive Vale were constructed for storage purposes.

In due course the Bourne Stream was covered in, apart from the area known as the Wilderness, from the top of the High Street to the Stables.

Because of the loss of the stream, the town supplied several water pumps for the people of the Old Town, this was then more or less a clean supply of water even though not a constant one, a supply of clean water was something that many of the inhabitants had not seen before, especially on tap!

At the same time the East Well was constructed in Rock-a-Nore Road, this was to supply an ever-lasting quantity of clean water that had been filtered through the East Hill. The Stream remained a place for the continual dumping of household rubbish and alike. In the summer sun, the ground would crack up and the smell emulating from the area was dreadful, in winter the ground became a quagmire. Many of the residents suffered serious health complaints, not from the foul waters that laid dormant in the so called stream, although

The bottom end of All Saints Street by what was the Salvation Army Hall.

these matters didn't improve their conditions, these were contributed from many sources, one obviously being the effects of drinking dirty infested water, another was that some of the cottages around the Bourne were rat infested and carried the usual diseases that followed the vermin, many suffered the effects of damp, rising and otherwise! A lot of the cottages had running water installed, but not from a tap! But from leaking roofs every time it rained, despite every effort to keep the premises dry with buckets and bowls under the leaks, the water still poured in. The properties were very cold in the winds mainly due to the fact that windows had glass missing and did not shut properly against the weather. Heating was achieved by normally a small open fire in what would be called the parlour, fuelled by what ever was available at the time, mainly wood from the wilderness at the top of the Bourne or from driftwood washed ashore at high tides. Coal was available but only to a few that could afford the luxury (unless you came across it by other means?) Chimney fires were a most common occurrence, due to the fact that all the wood burnt in the open fires caused large soot formations in the chimneys of which were rarely or never swept, hence from time to time this caught light and caused great concern from those living either side of the affected premise. Apart from chimney fires, sparks and burning embers spitting from wet wood out onto the hearth rug often caught light, this often caused sheer panic when papers laying on the floor caught light and flared up as well, there was always a bucket of water at hand for when this happened (Well most of the time).

If the fire was too great to deal with, someone would run to the combined police and fire station in Bourne Street and call out the pumper, but this was very rare.

Toilets (or privy's as they were more commonly known) were a non-starter, as in many cases a bucket in the back yard or the corner of the living room would have served the purpose quite well. After each use of the bucket the contents were covered with ashes from the fire, or soil, and only emptied when full to the brim! And where was it nearly always emptied I wonder?

Those, that were lucky enough to have the use of a privy, normally had to share it among several neighbours, when the cesspit that it was built over was full, it normally overflowed. Raw sewage commonly discharged into the streets finally found its way into the Bourne Stream where upon it was flushed away onto the stade and beach at the appropriate time. Waste products and slops were usually thrown straight into the streets, like out of the living room window for instance, and formed a foul smelling dung heap right under their noses, this enticed the formation of a large rat colony that roamed throughout the entire Old Town housing population.

The full to over-flowing cesspools remained over-flowing, as no one would take the responsibility to empty them. The liquids flowed through the streets and often in the houses themselves, the smells emanating were intolerable as the rotting sewage etc., gave off repugnant gases.

Despite the fact that many properties were being bought or even owned, a large amount throughout the Old Town were rented, and trying to get repairs carried out by the landlords (who ever they were?) was to the greater part a complete waste of time and effort. This is probably to why properties were left in such a deplorable run down state, animals wallowed in the stream and made the situation far worse. Hoggs (pigs to us) roamed the wilderness and polluted the waters even more, everything imaginable discharged into the Bourne stream at some point or other, so hence a desperate decision had to be made as to what could be done to clean up the Old Town.

A book written on the Public Health Act addressed to the General Board of Health by Edward Cresy; told how people of all ages were being taken seriously ill and often followed by death due to Cholera, Diarrhoea, Typhoid, Gastro-enteritis and Tuberculosis by the fact that the conditions that they lived in were extremely cold, cramped and damp.

The ground floors in many of the houses and cottages were constructed mainly of brick, consequently the dampness rose up through the bricks and made the atmosphere very cold and damp especially in the long winter months.

The floors remained wet nearly all the time, this was highlighted by the fact that the flooring bricks were laid   directly upon the soil and clay overlay, also the privy's leaked, as mentioned earlier, cesspools over-flowed soaking the flooring bricks to saturation point as well, and to add to the problems, the bucket covered with ashes stood in the corner of the living room till full, in all a wonderful recipe for disease.

Drainage throughout the Old Town was totally insufficient too, not only was the carrying capacity very low for the amount of properties connected to the inapt system where it existed, but sewer gasses were being omitted all over the Old Town though gratings in the ground and scullery sink outlets, (no traps then, just a hole in the floor to where waste water discharged).

Children playing in the alleyways were able to breathe in freely the foul smells being omitted from the gratings.

The older inhabitants easily fell ill before the children, although they took their fair share of illnesses anyway.

The population for the Old Town was far greater than over the whole of the Borough itself. Edward Cresy made a report in 1850 to the General Board of Health and submitted plans to lay down a drainage system to the Old Town by means of drainage pipes laid from each and every property connected to a central outlet. The system was never fully adopted within the complex of the Old Town as it was, until redevelopment had started to take place in the early 1920s, for when a moderate sewage system was then installed.

Edward Cresy found that the existing system failed in every sense, he reported that, at high tide, the sea water normally reversed the flow and carried the foul waters back up the land out-falls into peoples houses etc. At that point I shall let you draw your own conclusions to what happened next.

Even to this end the Old Town could still not be saved as a whole, demolition had to take place in areas of dense congestion and severe overcrowding even for the sake of better health conditions.

Guesthouses and boarding houses were filled to beyond capacity, built in areas of little light and extremely poor access, ventilation was also extremely poor as buildings backed onto each other and air changes were virtually non existent.

Gas was available to those that could afford it; its main purpose would have been for lighting only. Public lighting in the alleys and twittens existed in the form of gas lighting columns, but very few and far between though! Each of which had to be lit each night by the Hastings Gas Co, lamp lighter and then extinguished the following morning.

Should the mantle have burnt out or broken in the lamp housing, a fitter would turn up probably weeks after a request from the lamp lighter to rectify the fault. As each cubic foot of gas saved where a light was out, over time it would register and save the Gas Co, a few shillings over a period of time depending on the amount of lights out. Underground gas leaks were a very common occurrence, where poor quality iron pipes quickly rotted in the acid soil leaving the air constantly smelling of gas odours, or was it the stream?

Electricity was not installed in any of the cottages until much later; consequently, light had to be supplied in the form of oil lamps or candles, both of which were very dangerous when being moved from room to room, it wouldn't be the first time that a candle placed on a dresser by the open window caught the net curtains alight, because the breeze had wafted the curtain across the candle. Surprisingly though, not many cottages caught fire and burnt out., damage was very little surprisingly.

To take a bath was quite a rare occasion, you either did one of three things; (1) You didn't bath at all? (2) You paid a small fee and went to the public baths at the foot of Bourne Street and bathed in warm salt/plain water then onto the steam rooms. (3) Lastly you pulled in the tin bath that hung on the wall outside, placed it in front of the fire and filled with copious amounts of water taken from the public pumps, heated over the fire and then poured into the bath, pot at a time. When finished with, the great ordeal to empty the bath was on, pots, pans, saucepans, buckets anything that held water was used to empty the bath and where? Straight out the door and down the passageways, to drain where ever it could. When the water level was low enough, the bath would be dragged to the door and tipped up where the remainder of the water would flow away hopefully down the passage and not into a neighbouring house, this may explain the reason to why many did not take regular baths.

Many of the cottages were in a very sorry state of repair; landlords ignored pleas to rectify leaking roofs, broken windows, fallen weather boarding etc. This prompted the council to act, and in the early 1920s the town put forward a compulsory slum clearance scheme.

This was to involve the demolition of many of the cottages and shops in and around the Bourne walk; this would also lead to the permanent disappearance of many passages and twittens. (Listed later on)

The problem then arose as to where to put the people from the compulsory purchased houses, a further plan was placed before the council where council houses could be built on the old Bembrooke Farm site, and Halton area. Building then commenced on the erection of rows of council houses on the West Hill sites, this time all the houses and flats would have running water and sewerage connections, and electric light in moderate form.

The first road completed for accommodation of phase one was Hardwick Road on the Halton site.

By 1925 a vast area at the lower end of the Bourne had been demolished, and a 30-foot wide road was laid to no where. It terminated at what is now Courthouse Street. Its intentions were not for vehicular traffic but for pedestrian use only, it was re-named Bourne Street.

The motor vehicle had by now taken a firm but constant hold on the increase to the demands that it was taking upon the narrow roads through the Old Town, likewise with the trolley buses. This was now giving great concern for the flow of traffic in the High Street to where two way traffic had often become locked, or should we say grid locked!

Schemes were put forward to clear the slums and cut a road through the Bourne and redirect traffic away from the High Street as early as February 1876, but they all fell aside mainly due to the fact that the money for such a scheme could not emerge. The proposals were placed several times before parliament for government funding but each time were refused, so the scheme lay dormant for years to come until, February 1958 when the plans to push a road straight through the heart of the Old Town were aroused. This coincided with the council on deciding to fell 18 elm trees in and around the wilderness, stating that they had been affected by Dutch Elm disease, but only a few weeks later the work on clearing the wilderness had started. Funding by now had been sought and approved, the demolition of the remaining cottages and buildings in the path of the road into its final stages were well under way, the road had now started with vengeance and nothing was going to stop its completion. Bulldozers moved in, steam cranes with wrecking balls attached started to swing round and the remainder of the obstacles were quickly reduced to huge piles of rubble.

The Bourne Walk was now to become the Bourne Road, the final connection was made and a new road was born! (excuse the pun)

Roebuck Street was to become a reality when the Roebuck Inn was finally demolished to make way for the new connecting link between the Bourne and the High Street. This final stage of demolition tore the heart of the Old Town apart, the road carrying now all the coastal traffic has put a divider straight down the centre of what was a busy close knit society.

Many names of twittens and alleys have now been lost forever. Yes, the Old Town did need some modernisation, but not on this scale. Several different solutions could have been found as to where the traffic could have gone to relieve the pressure on the High Street.

One would have been to divert all coastal traffic over the West hill and straight into the town that way, or again over the West Hill, down Mount Pleasant Road, Queens Road.

The gap within the Old Town can no longer be filled! The damage has long been done and we can but only now make the most of it, make ourselves aware to any further destruction within the Old Town, remember it's our history and heritage that is slowly disappearing before our very eyes.

Demolition continued in dribs and drabs for many years to come, for when the matter was brought forward at a Council meeting in the December of 1937 by the local traders association.

Questions were asked about the many open spaces left by the demolition in All Saints Street and the Bourne, and to whether or not Mr. Sidney Little's scheme of a new road through the Old Town was still alive! and if so, when was it to be built? The Council replied, that properties still stood in the way of the scheme and continued negotiations were being sought.

Another question was asked to why such a long period of time had elapsed before John Street flats (Hastings Wall) were to be erected, since part demolition of the houses had taken place some 10 years previous.

The Council had now been left with a decision that answers were required soon.

Pleasant Row.

Leslie Badham's, The back of a romantic house in All Saints Street.

Hastings Borough Council sanctions Board of Health Report, 1850.

We have to now go back to the year 1850, as this is basically to where it all started in a report sanctioned by the Hastings Council into the general state of health as to the overcrowding within Hastings & St Leonards with special interest taken in the Old Town and a few other specific parts of the borough.

The Ministry's General Board of Health Inquiry had appointed a Mr. Edward Cresy one of their leading experts of the time in sanitation and diseases to inspect and write this protracted report on the general state of the borough with special emphasis on the Old Town, this was to form part of the Public Health Act of the same year.

Many facts were drawn from this 60 plus page report, with very strong emphasises on not only the state of the sanitation, but included the poor water quality, the lack of mains gas pressure, and drainage facilities whereby, many properties had no drainage facilities at all! And not let us forget the free air space much needed in such confined areas; this was really the start of what was to come later, believe it or not this was written 163 years ago!

At this present time the town did not have a Borough Engineer other than a Borough Surveyor. The first Borough Engineer came onto the scene in 1862 in the form of a Mr. W. Andrews, he continued to serve the borough until 1888 when Mr P. H. Palmer took over. The Borough Surveyor at the time of this report was written was not registered, but in 1851 a Mr. S. Putland was in charge of all redevelopments within the borough and he especially took a great interest in the overcrowded Bourne area of the Old Town.

For obvious reasons we cannot replicate the whole report, but we will look at some of the major factors, which were used to power the start of the demolition of the Bourne and Old Town as we knew it.

The report was very thorough, as every dwelling was visited in turn, the report went into precise detail of every defect found, from crumbling brickwork to springy floors, leaking roofs and so on as you will see.

When the report was read out to Council at the Town Hall it took eleven days to read through all the details including sketches made at the time and explain in precise detail all his findings. The Council made notes upon notes on the report, they now had what they needed to clear major parts of the town, not only restricting demolition to the area of the Old Town either! Reading other reports there just seemed to be one more problem ahead on themselves, and that was capitol, one for the demolition of the properties and the compensation to be paid out, but where to house these people that were just about to be made homeless? There was no surplus housing stock available at that time, and what there was didn't belong to the Council anyway; the Councils own housing stock was very few and far between at that time.

We hereby list some very odd statistics that came under the report for Health, this must have taken some while to compile all the measurements as listed!

The first to come under scrutiny was the roads and Streets of the borough, these were strangely mentioned as the report went on to say:

Roads and Streets are under the Hastings Commissioners, who are empowered to take all public squares and Streets under their management, after the owners or proprietors have made them to the satisfaction of the Commissioners.

The length and width of the roads at present under the control of their surveyors, are as follows:-

	Length	Width
High-Street	620 yards	10 yards
Court House-Street	83	7
Swan Lane	51	5
Croft-Lane and Church-Street . . .	170	6
George-Street	250	7
John-Street	100	6
East-Street	71	5
West-Street	163	5
Parade	314	7
All –Saints-Street	492	1
Bourne and Upper Bourne-Street . . .	160	10
Little Bourne-Street	38	5
Hill-Street	83	7
Priory-Road, Castle-Street, and York-Street .	540	10
Pelham-Street	150	7
Meadow Cottage and St Andrew's Terrace .	600	10
Castle-Lane	600	5
Castle-Hill to Gate	1700	7
Hastings-Hill from High-Street to the Gate .	1125	9
Winding-Street	90	8
Albion-Road	13	7

The superficial contents are 59,351 square yards, or 12 acres and a quarter.

The repairs of these roads, for the last two years, have not cost less than £400 per annum: Blue stone is employed, obtained under the cliffs; it is delivered for 3 shillings. per cubic yard. The breaking costs 2 shillings per cubic yard, to which must be added to the cartage and spreading. In the winter months the stones are laid over the roads about 3 inches in   thickness; thus a cubic yard and a half of broken material is sufficient for a square rod, or 30¼ superficial yards. Thus to cover the 59,351 superficial yards, or 2000 square rods, which are the superficial contents of all the roads, 3000 cubic yards of broken stone would be required in the course of the year. The cost of carting, breaking stones, and repairing the roads for a year ending December 1849, amounted to £683.17s 4d. beside the purchase of three horses for £103.5s.0d., and charges to wheelwrights, Smiths, etc. of £119. 7s.3d., with other items.

The scavengers work, and watering of the roads, formed a portion of the items as previously mentioned, so that about £800. is annually expended for the maintenance of the roads.

The footways are also repaved, flagged, or repaired by the Commissioners; and no one is permitted, without their consent, to remove or alter them, under a penalty not exceeding £5.

The present footways are:-

	Length	Width
Tackle-Way.	433 yards	2 yards
Crown-Lane.	80	1
East-Hill-Passage.	93	2
Bourne-Passage1.	240	2
Wellington-Court.	30	4
Waterloo-Lane	116	3
Bourne-Passage2.	126	2
Gower's-Passage.	26	2
Post-Office-Passage	92	3
Salter's-Lane	130	3
Tripe-Alley.	63	3
Church-Passage	58	3
Hundred-Steps	250	3
Light-Steps to the Dispensary. . . .	105	3
Market-Passage and Hooper's-Passage . .	50	2
Russell-Court	43	3
Literary Institution-Steps	13	2
Castle-Down-Path.	300	1
Tar-Hill-Path	500	1
Five-Gate-Field-Path	200	—

The footways are, in some places, flagged with square stone, or paved with brick; and in others laid with small pebbles obtained from the beach, or gravelled. Watering of the roads commences about the 1st March, and is usually continued till the end of October. The water is obtained from the Bourne and Priory Streams, where there is a small wheel and pump, which precludes the necessity for manual labour. There are two water carts constantly employed to water the 59,351 superficial yards of road.

The Commissioners, under their Act, have the power to cause any wells, tanks, reservoirs, pipes, pumps, and other apparatus to be made available for the purpose of watering the Streets, and to provide horses, water carts, and engines, which are necessary.

Scavengering. The Commissioners are required to provide for the cleansing of the Streets and other places, and to remove all dirt, dung, dust, cinders, ashes, filth, or rubbish, in and from the Streets and houses, if required to do so by the owners or occupiers: and to cart the whole away in scavengers' carts.

The foot-pavements are to be swept every morning by the occupiers of the houses, between the hours of six and ten, under a penalty of twenty shillings.

Privies are to be emptied between the hours of eleven o'clock at night and five o'clock in the morning, from Ladyday to Michaelmas; and between eleven and six o'clock in the morning, from Michaelmas to Ladyday.

In the year 1849, the sale of the ashes, bones, and rags produced a sum of £181. 18s. 5d.; as in the former year it was £112. 10s. 0d.

Slaughter Houses. Hogsties, boiling and melting houses, may be removed by the Commissioners, remunerating the proprietors, if deemed nuisances.

Whilst the inspection was carried out to a full and reliable acceptance, the above listed items were not forgotten about either, as the town to no matter of how many occupancy's were there, or to the area's concerned, they were to be kept clean and the Streets washed on a daily basis, along with privies etc.

Don't forget that we are still in the era of the 1850s.

The Gas supply was not left without comment either: as the report followed on to say in brief, the Gas works were situated in the Priory Meadows, water used in the plant was drawn from the stream that flowed from the hopgrounds, near Ore Church on route to the sea. The water that had been used in the plant was found to be contaminated as it rejoined the flow towards the sea, something the Gas Company had to deal with at once.

There was on inspection cast iron pipes in use to carry the gas to the consumers and the limited amount of public Street lighting in operation at that time. Leaks were found to be evident from various locations throughout the town, another problem for the Hastings Gas Company to solve on an urgent basis. Although the gas was hydraulically pumped around the town, the pipe sizes started off at 14 inch mains, reducing down to 8 inch, then to 4 inch, it was discovered that by the time the end of the line was reached (especially in the area of the highly populated Old Town) there was very little pressure left in the mains to maintain a flame on a burner, which constantly went out.

The recommendation was that, the Gas Plant had to be made more efficient and the production of more coal tar gas had to be made to fulfil all the requirements from the ever increasing consumers.

Water supplies. Both the Town of Hastings & St Leonards have their own water supply companies regulated by Acts of Parliament, which contribute to the chief supply to the inhabitants. The water works which belong to the town of Hastings were commenced soon after the passing of the Act, in 1832 at an original cost of £5,100. 0s. 0d. The waters of the Bourne, which neatly divides the Old Town, were collected, with several springs and rivulets flowing into it, at a short distance from the town, in the direction of Fairlight Down; where two reservoirs were formed, one holding 2,000,000 gallons, the other 800,000. These are situated at about 160 feet above the mean level of the sea, and are sufficiently high enough to supply the greater number of houses in the town. The number of houses that take water is about 700 besides 34 larger establishments. The houses generally pay a rate of 9d. in the pound.

The supply is upon the constant principle, and every house receiving water from the works is annually examined by an inspector. Three-quarter inch lead pipes, with brass shut off cocks, are found by the owners of the houses, who also have to pay the expenses of insertion into the iron mains.

In the beginning when the waterworks was first established, each person taking water was required to have a proper cistern installed with a ballcock to prevent the water running to waste; but this method was soon dispensed with, and the constant principle was adopted as the most convenient and economical. One reason assigned for this change was, that, when the cisterns were neglected for a period of time, the lead piping was found to become perforated with small pin like holes, to avoid this from occurring the pipes were coated in pitch. Carbonate of lead was also formed, producing, of course, many injurious results, such as simple lead poisoning!

Many of the houses in the town were supplied from private wells, or from stand pipes, these were provided for the poorer class of inhabitant, like a vast number within the complexes of the Old Town who just couldn't afford to have water laid on to tap.

Mortality. The amount of deaths were recorded in a register kept by a Mr. Harvey, Superintendent-Registrar of the district. Since 1847 and up to the year starting 1850, the rate had shot up by about 25%, this of course was truly not acceptable.

There were epidemics and epidemic diseases of the following numbers over the whole district, and they were:

	Recorded number in 1849
Measles	21
Hooping cough	7
Diarrhoea	10
Dysentery	1
Cholera	40
Influenza	2
Fever	4
Typhus	5
Small pox	2

Most of these deaths were recorded in the area's of the Old Town, diseases mainly brought about by the squalid conditions people were living in; cramped too close together, no proper ventilation, many living in damp, dark and dirty conditions, not by the direct fault of the tenants.

The number of crowded dwellings and the poverty of a very large proportion of the inhabitants, who depend upon a precarious subsistence, and whose food is chiefly fish, occasion maladies which frequently oblige them to apply for relief. The imperfect drainage, and the state of the Bourne, which was partly culverted in 1834, continue to multiply cases of diseases.

This brook, though frequently flushed by means of a head of water at the northern end of the town, is never free from those emanations which are injurious to health, and which, during eight hours out of twenty four, are pent up and cannot be discharged; and this must be the consequence of a large sewer at all times, if the flow of water is not sufficiently abundant to fill up the entire cavity and drive out the gases which float on the upper portions generally, and escape through the gratings and apertures of communication when not properly trapped.

The Bourne stream (brook) had even up till the time when the whole stream was culverted been a positive dumping ground for whatever! Household food waste, dead animals, basically if you can name it, it was in the stream over the long period of time; consequently a whole host of diseases were picked up from the foul waters by children playing in and around the water, this was certainly not a pleasant area.

A lot of properties in the Old Town were owned, buying, or rented, and those that were renting fell into the biggest trap of all by the standards in which their landlords failed to upkeep their properties. In many instances, the roofs were in such a poor state that every time it rained the water came down the walls. Broken or defective brickwork was yet another cause of rising damp. I did mention earlier on that these were picked up by the inspector along with floors that had too much spring in them, partly due to rotted floor members. The list was absolutely endless, very well written and thoroughly investigated, every bit to what the Council was looking for, but, were all the quotations correct?

Total deaths in the district. Over the whole borough the death rate was quite high in proportion to other areas along the coast, people here in Hastings & St Leonards were suffering from a variety of aliments, whereby, many resulted in premature deaths. The Registrar General recorded these figures over a one year period: Total deaths related directly to illnesses or diseases were 1,543., an annual mortality rate to 1000 persons living was 18.7%.

The figures revealed that 434 were from the Old Town alone.

An investigation was thoroughly looked into as regard the sick and to where they lived, it was discovered that many resided in cheap boarding/lodging houses, and there was of course the miserable overcrowded dwellings in which the poorer classes congregate. The cause is evident, and can be remedied by introducing habits of cleanliness, and such a supply of pure and wholesome water as shall be sufficient to scour and cleanse a properly constructed tubular system of drainage, and providing a discharge at all times of the tide.

The one area of course, which was to be so prominent in the report was the poor construction of many of the older properties within the complex of the Old Town; the report went on to say:

Overcrowding and the employment of improper building materials for the construction of the houses has done considerable damage, and requires the utmost attention on the part of the owners, as well as considerable outlay to improve. The greater part of the houses occupied by the poorer classes entirely without drainage, many without privy accommodation, and several without any supply of water, all which absolute requirements must be provided by the proprietors before any system of sewage can be rendered effective.

It was also noted that: The foundations of many of the superior houses are laid in sandstone, obtained from the cliffs, which, not being exposed long enough to the atmosphere before being laid, scarcely, ever becomes dry, resulting in breaking up under the pressures placed upon it. The wells and underground works lined with sandstone exhibit the growth of the polypodium, and the mosses which cover the surface indicate the quantity of humidity that this material will retain for many years.

The older dwellings, built of timber, with an overhanging chamber floor, were far better calculated to maintain their foundations dry. The projecting eaves and well-paved gutters underneath prevented any accumulation of water, and where these eaves drippings could not find a way, a gutter common to the adjoining houses poured the rain water from the roof, by the gargouilles, into the Street. A careful observation of the residences of our ancestors generally, will afford many useful lessons on drainage of every description. They had not many of our modern appliances, but the spirit in which they provided for the maintenance of their dwellings was a wise one, as their durability best attests.

Another serious comment was made as to many of the houses in the old part of the town are so constructed and placed that the sun's rays cannot ever reach them, and much needs to be done to introduce proper ventilation.

Not really any connection with the Bourne as such, but a few facts that made Hastings & St Leonards tick in the 1850s.

Within the last century, this town, like many others along the coast have been much resorted to by visitors, chiefly from the Metropolis, whereby, numerous groups of tradesmen have formed establishments to meet the demands of the ever increasing population that was being constantly demanded upon them in the borough.

In the town of Hastings, there were:

2 Bankers, 2 Physicians, 6 Surgeons and Apothecaries, 9 Chemist and Druggists, 3 Dentist, 3 Bathers, 5 Professors of music, 7 Solicitors, and 2 Surveyors, 2 Boarding houses, 54 Lodging houses for visitors, 6 Hotels, 2 Coffee houses, 45 Licensed victuallers, 3 Brewers, 4 Wine merchants.

3 Confectioners, 1 Flour dealer, 40 Grocers, 5 Dairy or Milkmen, 20 Green grocers, 1 Egg merchant, 3 Coal merchants, 1 Timber merchant, 1 Brick maker, 6 Builders, 29 Carpenters, 13 Bricklayers, 1 Sawyer, 4 Ironmongers, 1 Founder, 2 Paper hangers, 7 Painters, 4 Plumbers, 2 Plasterers and 6 Stone masons, 1 Carver and Gilder, 2 Cabinet makers, 1 House agent, 3 Auctioneers, 2 Furniture brokers, 6 Boat builders, 1 Shipwright, 1 Mast maker,

1 Sail maker, 2 Clog makers, 4 Coopers, 2 Fellmongers, 2 Leather sellers, 21 Boot and shoe makers, and 3 Saddlers, 14 Tailors, 17 Drapers, 2 Hatters, 2 Clothiers, 15 Milliners, 7 Straw bonnet makers, 3 Silk dyers, 1 Ready made linen warehouse, 2 Corset makers, 1 Furrier, 2 Printers, 2 Stationers, 2 Booksellers, 2 Bookbinders, 2 Newspaper agents, 2 Coach builders, 7 Wheelwrights, 1 Sedan chair proprietor, 3 Cartsmiths, 2 Corn dealers, 3 Licensed to let horses, 1 Coach proprietor, 3 Carriers, 1 Veterinary surgeon, 2 Shoeing smiths, 1 Livery stable keeper, 1 Gun maker, 1 Undertaker, 2 Jewellers, 4 Watch makers, 2 China dealers, 2 Lapidaries, 2 Dealers in shells, 1 Tonbridge Ware, 1 Toy warehouse, 1 Trunk maker, 1 Umbrella maker, 1 Basket maker, 4 Preparatory schools, 3 Academies, 5 Ladies schools. 2 Riding masters, 1 Portrait painter, 1 Billiard room, 1 Public Library, 2 Circulating libraries, 1 British and Foreign repositories, 1 Fancy ditto.

In St Leonards there were:

1 Banker, 24 Lodging houses for visitors, 9 Licensed victuallers, 5 retailers of beer, 3 Butchers, 6 Grocers, 10 Bakers, 1 Confectioner, 4 Green grocers, 5 Coal merchants, 2 Milkmen, 1 Wines and spirits merchant, 6 Builders, 2 Carpenters, 1 Brick maker, 1 Bricklayer, 3 Plumbers, 1 Painter, 1 Blacksmith, 4 Ironmongers, 4 Cabinet makers, 1 House agent, 2 Auctioneers, 1 Sail maker, 1 Dealer in marine stores, 3 Boot makers, 1 Milliner, 4 Tailors, 2 Hairdressers, 3 Shoe makers, 2 Haberdashers, 4 Shopkeepers, 1 Furrier, 1 China warehouse, 1 Watch and clock maker, 3 Physicians, 4 Surgeons, 3 Chemists, 1 Bather, 1 Ladies school, 2 Academies, 1 Drawing master, 1 Music master, 1 French master, 1 Library, 1 Fancy repository, 1 National school, 1 Bath; mechanics' institute, 1 Coach builder, 1 Licensed to let carriages, 1 Licensed to let horses, 1 Dealer in horses.

This list was compiled by Cresy for the reason to highlight the amount of trades people in both ends of the town and to what services they offered residents and visitors alike to maintain a humble service to one and all, and of course ultimately to make a reasonable living from their trades and services in feeding and housing their families, some of which were quite large.
We now have to return to the report with somewhat dismay, as many inconsistencies have been uncovered by the inspectorate as to the bare facts surrounding the squalor that unfortunately existed in the borough, with special emphasis on (yes) the Old Town area:
Tramp lodging houses. The Cinque Port Arms, in All Saints Street, at the back of which is a temporary building, under the charge of Ann Holt, who pays 12 shillings a week for it. There are two rooms, in one of which are eight steddles, (a means of a platform raised off the floor) and on four of them were beds. Men are only allowed to sleep here, who pay for lodging, washing, and cooking, each pay 2 shillings a week.

These premises are very badly drained and the privy cesspool overflowing, indeed to where people had to walk, and in many cases had no foot ware, so these people were walking bare footed most of the time through the filthy waters that constantly drained from this privy.

No. 12, Wellington Court, behind the Kings Head, St Clements. Mrs. Sarah Fuller pays 5s. 6d. Per week and all taxes: she makes up 12 beds, and never allows more than two persons to sleep in each. In this lodging house there is neither a sink, privy, nor a water supply. All refuse is thrown into the middle of a court yard measuring only 10 feet in width; this naturally is not only rotting, smelling, but is home to a family of rats.

The son of Mrs. Fuller was ill in bed and herself had been a victim of cholera.

East-Hill-Passage, All Saints. James Harris makes up 13 beds; he pays 5shillings a week rent and all taxes. One privy serves two houses, and is now full and overflowing. The floor of the room appropriated for these wretched lodgers to sit in during the day, was wet with the filthy water, which drained from the overflowing privy, again the stench was unbearable.

All Saints Street. Edward Paris makes up 24 beds. Here the privy stands upon the highest level, here you descend 13 steps to the living room; in fact the floor of the privy is nearly on a level with the one-pair window of the house in All Saints Street. The drainage proceeds from one platform to another and eventually finds its way into the Street. On hot days the smell was obnoxious.

Back of the Crown Inn, All Saints Street. John Huggett makes up 10 beds; he pays 7 shillings a week rent and all taxes. Here are 15 steps up to the yard, which is level with the chamber floor: No drainage!

Crown Inn yard, All Saints Street. James Huggett makes up 13 beds; the old stable loft had been converted into a sleeping area. The living room is 13 feet square, and in it 15 persons, male and female, were congregated in the middle of the day. In the loft were 12 beds, placed on a temporary floor laid upon the tye beams; the only light was admitted by two squares of glass introduced in the plain roof tiling. Mrs. Huggett's arrangements with the landlord of these premises is, that she does all the cooking, washing, and finding coals and candles for the lodgers, who in return each pay the sum of 2 shillings a week.

East-Bourne Street, All Saints. John Fisher makes up 16 beds and pays 7s. 6d. Per week, as well as all the taxes and rates.

There are in the above lodging houses as many as 100 beds, which on some occasions accommodate more than double that number of persons, the numbers being mainly made up from vagrants that visit them.

A simple suggestion that was included in the report reads as follows:

A building 130 feet in length and 25 feet in breadth, containing altogether 32 squares, could be constructed four stories high, furnished with every requisite for the accommodation of 200 persons for £5000.0s.0p.; the advantages to be derived by thus providing for the tramps cannot and ought not to be too highly valued. The general idea was not to provide good quality accommodation for those on the road, rather than for those that have fallen on hard times and were in desperate need of some temporary accommodation. The building would have been equipped with every modern convenience of the time, along with water on tap and most of all drainage and no overflowing privy's. Ventilation, and room to move about. The sleeping arrangements would have been divided between male and female on different floors, with simple beds and bedding supplied, a clean area in which to sit and talk, and another communal area to eat, not unlike Butlins really but again a clean area. Privy's would have been on block at each level, for both sexes.

But according to other reports I have seen and read, the scheme was never adopted and like many others was just put to one side to gather dust. It is thought that the council of the time just wasn't interested in an establishment as this, even though the council would have been the landlords with a constant revenue coming in especially when it had to cater for so many people that were either vagrants or those that had fallen on hard times and been made homeless for one reason of another, this seems to play a familiar tune throughout time with Hastings!

Returning to the poor state of the drainage in the area, the report clarified that the drainage throughout the Old Town was far from adequate, of poor construction, undersized pipes some of wooden construction and others in iron, which many leaked away into the ground before reaching the discharge point; but the fall was nearly always in the wrong direction and in some cases above the outlets from privy's and sinks as you will read.

Some did discharge directly into the Bourne stream, causing heavy pollution to the water and stank highly, especially even more so when the stream was penned up for long periods of time in hot weather conditions before being flushed, even then most finished up on the beach at low tide.

East-Bourne Street. Footway at the back of the Nelson. In the tan house lived Wenham and his wife, both of whom had been attacked with cholera, and a child with diarrhoea. The husband, wife and child died as a result of their illnesses. Four other families resided in this house, and several were under the medical attendant's hands, but fortunately recovered.

Bosham Square. There are four houses, one of which is occupied by Mr. Grisbrook, a bricklayer, who had recently recovered from an attack of cholera. Upon examination of his house, in which lived eight other persons, it was found to be without any form of proper drainage, a tub was substituted for a privy, without any covers, retained in each room, and only emptied when positively full and overflowing. There was a cesspool in the yard but this too was found to be full and overflowing, and 'no one would admit it was their business to cleanse it.'

Carpenters Passage. All Saints Street. In Mr. Chalfields house the bed was placed against a half brick wall which separated it from the privy.

Two persons that lived in this house died from cholera.

The list of defective properties was endless, the report went on page after page mentioning these sanitation defects.

Another important issue was discovered almost by accident, when fires were lit in grates in some of the closely coupled properties, it was found that due to the fact that some chimneys were much lower than their adjoining properties, and wind turbulence caused the smoke to fall rather than rise and be carried away into the atmosphere.

The end result was that court yards and interiors of properties were filled with smoke, that was trapped from being carried away no matter to how much wind there was; and of course if there were more than one fire in operation at the time, the area became totally smoke logged.

Most properties either singular or communal had a cesspool situated somewhere within their grounds, every property had been examined in detail, and it was found that all these cesspools were full to overflowing, with the water content seeping across the grounds and eventually finding its way into the Bourne stream. Classic remarks were made by the inspector of the foul smells that lingered wherever you went within the confines of the Old Town, he also commented on, wherever you walked you stepped into puddles of filthy water, foul water constantly seeped across footways, something that you couldn't avoid seeing let along smelling; action had to be taken against this dreadful condition, and the council had to act there and then and not in a few years time, people were dying frequently from diseases being picked up from the airborne smell and foul conditions that existed in this densely populated area, children played on the footpaths where they came into contact with this filth, it was the young and the old that were highly susceptible in picking up diseases and not being able to fight them off, as an adult was more capable of doing so.

Yes something had to be done to alleviate these deadly and serious health problems, condition upon condition had now multiplied by its self, mainly due to the fact of neglect not only from the individuals that lived in the effected properties but from positive action from the local authorities.

A separate report was conducted on the area of St Leonards, this too was very heavily criticized, as the sanitation conditions were no better than the area of Hastings main and the Old Town areas, some were even worse, and the most damming items to mention were the discharges of waste directly onto the beach from Warrior Square through to Rock-a-Nore. It was noted that many of the outfalls were undermining the seawall, causing collapsing in several places due to the ever increasing amounts of water and waste being discharged constantly, waiting for a high tide to carry the foul waters away on the tide, invariably, the tide did take the waters away only to bring them ashore again at the far end of the town due to the under currents and the way in which the currents flowed.

In conclusion, the report finished off by adding these recommendations which were made in the report for how the system should be set up to operate successfully. The system would have to incorporate a steam lifting pump, possibly of 3-4 horsepower only. Cesspools would have to have the capacity to store many thousands of gallons of waste-water against high tides and rough seas, for when it would be impossible to discharge the contents into the sea.

A period of about 8 hours in any 24, the system would have to penn back the waters in storage before discharge.

Two favourable sites were given, one being Bulverhythe, and the other being the far Eastern end of town (Rock-a-Nore). These sites would cope well with the extremities of the Borough.

Laid out below is a sample of some of the recommendations made as to the cleaning of the joint Borough of Hastings & St Leonards in 1850.

Being that there are several portions to the town and borough that call for major sanitary improvement and not being possible to lay down a proper system of sewers without the powers contained in the Public Health Act.

Edward Cresy stated, I quote; I most earnestly recommend that the Act should be at once applied to covering the entire town of Hastings & St Leonards, by which the Corporation will be the local Board of Health.

In furtherance thereof, I recommend that the powers be taken for laying down a system of main sewers, to collect all the drainage at the backs of all the houses, throughout the town.

For draining every house by the installation of tubular earthenware pipes, and for the establishing a proper water-closet, basin and sinks, with the means most efficiently to lead off all the sullage and wastewater into the common sewers.

Further recommendations were:-

1) For filling up of all cesspools, and preventing any drains from discharging into the Bourne stream, its tributaries, or any other watercourse, or onto the sands or sea-beach.
2) To adopt strict regulations with regard to the better construction of party walls and buildings that may hereafter be constructed.
3) To prevent any courts or alleys being set out, the width of which shall be considered inefficient for all the purposes of ventilation and cleanliness; and to prevent any being made the receptacles of filth.
4) To pave all courts and maintain their drains in an efficient order.
5) To prevent all interment within chapels and churches, and to provide a cemetery at a convenient distance from the town.
6) To establish one general slaughterhouse for the use of the butchers of the town.
7) To prevent the sands or the beach from being contaminated by the discharge from any sewer, or any other nuisance.

8) To maintain the groins, which protect the town, and maintain the sea-wall and esplanade in good order.
9) To provide some convenient baths for the labouring classes, to where they may bathe at all times without giving offence; and a better class of lodging houses for tramps and vagrants.

The said report herewith is for the pleasure of the council to pursue and ponder the remedies, of which were many.

      I have the honour to be,
       My Lords and Gentlemen,
        Your most obedient,
         Edward Cresy.

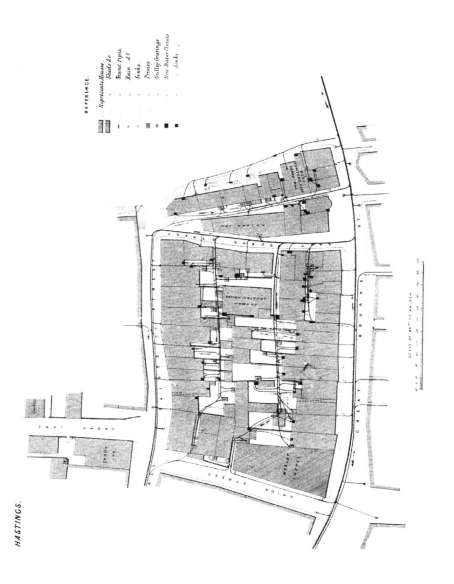

Part of Edward Cresy's proposed new drainage scheme showing the bottom end of All Saints Street only.

The after effects of the report when made public.

The local papers of the time were bombarded with letters of complaints, with various comments made as to what was recommended by Mr. Cresy:

SANITARY CONDITIONS OF THE BOROUGH.

The following copies of documents relative to the sanitary condition of the borough of Hastings, will not fail to interest our readers. Some portions had already been published in our columns; but others have not. We print the whole, in order to give a complete view of the case, and to qualify the articles for a correct record of the sanitary movement in this locality.

>The General Board of Health, Gwydyr House, Whitehall,
>13th November, 1850.

Sir, —- I am directed by the General Board of Health to transmit to you the accompanying copy of statements made to the Board, with reference to the Report of the Superintending Inspector on the borough of Hastings, deposited with you for public inspection pursuant to section 9, of the Public Health Act, 1845.

>I am, Sir, your obedient servant,
>T. Taylor,
>Assistant Secretary.

The Town Clerk, Hastings.

Hastings, 23rd July, 1850.

Sir, —- I am directed by the Commissioners for the improvement of Hastings to transmit to you, for the information of the General Board of Health, the enclosed objections to the Report of Edward Cresy, the Superintendent Inspector appointed by the General Board of Health, to inquire into the sanitary condition of Hastings; and to request the attention of the Board to the same in order that the inaccuracies therein noticed may be inquired into and corrected.

I am further desired to acquaint you that the Commissioners have, at their meeting held yesterday to consider the said Report.

"Resolved, —- that in the opinion of this meeting the application of the Health of Towns Act to the borough of Hastings is desirable, and would be of great advantage to it."

And I am further desired to request that if the General Board of Health should determine to apply the Health of Town Act to Hastings, the Commissioners may be made acquainted with their determination on as early a day as convenient to the Board, in order that I may be placed in communication with the Board before the provisional order be drawn, and be enabled to suggest provisions for insertion in it, which will meet the circumstances in which the Commissioners stand with regard to the rest of the borough.

I have the honour to be, Sir,
Your most obedient servant
(Signed)   John Phillips,
Clerk to Commissioners of Hastings.

Henry Austin, Esq.,
Secretary to the General Board of Health.

Statement made by the Commissioners for the Improvement of Hastings, with respect to matters contained in, or omitted from, the Report of Edward Cresy, Esq., on the sewage, drainage, and supply of water; and the sanitary condition of the inhabitants of Hastings.

In page 22 of his report, Mr. Cresy states that 3,000 cubic yards of broken stone would be required every year to cover the surface of the roads in Hastings; when one third of this quantity would be sufficient, as the whole of the roads do not   require to be fresh coated every year; and indeed, scarcely once in three years.

In page 37 of his report, he states that the number of houses within the borough, and the rates raised for poor and borough rate in the year 1849, as follows, viz:— Houses rated at and under £5 a year, 795; poor's rates, £12,876s.0d; borough rates, £3,468.0s.0d. When in fact there are only 52 houses in the borough at and under £5 a year, and the amount of poor's rates raised for the year 1849-50, was only £3,764.8s. 9d., and for borough rates £1,643.19s.11d.

It would appear that Mr. Cresy must have put down in the case of the poor rates, three years instead of just one; and in the houses rated at and under £5, all the houses rated up to £10; and these errors, added to the description of the drainage of the town, and without any reference to the extraordinary and temporarily over-crowded state of Hastings at the period of his visit, in consequence of the railway works, would make it appear to the General Board of Health that Hastings was a town full of small houses, highly pauperised, and exceedingly unhealthy. Whereas the Commissioners deny his calculations, and the conclusions derived from them; and assert the number of houses at the under £5 a year value, being only 52 out of 2,242, is remarkably small; that the relief for the poor instead of being £1 per head on the population, does not exceed 6s. per head, including establishment charges, which, as well as the rate of mortality, is considerably less than that of England — the deaths in Hastings in the table given by Mr. Cresy being 18.7 per 1000, and that of the Kingdom 22 per 1000.

That the Commissioners cannot place much dependence on Mr. Cresy's calculations, when he makes, in page 54, the interest on £5,000 to be borrowed for additional waterworks £295.16s.8d.; and on £6,000 to be borrowed for sewers (page 56) only £225; and provides no sinking fund for the liquidation of these sums; so that the small rate in the pound for which he states he could supply water and drain the town, must be at least in this respect under-stated.

Nor does it appear to the Commissioners that the quantity of water stated by Mr. Cresy, in pages 29 and 53, "can be procured at a height to enable every inhabitant to receive an abundant supply almost at the top of his house, without the use of engine power," at the sum of £5,000, stated by him.

And with regard to the system of sewerage recommended by him, and the expense of it, the Commissioners are quite unable from their own judgment, or the experience of other places, to form a sufficient opinion upon the efficiency or expense of so novel a scheme.

(Signed)   John Phillips
Clerk to the Commissioners of Hastings.

Sir,— I beg leave to transmit for the information of the General Board of Health, the following resolutions adopted at a meeting of the rated inhabitants of the borough of Hastings, held at the Town Hall, in Hastings, on the 17th instant, for the purpose of considering the Report of Mr. Edward Cresy, the Superintending Inspector appointed by the General Board of Health to inquire into the sanitary condition of the said borough, and the taking of steps as might be considered expedient with reference thereto.

"Resolved,— that it is the opinion of this meeting that the Report of Edward Cresy, Esq., is calculated to do a serious injury to the borough of Hastings, and regrets that gentlemen should have received such incorrect information."

"Resolved, —- that it is nevertheless the opinion of this meeting that the introduction of the Health of Towns Act into Hastings will be attended with great advantages to the borough; and that a committee of the following gentlemen, viz., the Mayor, and Messrs. Alfred Burton, Samuel Bacon, William Chamberlin, Robert Deudney, David H. Gabb, Thomas Hickes, James Mackness, Jammes Mann, Alexander Payne, Stephen Putland, Edward Norwood, James Rock, Thomas Ross, and Horatio N. Williams, be appointed a committee to procure the insertion of such powers in the provisional order as may be found expedient.

Adjourned Special Meeting of Commissioners.

Town Hall on Monday, July 22nd, 1850.

Mr. Bromley in the chair made a statement that on Wednesday, 10th July, it will be remembered that a special committee was appointed to examine Mr. Cresy's Report, and to report thereon at this adjourned meeting.

The clerk therefore commenced the business by reading the following:

(At this point I have decided to edit several pieces, as this only copies to what has already been mentioned prior to this report. We continue further into the Report and now detail other facts that contained massive errors.)

That whilst the committee feel it their duty to make these remarks on Mr. Cresy's statements, they cannot help drawing the attention of the Commissioners to the recommendations contained in his report, and to the benefits which would result to the borough by the application of the Health of Towns Act to it (and which the public meeting of the inhabitants on the 17th instant assented to); the principal of which would be, the centralization of the government of the borough as regards its police, lighting, management of markets, waterworks, and streets, and in fact its comfort and improvement, in the hands of one body instead of four as at present, that body too being a purely elective one; and by which, without going to the expense of fresh acts of parliament for increased powers for various parts of the borough requiring them, the Council may be invested by a mere provisional order of the Board of Health, to be confirmed by parliament, with more efficient powers for forming and regulating the public sewerage of the borough.

For compelling every house to drain into the public sewers, and to have a privy and ash-pit.

For suppressing private as well as public nuisances, and for enforcing sanitary regulations by cleaning houses and places, to prevent contagion and disease.

For regulating common lodging houses.

For paving and keeping in order private streets and places.

For regulating the width and level of all new streets and lanes, thus preventing the narrow and crowded state of many parts of the town from being increased.

For providing public walks and places of recreation, and keeping up and building sea defence walls.

And preventing interment in unfit places dangerous to health.

With extended powers of purchasing land and premises for all public purposes, besides the special clause which might be inserted to secure buildings from fire by party walls, provide a cemetery, and such others as might be required by local circumstances.

The opinion of the Commissioners was that they should not be too expedient to resist the introduction of the Health of Towns Act into the borough, then the committee would recommend that clauses should be inserted in the provisional order for giving powers to the local Board of Health to carry into effect all the recommendations of Mr. Cresy, as far as practicable, except by providing a public lodging house at the expense of the town for vagrants, as suggested by him. The Report also went on to say: That it was recommended to purchase the present gas works, or the construction of others; and also for preventing any house or building being erected without a party wall, if of brick, 9 in., and if of stone, 12 in. thick, up to 9 in. above the roof line. It also recommended that the Local Board of Health was given more powers to oversee the management of all the streets and public lighting and the collection of tolls etc.

The report then followed with a whole lot of facts and figures into the rating system, of which we feel is not totally relevant at this time, as we are looking at to why the Report was flawed in errors, and to how it was said to be damaging to the borough, in the effect that visitors and residents would suffer more if everything was implemented then; plus the fact that Hastings was in no position to take up grants to the value of the proposed recommendations.

Mr. Cresy, thought that this Report he had written was presented in all good faith as to what he had found, nearly all the figure work was his own from research, but he was also given statistics on financial matters from people who should have known as to what they were talking about, but having been given this vital information he either misconstrued, or was given the wrong information from the start. The Report was a catalogue of factual matters in statistics that contained a mass of errors from cover to cover, this was now a job for the Hastings Commissioners to read, study and try and put right to all those errors found.

It was a fact that something had to be done to try and alleviate the state of the living accommodation in the town and to the poor state of the drainage, whether it be surface water or foul. It was obvious that matters could not now be left to fend for themselves, a Bill had to be passed in whatever form.

But knowing to how much the last Bill on 'Local Acts' when passed cost the borough £1,500 to get through parliament, how much would this, a much more complicated Bill cost the town. As the Report was riddled in errors as to the sums needed for the proposed works to remedy the problems, the committee had to think a lot further ahead than once thought, as the final figures for all the works amounted to thousands on pounds above and beyond those quoted by Mr. Cresy, could the town really afford to borrow vast sums of money when their annual income from all the rates and various other sources wouldn't meet the repayment figures. There was not really enough capitol to keep the town running as it was in those days without the burden of extra loans.

The Bill was presented, but a much shorter version, thus giving the town more powers in the Health of Towns Act. It was nearly 20 years on before any real works to the drainage and sewerage started.

What the town needed was someone that could organise and plan to how the town was to be drained properly, and to draw up plans in to thinning out the densely populated areas of Hastings Old Town, and more so to where to house these families once made homeless.

Hastings in 1888 knew that they were completely out of their depth in planning for the future, so the position of Borough Engineer was born.

Mr. Philip Palmer, was appointed to the post and immediately started planning several different methods of thinning out the Old Town. Although drainage and sewerage was top priority, he started to demolish smaller properties, but was very spasmodic as you will read further on.

The Sanitary Struggle.

Our quiet borough is just plunging into a "Sanitary" contest, and for the next three or four weeks we bid fair to be swallowed up in a vortex of public and special meetings, motions, amendments, and legal enactments, *ad infinitum*.

Mr. Cresy's report has tumbled into the borough like a hissing bombshell, spreading confusion and dismay amongst those who were dubbed the other night by the ominous title of "Anti-Health-of-Towns" men, -- a name, moreover, given them by one of "themselves."

An independent comment made by a local newspaper of the time when the Cresy report was published in 1850.

An early view across the Old Town from the West Hill,
prior to the lift being built. Tamerisk steps had just been installed to aid the
workmen getting to the top of the cliff.

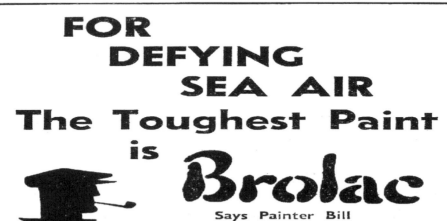

Cresy's report flawed from all sides!

The Cresy report was flawed in many ways as we have listed here, it showed up soon after, that his calculations were just a little out as you will discover.

Additional notes and corrections.

1850. The 'Classical wording' of Cresy's report possibly explains his apparent inability to compute estimates of cost, which bore any practical relationship to the volume of work required. The schemes carried over the 20 years, to comply with his recommendations, cost £51,000. His estimates concerning drainage were equally flawed, being set at £6,000; a major scheme in 1857, cost £18,000., and was found to be completely inadequate, necessitating a further expenditure of an additional £25,000 totalling £43,000., in 1866.

It seems doubtful whether any of these minor municipal schemes ever reached fruition, let alone started at all!

One of the main reasons as to why the drainage scheme cost so much more was, on inspection by Council employee's it was found that many of the pipes that took foul water away were constructed of hollow 'Elm Wood' pipes, (one pipe had tapered ends, which was then pushed into the other to make a seal and connection, found not to be water tight by any standards) very few pipe runs were constructed of clay pipes, and those that were had fractured severely over the years. Cresy, in his ultimate wisdom should have instructed a full drains survey not knowing what was laid underground, his assumption was that everything was constructed of clay pipes, this was just one of his major down falls, no calculations on his part or anyone else's for that matter were ever made for the replacement of the old wooden ones.

Now perhaps you can see the reason as to why the Council weren't able to start the Bourne demolition on a grand scale, all their money was tied up in Cresy's blunderous financial drainage scheme. The drainage scheme for the Old Town was never really thought out from the start, it was a case of start here and see where you finished up, plans of the old drain runs were totally inadequate, whereby, many had never been drawn on plans, so, one problem just led straight into another, and this is to why the expenditure escalated from day to day. All the Council at that time could do was to borrow vast sums of money from the Ministry, and struggle to pay the debt off over the next 30 of so years. From what we read today, the main sewer pipes and domestic connections were never really completed until the late 1950's, so it took 100 years to complete the pipe puzzle! I wonder to how much it has cost the Council from when it all started back in 1850, to the day it was completed sometime in the late 1950's? How many noughts would you like to place behind the initial figures?

Bottom of All Saints Street c1890

Keeping Hastings To The Front.

Taken from an actual letter sent to the newspapers of the time with regard to a persons visit to Hastings.

August 1894

Another instance of the good work of the Hastings & St Leonards Association comes under our notice this week, this time in the form of a entertaining article, entitled 'Happy Hastings,' which has appeared in the *Birmingham News* and several other papers circulating extensively around the Midlands.

In the notice the attractions of our watering-place are set forth in highly interesting fashion, and the publicity thus given to the borough in the thickly populated district of Birmingham cannot fail to confer material benefit on Hastings. We extract the following from the writer's observations:-

" Well what do you think of Hastings?" This was almost the first question that greeted me when I landed on the platform the other day, after a brief, bright sojourn at one of the most favoured spots on the South Coast. My reply was: "Well, all I can say is that it well deserves the designation Happy Hastings."

It is one of the sunniest, one of the healthiest, and one of the prettiest spots a man could wish to stay at. I looked around me on my dull, dreary, drenched surroundings. I had left Hastings bathed in all the beauty of a matchless sunny morning. That lovely ride through Sussex and Kentish hop gardens on my way towards London was a strange contrast to the scenes that had become so familiar to my eyes as typical of the toil and bustle of Midland business and life. The sparkling sea, the lapping waves, the invigorating breezes laden with ozone, the splendid length of promenade—all these pleasant memories of the morning served to intensify the feeling of complete change which had been one of the most notable features of a very pleasant holiday. A more perfect change it is hardly possible to conceive; certainly it is not easy to procure one more readily and more reasonably. The sea front is probably one of the most extended in the kingdom; certainly, it would be difficult to name another with great variety. The extremes of life blend in quaint yet perfect harmony.

The reputation Hastings enjoys as a winter resort has in some quarters been allowed to militate against it as a summer resort. Theoretically that may not seem to be correct; practically it is not so. It has it's warm, sheltered nooks undoubtedly. But it also has it's cool breezy heights. It may be said to have the unique advantages of two atmospheres. On it's upper roads, always within sight, and generally within the sound of the sea, the stronger bracing winds may always be enjoyed, tempered with the bright sunshine for which Hastings has earned a well deserved reputation. In fact, it may be questioned if any other district in the kingdom can show such a record of sunshine.

In illustration, it may be mentioned that for the last six years, for the first three months in the year it averaged considerably more than double the amount recorded in the Botanical Gardens, London. On some days, when there has been but one hours sunshine recorded in London, five, or even six, have been recorded in Hastings. No one who knows anything of the relation of sunshine to health will be surprised to find the death rate standing at so low a figure.

For the quarter just ended it reached only as high as 11.94 per thousand.

Compare these figures with the returns published from time to time of the thirty large towns. To estimate them rightly, too, it must be borne in mind that numbers go to Hastings from all parts of the kingdom as a last battle ground to fight against death. It is also a favourite spot for Convalescent Homes.

Yet with all these draw backs the mortality rate show it to be one of the healthiest districts in the kingdom. For rural beauty and picturesque loveliness the country all round cannot well be surpassed, yet for wild romantic grandeur the cliffs, including the famous Lovers Seat, excite the admiration of all judges of coast scenery. Hastings is a rare combination of the historic past, with a vital, active enterprising present, not forgetting the fishing boats, with that smell of freshly caught fish lingering in the air, also of all the quaint streets and alley ways encrusted in between the hills that nestle on either side, the area is known to the local people as the Old Town of Hastings. No visitor, whatever may be his tastes, need be dull. Not one of the least items in its favour is the fact that it is so easily reached from the great centres of life and business in the Midlands.

This little piece I found whilst researching all the other articles, will add just that little starting light to what might just be a sad story from here onwards!

Plans sanctioned for the demolition of the High Street and All Saints Street.
1894

The Council at that time had not given any consideration to splitting the Bourne, but the High Street and All Saints Street was a completely different solution. This seemed the easy way out, but many a calculation was misunderstood by so many.

Mr. Palmer thought that by clearing one side of the High Street and likewise All Saints Street, there would be less fuss and would be easier to control the situation, but again this was completely wrong in every direction. Far more property would have been lost by entering into this scheme and a whole lot more money would be involved too, as main drainage would have to be re-laid at a considerable cost to the council.

It seems that nothing was taken into immediate consideration as Mr. Palmer was therefore instructed to draw up plans to widen the High Street and All Saints Street, you might have thought that this may have been a reasonable request to demolish those on the lower level of the Street; but you would have been totally wrong! The demolition was to take place on the high pavement side of High Street, this would have resulted in many old building being lost for ever, and the gardens to some of them in Salters Lane and The Croft too.

The Old Town Police Station and Goal and once a Town Hall (now the Old Town Museum) would have been one of the culprits to be removed in the scheme, as the widening started right from the bottom end and finished at the Market Cross.

There would have been some valuable casualties when the demolition started, as the road was to be widened by some 20 or so feet. I can't find in any records as to whether some of the buildings would have been replaced for those lost but placed further back. As far as I can ascertain there would have been no buildings on the left hand side going up the High Street, but the slope would have been landscaped away from the new road formation to form a more gentler slope to join up with the back end of the gardens in the Croft, etc. The plan details all the moves that were originally sanctioned by the Council in 1894, but luckily for all those in the High Street it never got any further than the pen placed to paper!

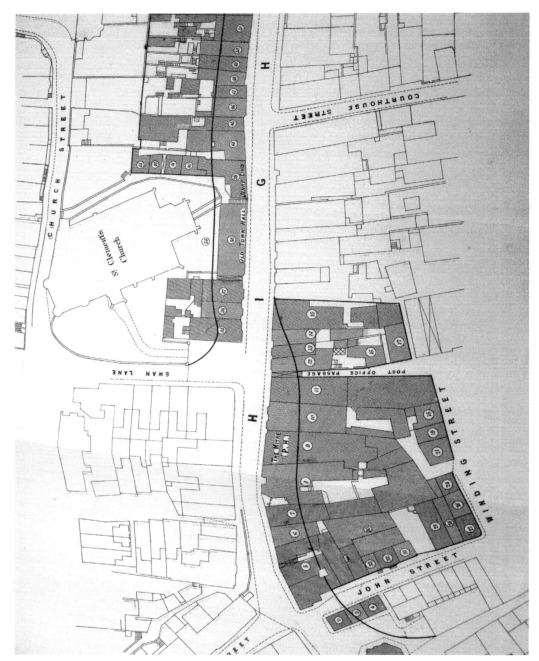

The following plans show to how much property in the High Street would have been lost forever if this demolition had taken place back in 1894.

The thick black line indicates the new line of the proposed road, whilst all heavy grey highlighted areas were for demolition.

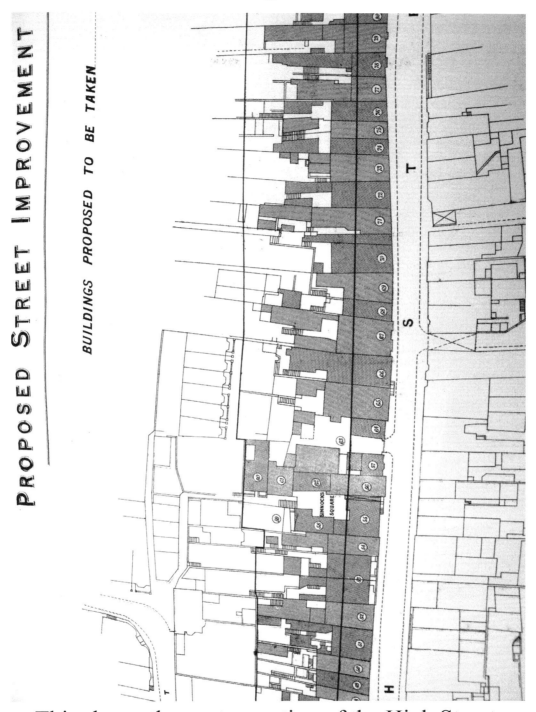

This shows the centre portion of the High Street.
Again, the thick black line shows the new width of the proposed road, and all properties marked in heavy grey were for demolition.

The top end of High Street
The same story repeats itself with the line of the new proposed road indicated by a thick black line through all the properties, and yet once more all areas shaded in dark grey were for demolition.

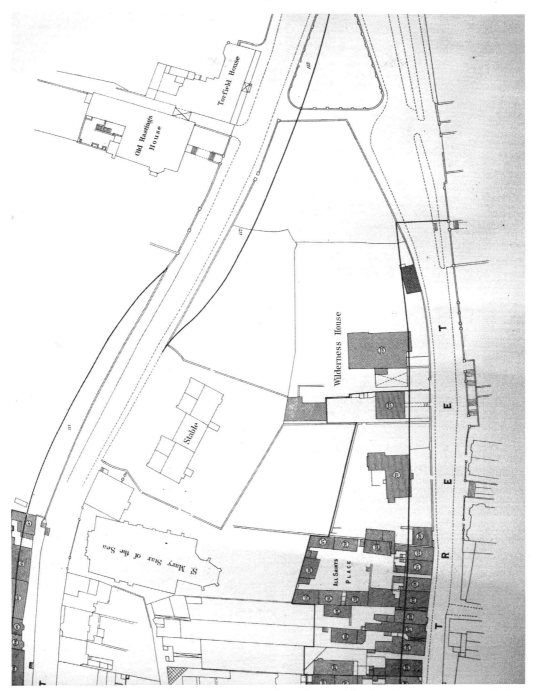

This shows to how not only the High Street would have been widened, but All Saints Street came under scrutiny as well in a road widening scheme.

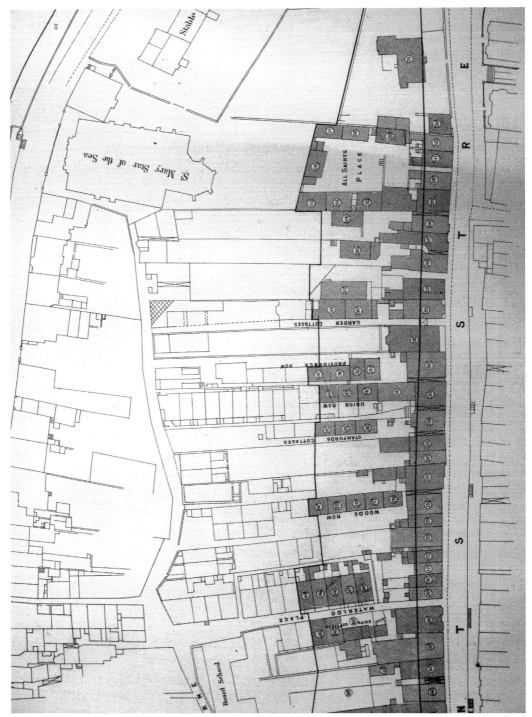

All these properties in All Saints Street coloured in dark grey were destined for demolition.

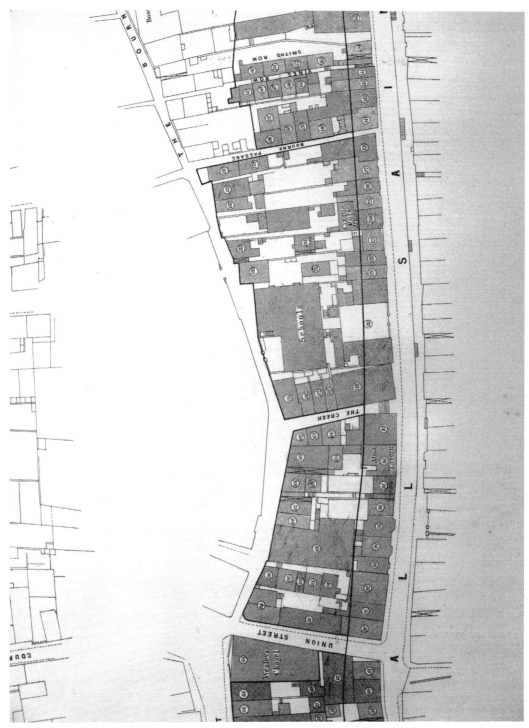

A large chunk of the Bourne was to be cleared
at the same time as All Saints Street.

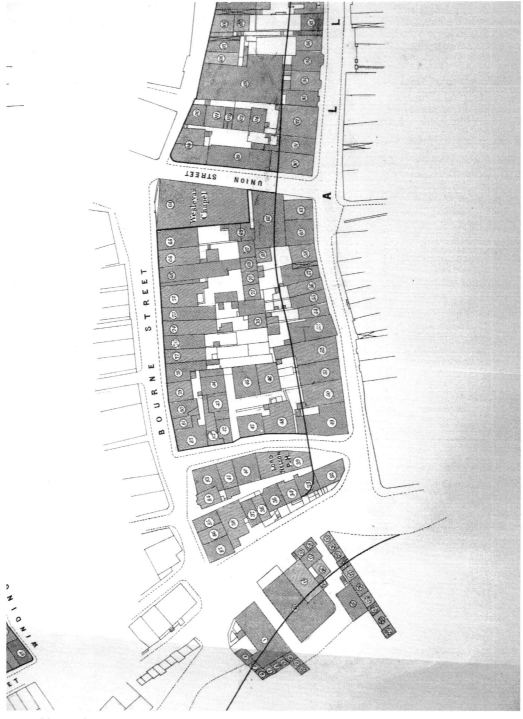

All Saints Street and extensive parts of the Bourne were destined for the big axe in the 1894 plan.

Extension to Clive Vale.
April 1894.

Some of the members of the Hastings Town Council have been amusing themselves by considering schemes for making a new roadway in the Old Town, so as to open up the improving district of Clive Vale and the pretty countryside to the northward of the town. That a new street is very much needed for the old town traffic is evident to the dullest capacity, but we are afraid the Town Councillors will have a difficulty in choosing between the three routes put before them, and a still further difficulty in getting the townspeople to accept, at the present time, any proposal entailing a very considerable burden upon the rates. If a project could be devised which would "pay it's way" in the end very little objection would be encountered from the ratepayers in the central or western wards; the objection would probably spring from those financially interested in the old town disagreeing with the route chosen. There are three routes selected:- (1) through the present High Street. (2) through the Bourne Walk. (3) and *via* All Saints Street.

In each case compensation would have to be given for disturbance, besides the market value of the property; and to whichever route was selected considerable expense would be entailed. In other towns the local authorities, we are informed, manage to carry out street extensions and improvements without entailing much cost upon the general body of ratepayers, but as we understand the new proposals, this is not likely to be the result in this instance.

All the more reason, therefore, for the Town Council taking plenty of time to get the best possible scheme in hand before presenting it for the acceptance of the ratepayers. We may add that no decision as a route, &c, has been arrived at by the municipal authority, which is still engaged in deliberation.

The natural line of street traffic is, of course, through the High Street; and it may be taken for granted that the tradesmen of that route would fight stubbornly against any divergence there from. This is very natural, and must be reckoned with by the promoters of the new project. But if High Street is the natural line it is likely to be the dearest one, for it contains the most valuable property. The Bourne Walk is the easiest route and probably would prove the cheapest project, for the property is mostly of a cottage character.

It would also give the best and widest approach to the new route from the sea end, with a good outlet to the north. All Saints is hardly in the running, and is hardly worth considering. We believe that some attempt has been made to arrive at an approximate estimate of the cost of the various routes; but the figures are hardly sufficiently reliable to be worth giving as an accurate index of the probable cost of any of the rival schemes. We should be very pleased to see a really practical proposal brought forward; but at present we are not in a position to announce the agreeable news.

A Committee Report in the October of 1894 made the following remarks.

The Roads Committee had received from the Borough Surveyor a report on a new sewage system for the Clive Vale district, and having given the matter the fullest and most careful consideration, recommended that the works specified in the Borough Surveyors report be carried out, subject, however, to the new piece of egg-shaped sewer from Winding Street to the Rock-a-Nore sewage tank being increased in size from 4ft. by 2ft. 8in., as proposed in the report and plans, to 4ft. 9in. by 3ft. 2in., that the system of ventilation be open, that the works be divided into two contracts, one for the repair of the Bourne sewer, and the construction of the new sewer at Rock-a-Nore, and the other for the remainder of the work as suggested in the report, and that application be made to the Local Government Board for sanction to the borrowing of the estimated cost of the work at £8,575.

One Councillor made comment to the fact that, it was necessary to put down new sewers in Bourne Walk, Bourne Valley, and Rock-a-Nore to save the main sewerage system from immediate overload. With respect to the Clive Vale estate, they considered it quite necessary to replace the old sewerage in most instances. Another comment to note was made from another Councillor who said that, this was a very serious matter in respect to the drainage of the Clive Vale estate. The estate was only laid out a few years ago, along with a new sewerage system, and now they had to replace it because the Surveyor had reported it to be in a most disgraceful condition. They thought it was not right that the promoters of the estate should have scamped the work in this way, and leave the ratepayers to pick up the ends and have the work done properly. Further comment was made about the sewerage system from the estate at Clive Vale, they were under the impression that when the new estates were laid out, the promoters should put in an adequate system for the drainage of such, and hoped that they had an official to oversee the quality of materials and workmanship. But, it was quick to point out that this was true if only the Council of the time were able to supply such a person, and dictate to the owners of the estate what materials should be used etc., but they were not in any state or condition to carry this out as they were, perhaps, at the present time. It was hoped that in the future that the promoters would properly put their estates in a proper state of drainage, and not having to ask the ratepayers to perpetually put it in repair. One particular Councillor said that, he had something to do with the laying of the drains on the estate. All the drains were laid before he came to the town, and he was under the impression that they were put down in accordance with the regulations as then in existence.

It has now been found that not only are the pipes very much undersized, but also have a vast number of leakages, and they must put them in repair at whatever cost to the ratepayer. Various new roads that had been laid out in the St Leonards area suffered the same faults with the sewerage system as Clive

Vale, whereby, they too were undersized and had many leaks, again all of which had to be rectified at public cost.

It appears that prior to the appointment of a proper Borough Engineer and Surveyor, planning applications were taken very lightly, whereby, rules and regulations were skimped upon or even ignored, as there was no one to follow up the works. This obviously was the path that lead to the poor state of the drainage system being installed throughout the Borough prior to this. But all this was to be at the heavy cost of the poor ratepayers, who ultimately had to finance the extra costs that the town wasn't able to sanction through a loan due to cost of repaying the sum in the period stated. Every project the Town Council took on had to be accurately estimated as good as it could be for sanctions to a loan, and put forward to Government for approval. Drainage wasn't the only project the Council were involved in, sea defence took vast sums of money away from other projects destined as important as this one too. Then came the big one, the road through or round the Bourne to link up with the forever expanding Clive Vale estate, and beyond, how much was this scheme going to set back the Council or should we re-phrase that as the ratepayers.

Leslie Badham's, Winding Street as seen through John Street.
Bottom: backs of houses in All Saints Street.

The problems just won't go away.

The whole idea to do something with the Bourne in respect of both road widening and dealing with the severe sanitation problems as well was quite a problem for the local council, which they had not completely foreseen until the Cresy report was published.

The question of what to do to eliminate or radically reduce the death rates recorded in the Old Town was a top priority, the figures recorded for Hastings & St Leonards were near to average for the whole of the country, but grave doubts were cast over these figures as untrue; many statistics had been laid down on paper but had these figures been altered in any way? As one report conflicted another, so all the council could do was to rely on the figures published by the local coroner as the true ones.

As Clive Vale was up and coming with building taking shape from Ore Village down to the Old Town, something had to be done about access from the seafront to the lower parts of Clive Vale and beyond, as the roads over the West Hill from the central part of Hastings was the main route to take. If trade was to prosper, then a new route through the Old Town had to be found.

The Old Town as it stood was very cramped with highly densely populated properties filling every gap possible. The road structure either side of the Bourne was not suitable for anything other than a pony and trap, and even then two had difficulties in passing each other especially in All Saints Street; the High Street was a little better, but still not up to standard.

The Borough Engineer Mr. H. Palmer was aware of these problems as one counteracted the other, his solution was if we were to reduce the number of properties in the Old Town then the sanitation problem will more or less solve itself! Build a new structure from the Old Town to link up with a more direct route into Clive Vale. This would allow people to move out of the area into a far less crowded environment, but which way would be the best?

The council were fully aware that for every property taken by compulsory purchase in a scheme to reduce the over crowding, would cost them dearly as there would obviously be a lot of protest, but could the council afford the damaging costs involved. As you will have read, there were several schemes to foot, all that would cost the council many thousands of pounds if implicated. Another problem came up before Council, that many of the drains in the Borough were old and needed immediate replacement, this problem didn't just sit within the boundaries of the Old Town they were wide spread all over the Borough, St Leonards probably had the worst drainage problems than Hastings did at that time..........New roads, Drainage, Sanitation, which one has to take priority over the rest, and in which order are these jobs prioritised?

Council sat time after time discussing all the problems that had really escalated since the publication of the Cresy report back in 1850.

As Councils from that era did nothing as such to try and alleviate any of the problems set out in the Cresy report, of course things didn't get any better for the time lapse from 1850 to 1893 when this was again picked up for immediate action.

Some 43 years later it was obvious to all concerned on the council that some form of immediate action for a cleaner sanitation was called for in the town.

Many forms were put forward, some which were to cost the council in excess of what they could legally borrow, and other solutions were just not feasible.

What the town had to do was to balance the books as to what was coming in though the rates and taxes, and to what they could comfortably borrow over a period of about 25 years without getting what one might call today as cash strapped, this was certainly a very tricky problem to overcome; but ultimately, a definite solution had to be found, one that would please everyone, not only the council but the residents of the borough also.

FIRST STEP TOWARDS FULL SCHEME. January 1924.

TENEMENTS PROPOSAL FOR
HARDWICKE ROAD

Town demolition scheme was considered at a meeting of the Housing and Improvements Committee of the Hastings Town Council recently. This part of the scheme provides for the demolition of a block of buildings beginning at the Roebuck Yard and continuing through to All Saints Street. Plans were shown at the meeting, and the Borough Engineer Mr. P. H. Palmer gave a full explanation of the scheme. A new 30 feet wide road will be provided when the buildings are removed, but as understood, it was not intended that this would be used for vehicular traffic. The intention is rather to keep the area as an open space with footwalks for pedestrians.

The Corporation cannot, however, dispossess any of the owners or tenants of the houses until other accommodation can be found to rehouse them all.

The Committee then considered a scheme for the provision of a number of tenement flats, which could be built upon a site at Hardwicke Road, which has just become available to the Council. Before either of the schemes can be started the approval of the Town Council, and the sanction of the Ministry of Health must be obtained. The plans of both schemes have been forwarded to the Ministry of Health, and they are to be presented before the Town Council for consideration at their next meeting. Another scheme, in a very embryonic stage, which the Housing Committee considered, is for the provision of a number of houses on the site adjacent to the proposed new Electricity Station at Broomgrove. It will be remembered that the Council purchased far more land on the Broomgrove site than would be required to build the generating station on, and the tentative scheme is to utilise some of the land to build houses on. In amongst all the houses that were built there, tin town arose from the ground in the form of steel prefabricated houses made from corrugated iron sheets, very nice, but you froze in the winter and cooked in the summer.
A report on tin town is further on.

The impression given out was, that the council thought very little of the original people that made the Old Town what it was, and that the new people coming in would improve the qualities of the Old Town to the Councils delight. Who would of ever envisaged the amount of heavy traffic that would thunder down through the Bourne valley today, would that have made any difference to the planners decision I wonder, if they could have read the future through a crystal ball?

The new Hastings Power Station built on land at Broomgrove purchased by the Council in 1922.

Old Town Improvements.
Feb 1924

The Housing and Improvements Committee reported that with reference to the order made at the meeting of the Council in the May of 1923, on the subject of representations received from the Medical Officer of Health as to certain unhealthy areas in the Old Town, they had before them a report from the Borough Engineer for the proposed clearance of the congested areas known as, Vines Passage area, Cinque Ports area, and the Alma area, from which it appears that considerable difficulties had been met in preparing the report, as the Old Town presented certain special features, some of which were the configuration of the ground on which the Old Town was built, and the scarcity of sites suitable for building purposes within a reasonable distance of the unhealthy areas, and the shape and extent of the area included in the schemes, all which features prevented any adequate scheme of rehousing on the insanitary areas being submitted in detail. The number of families proposed to be displaced in dealing with the three insanitary areas was 76, and the only available site within reasonable distance and which appears to be suitable for rehousing purposes was the partially developed portion of the Halton House Estate abutting on Hardwicke Road. It was proposed to acquire 2.575 acres of that land, and to erect thereon 56 flats in 7 blocks of 4, each two stories in height, such flats to be designed to give varying degrees of accommodation:-
1 living room and 1 bedroom, 1 living room and 2 bedrooms, 1 living room and 3 bedrooms, each flat being provided with a fixed bath.
It was estimated that 18 flats in 3 blocks of two, each 3 stories in height, could be built on the site of the present unhealthy areas together with two shops fronting onto the High Street, each having one flat built over, and the number of families which would therefore be rehoused on the site would be 20.
The proposed 30 foot wide road that was to be constructed to follow the route of the Bourne Passage would connect the High Street with All Saints Street, this roadway was considered to be a lung for the congested areas and do much to immediately improve the amenities of surrounding properties. The building of properties in Hardwicke Road would be completed before any demolition could be made in the unhealthy areas, the area of the site cleared was 5,333 square yards or thereabouts, and the value of the site was estimated at £1,333. 5s. 0d. The Borough Engineer had submitted a revenue account from which it appeared that the estimated net loss on the whole scheme would be £924. 6s. 8d. per annum.
For estimating purposes rents have been assumed as under: 1 sitting room, 1 bedroom, 4s. 6d. per week: 1 sitting room, 2 bedrooms: 5s. 6d. per week: 1 sitting room, 3 bedrooms: 6s. 6d. per week.
The Committee had pointed out that the Ministry of Health had allotted

£500 per annum towards the net loss of the scheme, or alternatively, to contribute 50 per cent of the net loss. The Committee did recommend that the scheme submitted accordingly be adopted, and that an application be made to the Ministry of Health for their approval.

Council made a point that, if there was any delay in the scheme being carried out, the fault would directly be with the Ministry and not with the Council or its Committee. A statement was made in Council that, as there is a new Government in power there would be no trouble in obtaining money for new housing schemes. Houses would have to come first before any pleasure scheme, and thereby making certain that capitol was readily available.

An important question was raised as to why this scheme was talked about some 35 years previously and nothing was ever done, in a reply, it was said that, when plans were first prepared and presented to the public, the people within the Old Town refused to move and there was nothing in power that could be done at that time to force people out of their properties, plus the fact that we, the Council had no where in which to rehouse them, money just wasn't readily available then as it is today, besides we weren't in a position to take a loan and pay it back in time prescribed.

The motion to build was duly carried, and just awaited a decision from the Ministry as to whether the grant was successful. But as we all know it was, and Hardwicke Road flats were raised from the ground and still stand there today as a monument to all those that were rehoused there from the Old Town between the years of 1924 and 1925.

Waterloo Place

Hollington Housing Site

1924

The Housing and Improvement Committee reported that the Borough Engineer had supplied them with details of the development of the Old Church Road Housing Site at Hollington.

It is proposed to erect 106 dwellings on the site, consisting of the following: 10 Parlour type houses, containing scullery, living room, parlour, 3 bedrooms, bathroom and W.C.; 52 non-parlour type houses containing scullery, living room, 3 bedrooms, bathroom and W.C.; and 44 two storey flats, containing scullery with fixed bath, living room, two bedrooms and W.C.; The cost of developing the site was estimated:- Erection of 62 houses and 44 flats, £51,199.; construction of roads and sewers; £7,248.

The Committee recommended that application be made to the Minister of Health to borrow the estimated cost and that tenders be invited for the work required to develop the estate. -- The report was duly adopted.

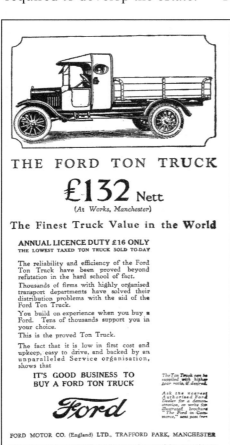

CLEARING THE OLD TOWN

----------:O:----------

MINISTRY OF HEALTH ENQUIRY--STRONG OPPOSITION FROM OWNERS.
"POKY" ROOMS AND BAD SANITATION STRIKING TUBERCULOSIS FIGURES.

1925

Strenuous opposition was forthcoming to the proposed scheme for clearing the Cinque Ports Area, Alma Area and Vine's Passage, at the Ministry of Health inquiry, which was held at the Town Hall on Tuesday. Mr. H. A. Chapman, F. R. I. B. A., conducted the enquiry, which lasted over four hours. There was a fair attendance of the general public.

Mr. Harold Glenister appeared for Mr. Lamb, 3 Bourne-passage, Mrs. Oliver, 6 Bourne Passage, and Mr. Henham, 28, High Street (Roebuck-Yard).

Mr. Percy Idle appeared on behalf of Mrs. Verrell's, Mr. Beney and Mr. White, occupying owners; Mr. C. W. Buckwell represented the Ancient Order of Foresters, 2, Bourne Walk. Mr. John Flowers, barrister, instructed by Messrs. Chalinder Herington and Pearch, appeared for the Hastings Cottage Improvement Society, whose property was 89, 93 and 94, All Saints Street, 1-5 Amphion Place, and 7, Bourne Passage. He also appeared for the executors of the late Mr. Stephen Starr, owners of 3, Bourne Walk. Mr. F. W. Morgan appeared for the owners of 50 and 12, Bourne Walk, 52 and 52a, Bourne Passage, and 7 and 8, The Creek. Major C. W. Buckwell appeared for the owners of 4, Bourne Walk.

Mr. J. B. Kelly appeared for the Town Clerk, and expressed regret that owing to absence in London the Town Clerk was unable to be present. The origin of the present application, said Mr. Kelly, was that the area concerned had been declared insanitary. For many years the housing conditions in the Old Town, mainly on account of the congestion and worn-out character of numbers of houses, had been a matter of anxious consideration to the Corporation.

The scheme affected 64 houses and 265 inhabitants. The cost of carrying out the scheme was estimated to be £33, 000. The main faults of the houses in the Old Town were overcrowding and congestion of buildings, lack of space in front and rear, with limited yards, bad lighting and ventilation, houses almost back to back, absence of water in houses, sinks, absence of washing accommodation and the scarcity of water closets. Many of the houses were worn out and the rooms small and pokey. Infantile mortality was more than double that of the remainder of the town as a whole, but the death rate of adults was not strikingly high.

No tenant would be disturbed until the Council were in a position to offer the tenant another house, provided at rents which the tenants could pay. Buildings included in the condemned area numbered 67, of which 62 were dwelling houses. There were 89.8 buildings per acre and 83.1 dwellings per acre.

The Old Town before it was touched.

The population per acre was 325.8. But for economic conditions many of the houses would have been condemned long ago. The fact that houses were still tenanted, and thereby profitable to the owners by reason of national misfortune gave the owners no new right neither did it give righteousness to their indignation. Dr. G. R. Bruce, Medical Officer of Health, said he had held a similar appointment at Willesden and at Jarrow, the former being partly an industrial area and the latter wholly industrials. He had visited every house in the condemned area, and examined houses externally and internally in the area it was proposed to clear. He made a representation to the Council that the area was unhealthy within the meaning of the Housing Act.

The main consideration which caused him to come to that conclusion was that from maps shown him when he arrived and from his own survey he formed the opinion that this area should be cleared. The witness gave particulars relating to the various properties, and added that the conditions which obtained in the area came under the claws of the Housing Act relaying to unhealthy areas. He regarded the congestion as very bad. There was no other way of dealing with the property other than under the Act.

Cross-examined by Mr. John Flowers –The premises in All Saints Street were in the congested area, but he agreed that if they did remove the other houses the All Saints Street houses would no longer be congested. He was not aware that Nos. 93 and 94 were bought in 1884 by the Hastings Cottage Improvement Society for £500, and that they were rebuilt in 1885.

One house in All Saints Street had not sufficient food storage. The "shells" were all right, but they were in rather a dilapidated condition.

A notice was served upon the owners recently to put the premises in repair. All the houses were brick built, and No. 89 consisted of a shop with a fairly large apartment house above, the rateable value being £70. The lavatory accommodation was inadequate. There were six tenants on three floors in the house, and there were seven tenants there when he first visited the premises. There was no water laid on indoors, and there was no proper cooking accommodation on the top floor. The yards at the back of the premises varied from 18ft. to 28ft. depth. His objection to Amphion Place and the Bourne Walk houses that they were in a very congested area.

By Mr. Buckwell-Nos. 2, Bourne Walk, was a clean house, main drained, and in front of the house was an open space. Across the road there was a brewery, which was a low building. On the south side of 2, Bourne Walk, was an engine shed, or cold storage, but that was equivalent of the size of a house. The house was three stories, but one was uninhabitable. He agreed that above the ground floor there was an open air space. On three sides the house was well built, and on the other side was a partition. There was a scullery on the ground floor. A fault with the house was that there was not sufficient air space at the back. The two rooms on the top floor were attics, and were built in the roof. They did not comply with the bylaws. On the first floor there was damp

Bourne Walk c 1920.

on the walls and ceiling. The kitchen on the ground floor was dark, and had no proper food cupboards.

The front parlour was all right, but it was dark. The size of every window in the house complied with the bylaws. The birth rate in the condemned area was bigger than average over the whole town.

The rate was 18.1 per thousand. There had been 45 births in ten years, and 37 deaths in the same period. The whole of Hastings death rate was 15.7 per thousand over ten years, and 14 per thousand for this condemned area.

The rate was uncorrected for age and sex. The children would go to All Saints Street School, but he would not say if it was a fact that in twenty years the school had never been closed.

By Mr. Kelly-To the east of 2, Bourne Walk, was an engine shed which was used for traction engines, and there were complaints of smoke.

Mr. Morgan cross-examined Dr. Bruce regarding 50 and 12, Bourne Walk, 52 and 52a, Bourne Passage, and 7 and 8, The Creek.   Replying to questions Dr. Bruce said he could give figures showing that there was more illness from tuberculosis in the area. The incidence was 4 per thousand as against 1.8 per thousand notified in other parts of the town. No. 50, Bourne Walk was in good condition but it was in a congested area. The house was comparatively modern. No. 12, Bourne Walk, was used partly as a store and the house was in fair condition. Nos. 52 and 52a, Bourne Passage, was small, pokey rooms, especially the kitchen used as a sitting room. In 52 there was a lack of light, air and ventilation. One bedroom was only 4½ft. by 8ft. In 52a there was a little more light than in 52. Nos. 7 and 8, The Creek, were two extremely small houses, suitable to accommodate small families. No statutory notices, so far as witness was aware, had been served on owners in the last ten years.

By Mr. Kelly-Nos. 7 and 8, The Creek, were shut in at the back by a school and at the front by a wall 12ft. high. The three rooms together in one of the houses would make about the size of the best room in a Council house.

Mr. Morgan asked for 50, Bourne Walk, to be excluded from the scheme, and for 52a, and 7 and 8, The Creek, to be coloured blue on the plan (for compensation).

By Mr. Glenister-3 and 6, Bourne Passage, and 28, High Street, were property close together. If the rag stores and warehouse, and 52 and 52a, were removed there would be considerable space, but he was considering the area as a whole. He did not admit the properties were up to the average working class house. There had been no illness in 3, Bourne Passage, for many years.

The accommodation was four rooms, small sized and pokey. It was in a moderate state of repair. He was not aware that the ages of the tenant's ancestors who had lived in the Old Town ran to 74, 84 and 94.

No. 6, Bourne Passage, was a four-roomed house.

No illness had been reported in the house and there was good drainage. At No. 28, High-street, were livery stables and there was a considerable space in front of it. It was in a fair state of repair but there was dampness in the ceiling. Mr. Glenister-Yes, perhaps a tile had blown off.

Mr. Idle questioned the witness with regard to 26, High Street, 110, All Saints Street, and Mrs. Verrell's property, consisting of marine stores and various buildings. No. 26, High Street, Dr. Bruce stated, that it was owned by Mr. Beney, who carried on a greengrocers business. The ventilation was very bad and there were other defects. One bedroom was unfit owing to the small window. Only three people lived in the house. It was similar to other houses in the High Street. The kitchen was large and the two main bedrooms were fairly large. Sanitary arrangements were in order.

Mr. White's house, 110, All Saints Street, was an oak-beamed house and he did not say anything against it except that it was in the area in question.

He dealt with Mrs. Verrell's yard by itself, but there were possibilities of danger to health from it. The place was insanitary, and it smelt.

The condition had existed for some years. There was no record of there having been any notice of nuisance served on the owners. The buildings were dilapidated, though he agreed no one lived in them. The general condition of the yard and buildings was unsatisfactory. Seventeen people used one lavatory, the houses being overcrowded. He was aware that the assessments of the properties were recently increased but that was because the assessment of the whole town was recently increased.

Major C. W. Buckwell, for the owners of 4, Bourne Walk, put some questions to the witness. The width of Bourne Walk at that spot was 15ft. to 18ft., there was a brewery opposite with buildings 15ft. high. No. 4a. was built against the back of No. 4. the w.c. was not ventilated, inside the house there was no washhouse, the attic was damp, the kitchen was dark and small, being only 6ft. 6ins. high. There was no sink and no pantry and the passage was very narrow.

Mr. Buckwell asked for the property to be marked blue.

Mr. Howell appeared for the owners of 15, Bourne Walk and two cottages at the back known as Fisher's Cottages. In Fisher's Cottages, said Dr. Bruce, replying to questions, there was no though ventilation, the houses were back to back, no pantry, the rooms were small and pokey. He had been informed that there had been infectious diseases in one of the cottages. He was not surprised to know that occupants of the properties lived to great ages. He was informed that in 5, Fisher's Cottages, there had been a good deal of illness, including typhoid and scarlet fever. Mr. Watson, representing the Western Counties and Southern Counties Evangelisation Trust, asked that a mission room in Bourne Walk on the plan should be marked blue.

Mr. Beney asked about 4a, Bourne Walk, and was told that the house was congested and jumbled up. Mr. Beney-Well that property is 13 per cent. of my living. I want £100 for it.

The Inspector replied, Oh very well, you shall have it coloured blue, Mr. Beney.

The Creek

Mr. Ben Meadows suggested that the doctor should have considered the state of the air in the Council Chamber.

Mr. Flowers, addressing the inspector, suggested the evidence of Dr. Bruce did not show there had been any detriment to health through this area; on the other hand the death rate had been less.

No evidence had been given to show that any of the premises were not perfectly fit for habitation.

He could not see why the premises in All Saints Street should be included in the scheme.

The rebuilding of Nos. 93 and 94, All Saints Street cost £900 when the Hastings Cottage Improvement Society bought them 1884.

Mr. Morgan said the properties did meet the demand for that type of house in which people were forced to live because they could not afford the rents fixed by the Council for their houses.

Henry George Vine, 46, High Street, builder, Chairman of the Hastings Cottage Improvement Society, said 93 and 94, All Saints Street, were bought in 1884 for £550 and the following year were rebuilt at a cost of £923.

The houses were occupied by six tenants. No. 89, All Saints Street was entirely rebuilt in 1884. The total rentals from all properties, including Amphion Place, amounted to about £73.

By Mr. Kelly-The object of the Society was to provide healthy and comfortable dwellings for the working classes. The Society endeavoured to do so and so far as he was aware they achieved their object. He did not see anything wrong with Amphion Place. The houses were not insanitary, the premises were not back to back. It was not true that considerable pressure had been brought to bear upon the Society to do repairs. Recent repairs had been done at 89, All Saints Street.

Percy Hunter Oxley, architect and surveyor, Havelock Road, said he inspected the properties on May 31st. Nos. 93 and 94, All Saints Street were substantially built, and were sound. The premises had yards 18ft. and 28ft. in depth respectively. They were perfectly good dwellings in good repair.

The same remarks applied to 89, All Saints Street, the Amphion Place dwellings were fit for habitation.

Mr. Kelly-Dr. Bruce's report says: No yard, no air space, dark, full of bugs. You have heard what the last witness says about the object of the Society. What do you think of it? I think they are quite fit for habitation.

Continuing witness said there were six tenants in 89, All Saints Street, and only two lavatories, but he considered that sufficient.

There were no pantries in the house. The yard space of 18ft. for a three-storey house was sufficient.

Mr. Ben Meadows spoke upon 107, All Saints Street, and said the yard, part of which it was suggested came within the area was not a common yard.

Mr. Buckwell, dealing with 2, Bourne Walk, said he did shut his eyes to the fact that surrounding properties would be taken apparently without opposition, and in order to make the scheme a success they must have 2, Bourne Walk. That the owners, were the foresters, working men who would suffer much injury by the loss of their house. He asked that the property should be coloured blue for compensation. How could they say, when the health statistics of the borough showed that the district compared favourably with the rest of Hastings, that the district was insanitary?

William John Stone said the Foresters owned the house. The two top rooms of the house were not let, and only three persons lived in the house.

By Mr. Kelly-There was sufficient air space in the house.

Harold Burleigh, London Road, St Leonards, architect, said from a sanitary point of view the premises were entirely satisfactory. The ground floor front room was well lighted and the back door was also well lighted, but not so much as the front room. The place was 'superlatively clean.'

By Mr. Kelly-The rooms were quite large enough. On the first floor they were 10ft. by 10ft. and 9ft. by 7ft. The sizes were not prejudicial to health.

Mr. Harold Glenister said the Old Town had brought up a race of very healthy people going back hundreds of years. As a matter of expediency it was necessary that a large number of people should live close together. Let the Corporation build houses and see if the people living in the Old Town would go to them: these people chose to live there as they had always done.

Harry Lamb, replying to Mr. Glenister, said, his family had attained to long life. He was a fishmonger and stabled his horses in Mr. Henham's stables. The family had enjoyed good health, and witness had never had a doctor in his life. He bought the house out of prize money he got after minesweeping during the war.

By Mr. Kelly-Everyone in the Old Town was not as healthy as the witness.

Mr. Idle said the Council sought to say that the site was such that the property upon it could be of no value, and that they should therefore pay only for the site. No one could suggest that the properties on this land were absolutely of no value. With regard to Mrs. Verrell's property, it was a very big business which employed regularly 18 persons. The husband and son of the owner were also engaged in the business, and there were also 20 to 30 persons casually employed by reason of the fact that through the business they were able to dispose of goods they collected. To seek to get rid of that business was iniquitous.

Major Buckwell dealt with the property at 4, Bourne Walk.

Mr. Kelly, replying to the opposition, said if they talked until Sunday it would not bring another ray of sun in to this area. It had been found that of 249 persons in the area 28 persons only worked in the Old Town.

The Inspector, in closing the enquiry, said he would make his inspection of the property on the following morning.

Leslie Badham's, Bourne Passage looking westwards.

Leslie Badham's, A glimpse through Bourne Walk.

Leslie Badham's, The East Side of Bourne Street.
Bottom: Part of Bourne Walk.

Slum clearance
Scheme approved by the Ministry
Clearing an Insanitary Area.
1925

The town clerk has received notification of the approval of the Ministry of Health to the scheme for the clearing of a portion of the slum area in the Old Town.

The area includes Vine's Passage and the Cinque Ports and Alma areas, and the whole of the existing property on the site is to be demolished. Seventy-six families will be displaced and when the rebuilding of the area is completed there will be accommodation only for twenty families.

Before any property is pulled down, a new block of flats will be built in Hardwicke Road. There will be 56 flats altogether and they will be occupied by people displaced under the clearance scheme. A new road, 30ft wide will be laid out following the present line of Bourne Passage connecting All Saints Street and High Street.

Steel Houses

The sub-Housing committee appointed to consider the matter of the provision by the Council of steel houses report that they have received an invitation from the makers of the houses, Messrs Braithwaite & Co. to inspect two houses, which they have constructed at West Bromwich, and the company have informed the Borough Engineer that a number of Local authorities are sending delegates to inspect the houses. The sub-committee have deputed their chairman (Alderman Cox) their Vice chairman (Councillor Paulson) and the Borough Engineer to visit West Bromwich for the purpose of inspecting the houses on Monday next and recommending that payment of their expenses in accordance with Standing Order No.35 be sanctioned under Instructions to Committee No.13.

Alderman Cox said there was a very real shortage of houses. They had a communication from a firm erecting steel houses, two of which had been built at Birmingham. They could be put up in 14 days. He moved the adoption. The price was £425 complete with foundations, or £390 without foundations.

Councillor Paulson seconded. What they could provide at a rent working people could pay. When people were obliged to sub-let in order to pay their rent it only created fresh slums.

Councillor Burr said he had attended the previous night a meeting of the Building Trades Operatives. One man told him that the only advantage of steel houses was that if you lost the key and had a tin opener you could get in easier. There was no steel in these houses. Lord Weir's houses were doomed, but these were only imitations. The deputation would have a nice little joyride for no earthly good.

The steel houses were sure to be a failure. Lord Weir had said they had yet no means of stopping rust.

Councillor Payne said there was a chance of getting a £200 subsidy on all these houses. What was hindering the demolishing of houses was the time it took to put up brick ones. He proposed to accompany the deputation at his own expense. The Public Health Committee knew they must have houses quickly and cheaply. It would be well worth the expenditure if only to get people out of their rookeries until more substantial houses were available.

The Mayor said Councillor Burr ought not to call this a joy ride. Councillor Paulson would go not because he wanted to but for a sense of duty. They had been told that the houses were rust-proof; but Councillor Paulson would go to satisfy himself of that.

Alderman Smith said the house might look remarkably nice, but he was afraid they would not get many tenants for them. Until they had an opinion from a tenant he hoped none would be erected in this borough.

Alderman Chesterfield said he thought it was a valuable suggestion that the deputation should go to view the houses. Deeds and not words were needed. The houses could be built in three weeks instead of nine months.

Alderman Dighton asked if Councillor Burr know of any Building Society that would not advance money on a steel house? Councillor Burr stated I'm not a director of one of these societies.

Alderman Cox said the houses were all steel with asbestos interiors.

What was proposed was to see them and perhaps erect three or four as an experiment. They were to have a life of sixty years.

The report was adopted.

Purchase of Steel Houses

The Housing and Improvements Committee reported that their Chairman and Vice Chairman and the Borough Engineer visited West Bromwich to inspect steel houses and in their report consider the houses quite suitable for erection in the borough. The committee thereupon instructed the Borough Engineer to interview Messrs' Braithwaite and Co with reference to certain details in connection with the method of construction and the ministry of Health on the subject of the granting of loans and subsides for such houses, and they had now been informed by the borough engineer that Messrs' Braithwaite and Co. were prepared to erect eight houses within eight weeks of the date of the order to commence the work, and that the cost, including the provision of bay windows to the two rooms on the ground floor would be £850 per pair of houses, which sum did not include the cost of construction of the concrete foundations and that the houses would have the following accommodation: Living room, scullery, bath room, larder, coal store and w.c. and 3 bedrooms. The committee recommended that eight houses be purchased and erected by Messrs Braithwaite and Co., at a cost of £3,400 – that four of the houses be erected on a portion of the Eversley Road Housing site abutting upon Beaufort Road to be constructed with tiled roofs – and that the remaining four houses be erected on portion of the land at the Broomgroove Estate not required for electricity purposes – that the Borough Engineer be instructed to prepare and lay the concrete foundations for the eight houses at an estimated cost of £320, and that application be made to the Ministry of Health for sanction to the borrowing of the total cost of the houses, £3,720 and for the appropriate subsidy under the Housing, etc. acts in respect of the erection of the houses.

Alderman Cox moved the adoption and said the deputation was considerably impressed by the houses and all the reports of the members of the deputation were satisfactory, except in one or two details. The houses would be superior to anything the Council were building today. When they knew that £1,300 had been spent in two years in keeping the existing Council houses in repair they realised what the upkeep was. The cost of upkeep of the steel houses was 70 per cent less.

Councillor Paulson seconded, and said he was agreeably surprised to find such commodious and well built houses. The steel used, he was informed, was practically rust less and a bitumen solution was used to keep all the damp away from the steel. A novel contrivance was used to heat the houses, by means of pipes which went through the whole building. The houses would last for 100 years or more. Eight men could put up a house in a fortnight and the house was dry and ready for occupation the moment the workmen finished.

Councillor Blackman hoped that the Borough Engineer would make quite certain of the restlessness of the steel.

Councillor Walters asked for four of the houses to be put up at the Bulverhythe end of the borough, where there was a great need of housing accommodation. He moved that in addition to the eight houses mentioned in the report, four more houses be erected at Bulverhythe and a suitable site. Councillor Breeds seconded.

Alderman Collins said the Council owned no land at Bulverhythe suitable for the purpose.

Councillor Burr said the manufacturers of the houses would not give them a longer life than 60 years. If men had been on making concrete blocks they could have had concrete houses just as quickly as the steel houses.

Councillor Breeds said sea air would affect anything that was why he wanted one of the houses to be put up at Bulverhythe as an experiment.

The Borough Engineer said the houses looked good and sound. There was practically no risk of deterioration from rust.

Replying to councillor Henbrey, the Borough Engineer said the steel houses would not be affected by lightning. They would be perfectly safe. Councillor Miss Lile hoped the eight houses would grow into eighty, if not eight hundred. Alderman Cox said the houses were not "Lord Weir" type of houses.

The amendment was lost and the report adopted.

The old Dymond Inn at the corner of Roebuck Street.

Roebuck Street at a much later date.

ASSISTANCE FOR ERECTION OF HOUSES.

The Housing and Improvements Committee had received applications for financial assistance in connection with the erection of eight houses, five bungalows, etc. under the scheme adopted by the Council, and recommended that £75 be paid to the owners upon completion of each of the premises, subject to their being commenced before June 30th and completed before December 31st next. – Adopted.

FIFTY STEEL HOUSES

The Improvements Committee reported that they had been informed by the Borough Engineer that he estimated the cost of constructing the roads and sewers at the land at the Broomgrove Estate proposed to be utilised for the purposes, when fully developed of a housing site for 96 houses at £4,530 and £2,300 respectively. The Committee had before them a letter from Braithwaite and Co, Engineers Ltd. Stating that they were prepared to supply and erect on foundations to be provided by the Corporation, 50 standard non-parlour type houses of steel construction, each house consisting of a living room, scullery, larder, bathroom, w.c, coal store and three bedrooms, at the sum of £24,337. 10s., and pointing out that the price included a Workwell range, bath, sink, a 40 gallon galvanised iron tank and high pressure ball cock, with necessary connections fixed in the roof, seven electric light points and two electric light plug points for cooker and kettle to each house, internal door to living room, hot water supply and bay window. The committee recommended: (1) That land acquired for the purposes of the electricity undertaking and not required for such purposes be laid out as a housing site in accordance with the plans now submitted. (2) That the roads and sewers be constructed in accordance with plans submitted by the Borough Engineer. (3) That the Borough Engineer be instructed to carry out in due course the construction of the foundations for the erection of 50 houses, and the necessary footpaths, fencing, gates, etc., at an estimated cost of £2,563. (4) That the quotation of Braithwaite and Co., Engineers Ltd., for the supply and erection of 50 steel houses, as above mentioned, for the sum of £24,337 10s., be accepted and that the Seal be affixed to the necessary formal contract with the company.
(5) That application be made to the Ministry of Health for sanction to the borrowing of the following sums: for the construction of road and sewers, £6,830; for the construction of foundations, footpath, fencing, gates, etc., £2,565; for the supply and erection of 50 steel houses, £24,338; total £33,733. Alderman adoption and Councillor Payne seconded, and the report was approved without comment.

Traffic in the Old Town

Councillor Burr moved, that owing to the congested and dangerous state of the roads in the Old Town, consequent upon the large and increasing volume of motor vehicular traffic using these roads, a Committee of ten members be appointed to consider the desirability of carrying out the plans already prepared for the construction of a new road through the Old Town, to prepare an estimate of the cost thereof with a view to the work being put in hand at an early date and to report to this Council at their meeting on the 31st July 1925. The Improvements Committee, had so much in hand that they could not take on the extra work entailed. In ten days there had been eight minor accidents in the High Street alone. Fifty-two years ago a scheme for the improvement of the Old Town was got out, but it was turned down. Again, 31 years ago a scheme was turned down. There were now two schemes of improvement in the Old Town in existence. The time had arrived when they should have an adequate road to take the traffic, and he thought the new Committee could work in connection with the clearance scheme.

It was stated that there was an enormous amount of motor traffic coming into the town and a lot depended on the first impression people formed of the town. Alderman Cox said Councillor Burr's motion, if carried, would speed up the matter generally. Councillor Burr, however, was trying to do in two months what the Council had been trying to do for 54 years. He moved an amendment that the report of the special Committee should be made at the earliest possible moment; it was impossible to do it in two months.

Councillor Payne said he could not get the Chairman of the Improvements Committee to move in the matter.

Councillor Morgan said there were more important matters than the widening of the High street. The water supply was most important and the Council ought to know what they had to spend on the water before they embarked upon this matter. The motion was carried.

High Street Traffic

The Town Clerk was asked the Town Clerk "Did you receive a communication some time ago from a group of interested ratepayers, in which it was suggested as a partial solution of the congestion of traffic in the Old Town that vehicles should be compelled to go up the High Street and down All Saints Street? That no up and down traffic should be allowed in these two streets? And if you received such a communication what has been done in the matter?" The town clerk replied "Yes," it was intended to lay the communication before the Transport Committee before their vacation, but it was found impossible to call a meeting. I am informed by the Mayor that he proposed to call this Committee within the next ten days and the communication will then be considered.

Houses at Halton
1925

The Housing and Improvement Committee recommended that the tender of Messrs. Simms, Son & Cooke of Nottingham at £21, 279 be accepted for the construction of the seven blocks of flats on the Halton House Estate, Hardwicke Road. The Council stated that the accepted tender was at a considerably lower figure than that originally estimated by the previous Borough Engineer Mr. Whitaker.

It was understood that a consideration as to a time limit was to be imposed before the tender was accepted. The amount of time taken with the Hollington houses was in excess of that fixed by the tender, and many of the houses were still unfinished. Council said that, the contractor was prepared to pay a higher rate of wage, in order to recruit more men. It appeared to have been the case in the past that the highest bidder got the men. Another builder had gone to the Hollington site and offered the men working there another 3d. per hour more than they were getting above the Union rates. The contractors were determined not to lose their reputation as builders, and were now offering London rates of pay. The local Trades Union rate had always been paid and accepted. The contractors for the Halton houses were prepared to carry out the work in the time specified in the contract.

Broomgrove Housing Site.

The Housing and Improvement Committee reported that the receipts from the Borough Engineer of a layout of the land at Broomgrove and recommended that it be approved, and further, that a quotation be obtained for the erection of fifty steel houses by Messrs. Braithwaite and Co. to be submitted to the Council in due course. There was a keen demand for houses in the district. The land really belonged to the Electricity Committee but, in passing the report, would only get quotations as to the cost of erecting the steel houses.

A letter received from the Allotments Association was read out urging the Council to allow any diminution in the land available at Broomgrove for gardens, or if the land was required to provide suitable land elsewhere.

The housing conditions for the poor in Hastings was appalling to say the least, if it were not for the difficulty of building with bricks and mortar, we would not have steel houses at all, but the conditions were such that the steel houses must be erected. The Electricity Committee were paying the interest and sinking fund charges on the loan for the purchase of the land, and we would like the Improvements Committee to take over complete control of the situation. The Council were told that, they must build these steel houses if they were to deal with the huge demand from applicants for houses who came before the Selection Committee. In addition to the Broomgrove site, the Housing and Improvements Committee had a site which would shortly

MASTINS

FOR
HEAVY WINTER CURTAINS

GREAT OFFER OF FADELESS
CURTAIN VELOUR

Very Heavy Pile and Rich Appearance. Width 47 ins.

- RICH COLOURS
- DRAPES PERFECTLY
- HEAVY QUALITY

FADELESS VELOUR FOR CURTAINS

A new width in Curtain Velour for modern homes. Casements do not usually require full width material. Here you can save considerably on account of the narrower width, and yet maintain the quality. In all good shades.

36-inch Per yard **2/6¾**

Let us quote you for your curtains complete

WRITE FOR PATTERNS NOW

SUNDOUR GUARANTEED QUALITY VELOUR

THE SUNDOUR COMPANY have never before offered a Velour at anywhere near this price. Here you have the full guarantee of quality and colour really worth making up, and yet at such an economical price. The shades are typical of the beautiful Sundour range. Patterns and estimates free

50-inch **3/11½** Per yard

Art Serges & Plushettes

HEAVY ART. SERGE. 48 in. A really remarkable purchase. Extra weight, full width, and equal to last season's 2/6¾ quality. Red, Green, Brown, Blue.
Now only, Yard **1/11¾**

COLOURED CHENILLE. 46 in. Never before have we offered this attractive cloth at such a price. In Green, Gold, Blue, Red.
Now only, Yard **1/11¾**

REVERSIBLE PLUSHETTE. The heaviest reversible cloth at a low price. Specially suitable for strong, draught-proof, inexpensive curtains. 48 in. In usual colours. Yard **2/6¾**

CHENILLE PORTIERE CURTAINS. Good colours with attractive borders. Sold singly for doors or windows. Extremely good designs. Each **5/-**
12/11, 10/11, 8/11 to as low as

PORTIERE RODS from 1/11¾ to 5/6

SPECIAL CARD TABLE OFFER
Strong frame. Each **2/11¾**

We Specialise in LOOSE COVERS

SPECIAL OFFER JACOBEAN LINEN UNION—HALF PRICE
One of the famous "KNIGHT-RIDER" Fabrics, secured from liquidation stock, and guaranteed 2/11 quality. Special prices this week for making covers from this cloth. May we estimate?

1/6¾ Yard

7, 8, 9, 10 BREEDS PLACE
1 & 2 CASTLE ST.
HASTINGS
Telephones 596-597

The Clive Vale Hat Shop
A. RELFE   PHONE 2449
195 Harold Road, HASTINGS

The Cash Discount Shop
PHONE 4430
147 Battle Road, HOLLINGTON

SPEND to SAVE by SHOPPING at the DISCOUNT SHOPS
GIVEN **1'6** AWAY
on each £1 you spend for cash.

Smart Wool Afgalaine Dresses
10/11 WMS.
Also in W.X. & O.S.
12/11 X.O.S.
15/11
New Shades, Rust Petrol, Navy Black, Wine, etc.

Navy Nap Coats from
10/11
Size 24
Rise 1/- per size
Also in Better qualities from
14/11 to 25/6
Coat and Hat Sets **4/11**
Better Quality **8/11, 10/11**
Smart Girls' Coat and Hat Sets from 12/11 to 21/9

become available at Red Lake. Mr. Braithwaite had said that, some of the steel houses could be erected within 12 weeks, and 20 pairs could be erected in 22 weeks. It had been considered whether to erect some the steel houses on the newly acquired sites at Red Lake, whilst money was sought to build brick houses. But this plan never came to fruition, as all the steel houses were only erected on either the Broomgrove site, or the one at St Leonards Eversley Road.

Steel Houses
Completion within six weeks.
Inspection at Eversley Road.

One of the new steel houses erected at Eversley Road building site has been completed, and will be open for inspection for a period of one month.

In outward appearance the houses are scarcely distinguishable at a short distance from the ordinary brick and mortar houses.

They are erected on solid concrete foundations into which long bolts are embedded into the base to hold the steel plates which form the walls. A length of steel also passes through the concrete to the earth beneath and acts as a protection from a lightning strike. The steel walls are nearly half an inch in thickness, and are dressed with a thick sprinkling of pieces of cork, so that if there is any sweating when the plates are in position the moisture is absorbed by the cork. The girders which hold the upper floor are composed of two strips of timber between which thick steel plates are bolted. Each plate is flanged, and between each flange in the process of erection is placed a strip of rubber dipped in petrol, to prevent any possible leakage between the two plates. The roof, also of steel plates, is absolutely waterproof, and efficient drainage for rainwater is provided with gutters and stack pipes bolted to the roof and walls. The total weight of the steel is about 27 tons, and precautions are taken to ensure the bolting of the walls to the foundations to prevent any movement in the strongest gale. Provided the proper care is taken in having the house repainted at definite periods, the life of the steel house seems to be unlimited. The house inspected consists of a large front room, on the ground floor, kitchen, scullery, bathroom, pantry, and coal store. Hot water is supplied from a tank heated from the front room fire. The walls inside are composed of strips of asbestos, treated with light colour distemper. Strips of beading are nailed at intervals, and the ceiling, which is also of asbestos, has a square beading pattern. The floors are of timber in the usual style. Upstairs there is a front bedroom, second bedroom, and box room, the two bedrooms have fireplaces fitted, and gas is laid on in every room. The front rooms are airy and bright, and a special type of window enables easy cleaning of both sides of the glass panes from inside the room. So far, the steel houses erected at Eversley Road are concerned, they cannot be said that they are "Tin Boxes."

Hastings Grows out of the Old Town.

Roadmaking on the new housing site at Ore, (Redlake Road) where a number of houses are already occupied.

Wireless For All.

The "*Marriott,*" unequalled for quality, workmanship and purity.

1 VALVE	£8 : 8 : 0
2 VALVE	£14 : 12 : 6
3 VALVE	£20 : 0 : 0

All complete (but it does not include erection of aerial, pole, etc.).

LOUD SPEAKERS from 25/-

☞ Mr. Marriott will give demonstrations any evening at his private house, 22, White Rock, if due notice is given.

Marriott's Wireless Stores,
38a, ROBERTSON ST.
'Phone extens. 933.

Slum Clearance Scandal.
1926

Amazing Demand on Property Owners
poor people in Old Town threatened with ruin.
Six pounds offered for £100 house.

Cases of great hardship and extreme injustice are occurring as a result of the system of compensation, which the Corporation rebound to adopt in connection with the Old Town clearance scheme. This scheme, passed by the Town Council two years ago, provided for the clearance of an insanitary area in the Old Town and the making of a new and wider road through from the High Street to all Saints Street. In order to provide accommodation for those who will be dispossessed of their homes by the clearance scheme a number of tenements and houses are now being erected at Hardwick Road.

The owners of property in the area declared to be insanitary are finding that the amount of compensation they are likely to get is extremely small.

The method of the Ministry of Health is to hold a public inquiry, and then to mark certain properties red, and others blue. The properties which are marked red are those for which compensation will be paid only on the site value, whilst for those marked blue compensation on the property erected upon the site will be allowed at fair market prices. In the Old Town scheme there are only a few properties, which have been marked blue on the plan.

The remainder will receive from the corporation only the value of the land upon which the property stands. They will not receive one penny for the property, which will be demolished, although the house or tenement may in itself be quite sanitary. In certain cases the corporation can take land WITHOUT PAYING FOR IT AT ALL!

In other cases they can take a portion of the land on which a house stands, and can leave the owner with for instance, the area of land sufficient only for one back room. Even if the house is in itself quite sanitary, the fact that it is in an unhealthy area renders it insanitary under the Act.

An impression seems to exist that the procedure is adopted because certain officials in the corporation have persuaded the Council to adopt the scheme under an Act through, which, it was not necessary for them to operate.

This view is entirely incorrect. If the Council did not proceed under the Housing Acts, and the terms laid down therein, the Ministry of Health would decline to make any grant in respect of the scheme, and further, would not have sanctioned the scheme at all. This would mean that there would be no slum clearance in the Old Town. The Corporation is proceeding and can only proceed under the Acts of Parliament which are general in application, and only an alteration of the acts can help those who are unjustly penalised by the small amount of compensation payable.

The position created is one of considerable technical difficulty.

The Corporation by the Housing Act, 1925, is empowered to pay only the site value for the land, and nothing at all for the buildings which, have been erected on it. The Act consolidates, but does not amend the Housing Acts 1890-1919, and it is under the terms of this Act that the Corporation are required to operate in the clearing of slums. Sec.46 of the Act states: "The compensation to be paid for the land including any buildings thereon, shall be the value at the time the valuation is made of the land as a site cleared of buildings and available for development in accordance with the requirements of the building by-laws for the time being in force in the district."

In many cases, however, the owner of the property may not get even the value of his land.

Most of the properties included in the insanitary area were built before the building by-laws were in operation, with the result that they are not set back 24ft, from the property opposite, or, at the back are not a minimum of ten feet from the house behind. An illustration of the effect of this will show how the process of SQUEEZING OUT THE OWNER has been accomplished.

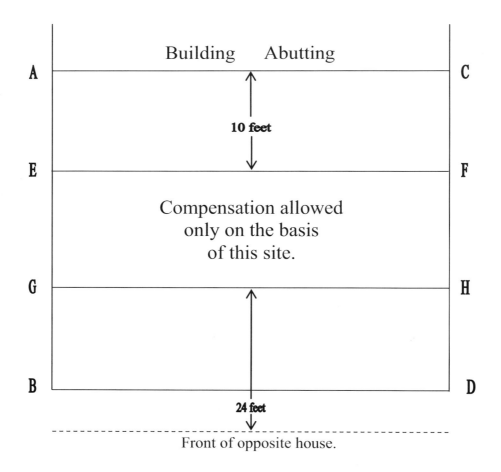

In the sketch the square, A B C D, represents a house within the scheduled area. It stands, let us assume, in a row with either houses on each side of it. The frontage B D must, to comply with the building by-laws be put back until it is 24ft. from the building opposite. In order to do this the frontage would be on the line G H. The Corporation take the strip of land B D to G H without any *payment to the owner whatsoever.* The rear of the premises abuts immediately onto another house. To comply with the by-laws the rear must be brought back to the line E F, and the Corporation takes without payment the land between A C and E F. The only sum paid in compensation is in respect of the land only (not the building) in the centre.

Although Corporation officials state that the land clipped off under the building bye-laws is paid for, yet in practice it is not so. The basis of valuation is that of the whole site as a *building site.* Thus; if the area of a site upon which a building stands today is 40ft, square, in actual building space of a new building in compliance with the bye-laws were erected upon it, might be only 20ft. square. Compensation is paid technically on the whole site, yet it is on the basis of its value as a 20ft square building site that the owner actually receives recompense. The extent to which the building sites of some of the existing plots have been curtained, may be judged from the fact that in some cases the amounts owners will receive vary from as low as £6 upwards, and there are many owners who will receive only about £10. No compensation is paid in respect of the good-will or premises of any business. Many of the properties affected are comparatively new, and are in good tenantable condition and repair. The natural effect of the scheme has been to cause people to withhold mortgages on property in the Old Town, and an official of one local body (not a building society) informed an 'Observer' reporter that it was probable that the mortgages already granted on certain properties would be called in. It is certain that few, if any, of the Councillors who voted for the scheme, knew what its effect would be upon the owners of the properties. Many of them have been surprised and dismayed to learn of the serious injustice inflicted upon the small owner-occupier whose life savings have been absorbed by the purchase of his house.

The main object of the section of the Act is to defeat the syndicates who in London bought up large blocks of insanitary and tumbledown slum property with the express object of selling at a high figure when the Borough Council decided upon a clearance scheme of the area. The granting of compensation only on site value defeated this type of speculator entirely, and, of course, another argument which might be advanced is that because the property comes within an unhealthy area it is insanitary and therefore of no value to anyone.

It cannot be held that in Hastings there has been any speculation with the deliberate object of forcing the Corporation to pay high prices for the property, but there does seem to be the strongest possible argument for consideration of the owner who has owned and in many cases occupied houses for a number of years, certainly long before the slum clearance scheme was mooted. It does not appear that there would be much difficulty in inserting in the Act an amending clause, whereby, full compensation would be payable on a property, which has been in the owner's possession for three or more years, provided it has been kept in a reasonable condition of sanitation. The speculator would be precluded from benefit under such a clause, and the owner who did not keep his premises in proper repair would also be excluded.

The effect upon the owners of property is, of course, very serious. In some cases the compensation allowed on small properties, which in the open market would fetch £150 to £200, is but £6, whilst on better properties of the value of about £400 to £500 the compensation offered is only £80.

The very great hardship which such an action inflicts upon the owner-occupier can well be imagined.

SOME PITIFUL STORIES were told to an "Observer" reporter who made investigation within the area which has been declared to be insanitary.

In the combined living and front room at 3, Bourne Passage, Mr. Henry. Lamb, the owner, frankly told our reporter that, if the Corporation could offer him no more compensation he could see nothing ahead of him but the Poor Law Institution. "The compensation I have been offered," said Mr. Lamb, who is a fish hawker by trade, "is £6. It will not even pay the costs of the solicitor I have had to consult. I bought this house three years ago for £100, and £72 of that money was sent to us by my boy's mates on H.M.S. Ramilles after he died. My boy was taken ill when his ship was on the way to Gibraltar, and he died before reaching shore. His mates on the ship made a collection and sent us £72. We also had £10 from the canteen on the ship and £8 from Chatham. Then I added to that three lots of prize money which I got for being on a minesweeper during the War. All that money was put together, and we paid, bought the house three years ago, and paid the solicitor's cost. It was all we had then, and since then we've spent money in repairs and keeping the place in order. It just hits me right down. I haven't any money; it's ten thousand to one we shall be summoned for our rates now, yet all I'm to get is £6 for this house. It's taking my boy's death money. How can I go up to Hardwicke Road, right away from the Fishmarket, and with a higher rent than I can afford?" Mr. Lamb has two sons dependent upon him. His earnings are augmented with the efforts of his wife, who takes what work offers itself. "When that letter came offering us £6," said Mrs. Lamb, "I just sat down a and cried to think after all our struggling to make ends meet that is all we shall get." Mr. Beaney, the owner of a fruiterer's and greengrocer's business in the High Street with shop and house, is probably one of the most severely hit by the system of compensation. In 1920 Mr. Beaney bought the property for £300. He paid £100 cash and obtained the remainder on a Building Society mortgage. He has paid the instalments on the £200 regularly, and there now remains about £100 to be paid off. He has been offered the sum of £80 as compensation so that he will have to pay that to the building society under the mortgage and £20 besides. Having done so he will not own a single brick or inch of land, and he will be dispossessed of his business without any compensation whatever, although he paid £100 for the goodwill and stock when he took it over. Upon the death of his wife two years ago Mr. Beaney had the property valued. The Valuer informed him that the market value was £375, but that he would have no difficulty in getting £450 to £500 for it.

Mr. Beaney who has a widowed daughter and her child dependent on him, is an elderly man, whose whole life savings were put into the property.

Upon question of the ownership of the material upon the land purchased, we are informed that the Corporation will carry out the demolition of the premises upon a pre-arranged scheme, and that the owners will be allowed to remove the bricks and other material if they desire to do so. Certain owners had received a letter from the District Valuer, which, appeared to suggest that the Corporation could not agree that the owners should retain the material.

The Town Clerk explained to an "Observer" representative that it would not be practical to allow owners to pull down their premises at their own convenience; otherwise the whole demolition scheme would be brought to a state of chaos. When, however, a property had been pulled down the owner would be given an opportunity to remove the bricks, slates, and other material.

Established 1885   *Has Stood the Test of Time*

BRADFORDS' STEAM LAUNDRY

——— HIGH - CLASS WORK ———
FAMILY & SCHOOL WORK A SPECIALITY

Vans Collect and Deliver in Battle, Bexhill,
Cooden and District

Bexhill Road, St. Leonards - on - Sea
——— 'Phone Hastings 325 ———

Land at Hardwick Road
1926

The Council in Committee at their meeting held on the 5th March 1926, had received a report from the Town Clerk with reference to his negotiations for the acquisition of the land required to be purchased at Hardwick Road, from which it appeared that he had agreed to purchase 7 building plots from Mr. J. Burton for the sum of £50, that he was unable to agree terms for the purchase of Plots 32 to 37 and 19 to 27 and that the owner of Plots 44 to 52 and 81 and 82 and a portion of Plots 53 and 54 could not at present be found. The Committee recommended that the action of building plots for the sum of £50 be approved, that he be authorised to submit the matter of the price to be paid for Plots 32 to 37 and 19 to 27 to arbitration, and that the District Valuer be requested to value Plots 44 to 52 and 81 and 82 and a portion of plots Nos.53 and 54, and that the amount of his valuation be deposited in Court. This was adopted.

Old Town Property
1926

The Housing and Improvements Committee reported that the owners or other persons interested in the freehold of certain properties in the area of the Old Town Improvements Scheme (Vines Passage, Cinque Ports and Alma), had expressed their willingness to accept the valuations as fixed by the district Valuer as follows: Water closet in yard at rear of No.9 and 8b Bourne Walk, £1., and vendors' costs. Passageway (Vines Passage) open yard, two water closets, wash-house, dwelling houses Nos.5, 4 and 3 Vines Passage; dwelling house, No.111, All Saints Street, water closet and wash-house at rear, £45, together with £5. 5s. Surveyor's fee and vendors' costs. Bourne Mission Room, adjoining No.4 Bourne Walk, and passageway, No's 5a and 5b Bourne Walk, £300 and vendors' costs and £5. 5s. Agent's fee. The Committee had instructed the Town Clerk to proceed with the purchase of the properties and recommended that their action be approve. – Adopted.

Rents for Steel Houses at Broomgrove.
1926

The Housing and Improvements Committee have had before them a report from the Borough Accountant showing that the total cost of the 54 houses, including the cost of roads, sewers, land, drainage, foundations, footpaths, etc., and the payment of compensation to certain allotments holders who had been displaced was £33,535, being an average cost per house of approximately £621, and showing the following comparison with the cost of other non-parlour type houses erected by the Council: Barley Lane and All Saints Crescent (assisted scheme houses), £971 per house; Eversley Road site (£6 subsidy houses), £398 per house; Eversley Road site (£9 subsidy houses), £517 per house; Eversley Road site (assisted scheme houses), £419 per house; Hollington site £536 per house; Broomgrove site £621 per house; and stating that the economic rent of a Broomgrove house is 19s.7d. per week, that after allowing for the £9 per an annum subsidy and the rate contribution of £4. 10s. per annum the rent to be charged per house is reduced to 14s. 2d. per week and that any reduction below that amount will have to be borne out of rate account, in addition to the charge of £4. 10s. per annum per house, and that the rents now charged for non –parlour type houses on the Council's other housing sites are: Barley Lane and All Saints Crescent, 10s. per week; Hollington and Eversley Road sites, 9s. per week. The Committee recommended that a rent of 10s. per week (exclusive of rates) be charged for each of the houses, the same to operate as from the date upon which the respective tenants first   commenced to occupy the houses, with the exception of the first four houses erected on the site, and that the rent of 9s. per week, which has hitherto been charged for those houses be increased to 10s.per week as from August.

Alderman Cox moved the adoption of the report and pointed out that even with £9 per house from the Government, and £4. 10s. from the rates there was still a difference of 4s. 2d per week, per house to be borne by the ratepayers.

Councillor Beck opposed the report, and said the Council has to consider something else besides the economic rents. He would rather see the houses built by direct labour, which was much cheaper than when built by contract.

Councillor Shoesmith said, Councillor Beck had not read the report or he would see that the Barley Lane houses were built by direct labour at a cost of £971 per house, whereas the Eversley Road houses, put up by contract, cost £598, £517 and £419 according to the class of house.

Councillor Payne hoped the Council would never put up any more steel houses. The contractors said the houses would be cheaper and would be put up more expeditiously than brick houses. Was that so, when the price was £621, and even now the houses were not finished? He had inspected the houses and could not speak favourably of them. The report was adopted.

Purchase Price of Council Houses.
1927

The Housing and Improvements Committee reported that they had considered the matter of the advisability of offering for sale the houses erected by them under the Housing Acts. The Borough accountant reported as follows:

Barley Lane and Rectory sites – Parlour, suggested selling price, £650; average cost £1074. non-Parlour, suggested selling price £525; average cost £971.

Eversley Road – Parlour, suggested selling price £550; average cost £496. Non-parlour, suggested selling price £470; average cost £445.

Hollington site; Parlour, suggested selling price, £520; average cost, £600. Non-parlour, suggested selling price £450; average cost £536.

Broomgrove site (Steel Houses Non-parlour, suggested selling price £435; average cost £621.

In March 1923, the Committee instructed the Town Clerk to enquire from the Ministry of Health as to the figure which, the Minister would be prepared to approve the sale of the houses erected at the Barley Lane Housing site, and at All Saints Crescent, and the reply was that the Minister would be prepared to sanction the sale of the parlour type houses at £600. per house.

The Committee recommended that the houses be offered for sale to the tenants, or prospective tenants in the case of vacant houses, at the various prices. After the report had been moved and seconded, Councillor Morgan urged that the Council should not part with the property at all.

Councillor Burr asked if it could be made a condition that tenants should not be allowed to sell the houses for a certain period.

Alderman Cox said under the Act the tenants must live in the houses for at least three years. The report was adopted.

Purchase of 75 All Saints Street
July 1927

The Council in Committee reported that they had authorised the purchase of 75, All Saints Street, and adjoining premises in East Bourne Street for the sum of £1,500 under the provisions of Section 49 of the Hastings Corporation Act 1924, and recommended that their action be approved and confirmed and that application be made to the Ministry of Health for sanction to borrow the purchase money.

Councillor Burr contended that the price was far too high and Councillor Tingle agreed.

Council Morgan said it was not an old building, and eventually the road there would have to be widened. If somebody bought the houses and started a business there the Council would have to pay much more.

Councillor Stevens urged the Council to wait until some later date.

Alderman Fellows said the matter had not been before any Committee. It had been brought to the notice of the Mayor by Councillor Morgan. The Mayor had counselled with Alderman Chesterfield and himself. It was thought unwise to let the news leak out, and the Mayor acquiesced in the suggestion of getting the property at the lowest figure. The property was put up for auction with a reserve price of £2,000, and withdrawn at £1,500. The recommendation was adopted.

Rents of Redlake houses.
July 1927

The Housing and Improvements Committee reported that they referred the matter of the rents to be charged for the 50 houses now in course of erection at Red Lake to their sub Housing (Selection) Committee for consideration with power to submit a recommendation to the Council thereon.

The sub Committee had had before them a report from the Borough Accountant that the all in cost of the 50 houses was estimated at £30,000, which makes the average cost per house £600; that the economic rent of such houses might be taken at 17s. per week, and after allowing for the £9 per annum subsidy and the rate contribution of £4. 10s. per annum per house, the rent to be charged per house was reduced to 11s. 10d., and pointing out that if the rents were fixed below that amount the difference would have to be borne out of rate account in addition to the rate contribution of £4. 10s. per annum.

The sub-committee had carefully considered the matter, and recommended that the following rents be charged: for houses with a bay window, 11s. 9d. per week; for houses without a bay window, 11s. 3d. per week; in each case exclusive of rates.

Councillor Holloway asked the Chairman of the Committee on what basis he estimated the value of a bay window at sixpence a week. Councillor Shoesmith pointed out that there was a considerable difference in the cost of building the two types. The report was adopted.

Excessive Overcrowding.

Councillor Burr moved: "That owing to the proved shortage of housing accommodation and a grave excessive overcrowding in this borough, and owing to the great delay in connection with the carrying out of the Old Town Improvement Scheme, this Council authorises the Town Clerk to make immediate arrangements to transfer tenants from properties certified by the Medical Officer of Health as unfit for human habitation to one block of the existing flats at Hardwick Road that are now vacant.

Councillor Burr declared that the Sub-Committee of the Housing Committee had considered the question of providing alternative accommodation, and, he regretted, had scarcely done anything. He read letters from various people in the Old Town. One writer complained that four were sleeping in one room overrun with rats. In another case, a father and mother, with children, were living in two rooms. A Corporation employee living in a cottage said ten were sleeping in two rooms measuring 9ft. 4ins. by 8ft. 10ins. Again, 11 people were living in a four-roomed cottage. He asserted that the Council could take over one of the sets of flats, legally, and put some of these people in there.

Councillor Beck seconded. "Whatever the legal position is." He argued, "Go ahead. If it is necessary to get another grant to put up more flats, it can be done. I've seen the state of some of these people are living in. We dare not let it go on. Do something tonight before we go on the vacation."

The Mayor said he could find no strong objection to the proposal, and thought it might be passed without further discussion. The Town Clerk said any deficiency with regard to the one block would fall on the Corporation, and they would not get the 50 per cent, from the Ministry of Health.

The resolution was formally adopted.

Rents of flats – Hardwick Road
September 1927

The emergency committee had a letter from the Ministry of Health stating that the Minister felt great difficulty in departing from the rents of the 48 flats erected at Hardwick Road under the Old Town Area Improvement Scheme already agreed upon on the initiation of the Council, but in view of the fact that the Council's choice of tenant is to some extent limited by the necessity of giving first offer to the tenants of the area to be cleared, he was prepared to agree that a reduction of 6d. per week might be made in the exclusive rents hitherto agreed, reducing them to the following: One living room, 3 bedrooms, 8s. 6d. per week; one living room, 2 bedrooms, 6s. 6d. per week; one living room, one bedroom, 4s. 6d. per week. The Committee had authorised the Town Clerk to offer the flats to tenants at the reduced rents and to alter the rents to the present or existing tenants of the flats, and recommended that their action be approved and confirmed. The report was adopted.

SLUM CLEARANCE
October 1927

CORPORATION TO BE RECOMMENDED TO GO FORWARD.

We understand that at a meeting of the Hastings Town Council in Committee, it was decided by 14 votes to 11 (15 members of the Corporation not voting) to recommend the Council to go forward with the slum clearance in the Old Town. This is the scheme by which owners of property will be dispossessed with absurdly inadequate compensation. We venture to express the hope that when the Corporation discusses this recommendation, it will decide on a plan by which the owners of the property will be fairly treated.

Some of these owners practically depend on the income from the property, and it is manifestly unfair that they should be deprived of their means of living without reasonable compensation.

Big Trouble with Hollington Houses.
1928.

A statement was read out at Council concerning the conditions of the foundations of the Council houses at Hollington. The wet season had had a disastrous effect on them, and in some places the tenants had to walk through a seething mass of mud. A deputation of tenants had called on the Council and complained that there were some inches of water beneath the floor of many of the houses. In one case there was already dry rot, and the health of the children was suffering considerably. The Borough Engineer had been authorised to get the water away by whatever means. In the case of one house, where a channel was opened to drain away the water from beneath the boards, a strong flow of water continued for hours, showing the pressure of a spring.

The matter had to be dealt with at once, not only the condition of the houses, the pathways, too. The Borough Engineer had estimated it could cost about £1,200,. A Councillor demanded that this work be put into hand immediately without having to wait for the next full Council meeting.

The Mayor asked to whether this amount of money would cure the faults? In a reply, it will provide for draining away the water, and provide decent paths.

The Council had heard very little of this trouble with regard to the water logging at Hollington, but a full comprehensive report was called for from the Borough Engineer as to what was required, as they had just been informed that the Red Lake houses were nearly as bad - so were those at Eversley Road.

One Councillor that had visited all the effected houses, feared that £1,200, would not see the end of all this trouble. There were so many things needing immediate attention. In one house the tenant pulled up the carpet which was wet, but the real problem was the worms underneath the carpet, which were actually crawling up through the boards! The water trapped under the house was absolutely stinking, so much that the tenant and himself had to put their pipes on (rubber boots), and children were living over that water.

Many Councillors demanded a public enquiry by the Ministry of Health and only this would satisfy public opinion. In a reply, it was stated that, it was the outcome of the Ministry interfering with public authority matters before that had cuts made to Mr. Little's plans time and again, and this is what you get for having them interfere in our Council matters.

The Council recalled that that the Housing Committee had had to face great difficulties in getting the houses erected at all. Some weaknesses were invariable found in new houses; it was unfortunate that in these cases the weaknesses should have been found in the houses of poor people who could not afford to have the troubles corrected. The Ministry of Health had not done quite the right thing, should they not be asked on this occasion to advance a loan for about 20 years to cover the cost of repairs?

The Town Clerk said, there would be little doubt that the Ministry would grant a loan of £1,200. there had been gross exaggerations that enormous sums would be involved. An independent enquiry had been called for to sift the matter to the bottom, and to find out exactly what went wrong, and to why the houses became flooded as they were. There were suggestions from the floor that the specifications were at fault, but, it was conclusive that the Ministry had some dealings with the specification and made alterations. If a Ministerial enquiry was to be called for, this would hold up the building process for months to come and these houses were needed now. It was an extremely difficult time for the Council, as they had to deal with one particular house where the floors were giving way to dry rot, and others were suspect also.

The water under the floors was eventually drained away, and the Borough Engineer devised plans to redirect the water from the natural springs in the ground, which no one had ever taken heed of when the foundations were laid.

Although, we were told that the original specifications sent out to the Ministry for their approval, stated that there was positive evidence that the grounds contained live springs within the area to where the buildings were to be erected, it now appears that certain parts were either altered or removed from the specifications that the builders were in receipt of. This I have to say is only the word of someone to whom I had spoken to, who was connected with the building at Hollington. But I don't think it takes too much working out that some things may have just been tampered with before the contractors read the final specification.

Hastings Old Town c1920s

Old Town Improvement Scheme
March 1928

The Hastings and Improvement Committee had received a report from the Town Clerk to the effect that the owners and other persons interested in the freehold of the under mentioned premises in the area of the Old Town Improvement Scheme, had expressed their agreement to accept the valuations fixed by the District Valuer, subject to the additional conditions mentioned in the schedule below with regard to materials:- No. 3. Bourne Walk, £15, the vendor to demolish the building and take the materials, and vendor's legal costs. No. 2. Bourne Walk, £14, the vendor to demolish the building and take the materials, and vendor's legal costs. Nos. 52 and 52a, Bourne Walk and garden at rear, £25, and vendor's solicitors' costs. Vendor's to be allowed to take such materials as they may require, the purchase to be completed as soon as Corporation are in a position to demolish. Nos. 7 and 8, The Creek, £15, ditto. No. 5, Fishers Cottages and Passageway, Fishers Cottages, and Smiths Row, £10 each respectively.

March 1928

45 & 46 Bourne Walk

Corner of Roebuck Street. Aug 1928.

Proposed New Thoroughfare.
April 1929.

Councillor Dymond stated that, "The Borough Engineer prepared plans for the Carlisle Parade improvements, and for a new highway to connect the Parade with the bottom of Old London Road, in order to provide a thoroughfare for East and West traffic, with estimates for the cost and that the Town Clerk ascertains from the Unemployment Grants Committee, whether a grant of 75 per cent of the cost would be made if men from the depressed areas were employed for the work." The purchase of property at Beach Terrace was so far complete as to enable them to go straight ahead with the work. One of the great reasons for the improvement was the increase in traffic difficulties in Robertson Street and Castle Street. There was a chance of getting a large Government grant towards the cost. The Borough Engineer and Cllr Dymond had been considering if they could not use Tackleway as a thoroughfare through the Old Town. A tunnel would have to be made from Rock-a-Nore up to the Tackleway level. This would be very steep, and to obviate this it would be possible to make the tunnel extend to the junction of All Saints Street and the High Street. This appeared at first sight an expensive scheme, but it was a scheme which had been successfully carried out on the continent. The cost of the tunnel would not be more than one third of the entire cost in the widening of the High Street. Councillor Burr supported the resolution in part, but he was in complete favour of the scheme for taking the thoroughfare through the Bourne. He did not want a tunnel, but an open road, where the Corporation could recoup the cost from the frontages.

Alderman Cox was convinced that the right scheme was the Bourne scheme. He put forward a motion that an amendment should be referred to the Highways and Improvements Committee for a final decision.

Councillor Morgan thought that the Borough Engineer had already enough work in hand. He did consider the suggestion of a tunnel absolutely fantastic. The Bourne scheme would entail a considerable rehousing project if no road was to be built here.

Alderman Blackman said that he had always favoured the Carlisle Parade scheme, but not if it were to just stop there. It had to be continued to give an outlet through the Old Town, it would only be half doing the job. He did not see why a tunnel should be considered extraordinarily. Other Councillors said that the only course of action to take was for a road through the Bourne.

Alderman Collins hoped that the Council would throw out the schemes, as the town was not in a position to spend money on them.

Councillor Dymond wished to point out that the suggestion of a tunnel was not one of his resolutions.

Alderman Cox's amendment was carried by 15 votes to 14.

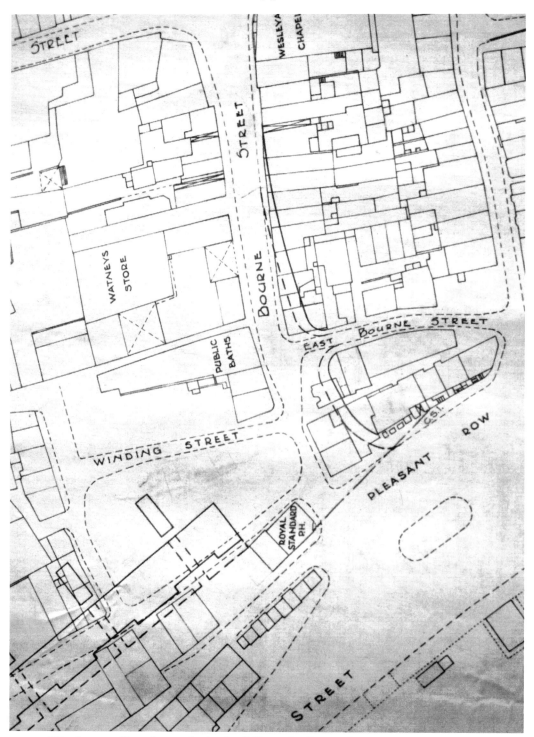

The heavy line through the buildings indicate the area to be cleared, dotted lines remain.

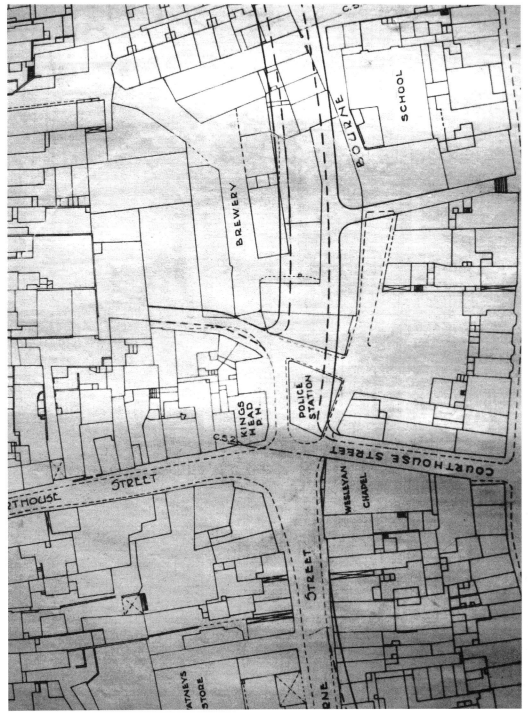

This plan of the early 1920's portrays a vision of what was hoped would be a final road layout through the Bourne.
The dotted line indicates the proposed route

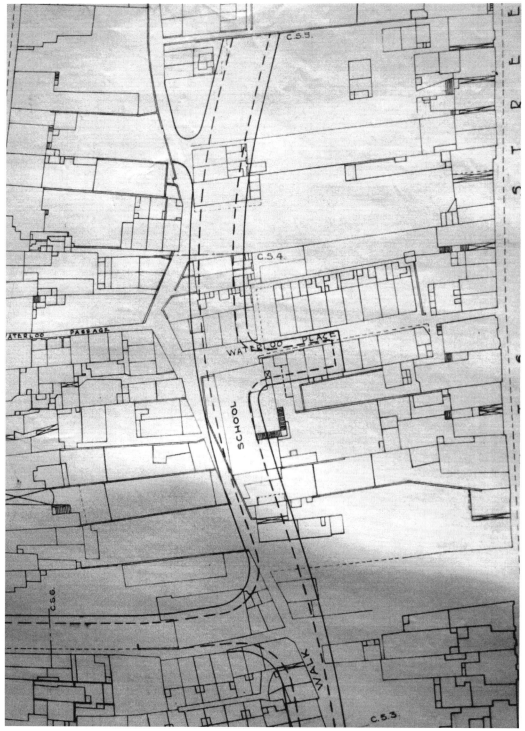

This shows the proposed route of the road further up the Bourne, with a turning into Waterloo Place indeed!

Old Town Road Proposal.
June 1929.

One Councillor stated, "That there should be an instruction made to the appropriate Committee of the Council, to at once proceed to acquire, by agreement, the necessary property in All Saints Street between Courthouse Street and the bottom end of All Saints Street to enable the Corporation to adopt a one-way vehicular traffic policy, and so ease the present periodical congestion within the High Street, and that if the Committee are unable to acquire the property by agreement, that the Town Clerk take the necessary steps to apply for a Provisional Order to enable the Corporation to acquire the property by compulsory purchase." Another Councillor rose to suggest, that the increase of transport had made it imperative that something had to be done and quickly to reduce the congestion in the High Street. It was contended that, if All Saints Street was widened as suggested, it would be adequate for one-way traffic. Other Councillors said that, they too had experienced problems in the High Street when travelling in one direction and meeting a bus in the other, whereby neither could pass. The Council in general said that, it was a matter that could not be solved in any casual way, it was of general consensus of the Committee that a new arterial road should be cut through the Bourne. There was much dilapidated property, and there would be no more difficulty than acquiring property in All Saints Street. They declared that this improvement scheme was deliberately being hung up because they could not afford to pay the adequate compensation being asked for from the tenants of the property that was sanctioned by the Ministry of Health as being in an insanitary condition. One Councillor (who shall remain nameless) described the scheme as palliative. He suggested that an amendment put forward earlier by a college of his be carried through under the Town Improvements Act, by which full value could be given to the property acquired. This has been all our doing he said. We did not oppose strongly enough the powers for the trolley buses to run through the High Street when we had the chance, and I will go as far to say that, as soon as the road is widened, the trams will start running through it. It will be a golden opportunity to pay back to the people the fair value for their property, instead of stealing it from them. Alderman Shoesmith did not think that many members of the Council actually realised what number of people in the Bourne area would have to be dispossessed . He also added that the Council were not proposing to take property without paying for it at a proper and reasonable price. If the south end of All Saints Street was widened they could give up the Bourne scheme for a long time to come. It was questioned as to whether All Saints Street was suitable for one-way traffic. The houses would probably come down on their own accord by the sheer volume of traffic that would have to use this street.

Think of the danger of accidents, all day long the streets are swarmed with children who have no where else to play. A radical statement was made to the fact that we declare that All Saints Street and High Street were two of the tiniest street in England from the picturesque point of view. He believed that the only solution with traffic coming into Hastings was to construct a wide road through the Bourne, thus retaining the picturesqueness of the other streets. Councillor Tingle, who supported the Bourne scheme, paid a generous tribute to the Press, declaring that it was mainly due to the local newspapers that the matter had been brought before them today. He declared that at one point All Saints Street only measured 14 feet in width, this would certainly not accommodate a large vehicle such as a bus. The Council in whole supported the claim that they were wasting human life, and human life was far more important than a road. Alderman Chesterfield added that in his opinion the Bourne scheme was an impossibility. Councillor Dymond said that he was astonished by the fact that there was so much indifference within Council to the schemes put before them, and asked that the question be deferred until the Council could get a full report from the Borough Engineer. Carried.

Within the same time scale as the above, the Press received many a letter for and against the schemes proposed in driving a wide road through the heart of the Bourne. Many were for a new road, but were uncertain as to where it should really be, one letter described that a roadway should connect with the centre of town through a new route over the west hill and down through Wellington Square, whilst there were several brain storm schemes offered by the public, but with no appreciation as to how much their brain wave schemes might cost the public at large, and to the total destruction of other areas in the town, and where to place all those including valuable businesses that would be lost. Many a criticism was passed over the narrowness of the High Street, as drivers were complaining daily that they were unable to pass certain vehicles, and even the Constable that was on point duty at the foot of High Street would have been powerless to intervene. Obviously, All Saints Street took a full strike in regard to this being used as a portion of the proposed one-way system for traffic coming into Hastings from the Ore end of town. Where comment was made in Council that the traffic would do the work of the Council in bring down the houses from their sheer size and ever increasing weight, there was great opposition to the scheme and a host of protest from all quarters.

Week after week the letters flowed in, and many were published by various newspapers of the time, some were even read out in Council.

These letters had a great influence upon the final decision made by the Council, later on. One said, "Take heed, we are not going to sit back and let you take our houses from under our noses without a good fight just for the sake of a roadway." Did this work or not?

Old Town Road
Councillor Morgan explains parts of The Bourne Scheme.
And calls for a full investigation.

We append a letter we received from Councillor Morgan on Wednesday. "Vigilant" refers to it in one of his notes today:-

Sir, Just 20 years ago the water Company sprang upon an astonished Borough a new and costly water scheme and the Council accepting a plea of urgency and failing to bring its critical capacity to bear upon it passed the scheme. The ratepayers took the matter in hand and by a 10 to 1 majority rejected the scheme, and in a except in a much attenuated form the scheme has not again been put forward. I trust that the Council of 1929 will not, in regard to the Bourne Road Scheme, make the same mistake as the Council did in 1909.

In traffic matters it is necessary to look some years ahead. So looking, one is bound to recognise that sooner or later a new road in the Old Town district must be constructed joining up Old London Road with a new road from the baths to the cinema. Large issues are involved in the scheme now before the Council, and the cost (estimated at between £83,000 and £93,000) is heavy.

A critical examination both of the merits of the scheme and of its finance is essential. The Council should in this matter as those in the Music Pavilion, the Great Sanders Scheme educate the ratepayers and obtain their whole hearted support for any scheme ultimately adopted. For this time is necessary.

The congestion of traffic in the High Street occurs only at certain hours.

It is almost due to the stupidity of some drivers or the owner of some standing vehicle. Two simple expedients will do away with it.

- Let a Constable patrol the southern half of the street at certain hours.
- Make a passing place adjoining the Corporation Yard.

But these measures will not provide for the traffic difficulties of the future 10 years ahead.

I state below some matters connected with the road scheme, which need most careful consideration.

1. Housing. The scheme itself proposes to dislodge some 400 to 500 residents; if the land adjoining the new road is to be built upon, a very substantial number of persons living just off the line of the road will also be dislodged. These two classes of residents are living in low rented properties; they cannot pay such rents as the Council charges for houses such as those in All Saints Crescent, nor do they want such houses. They will be dislodged not in their own interest but in that of the owners of vehicles intruded into their area against their wishes.

   Unless the Borough provides housing accommodation such as they wish for and at rents within their means they will be (as has happened frequently under clearance schemes) be compelled to shift into what

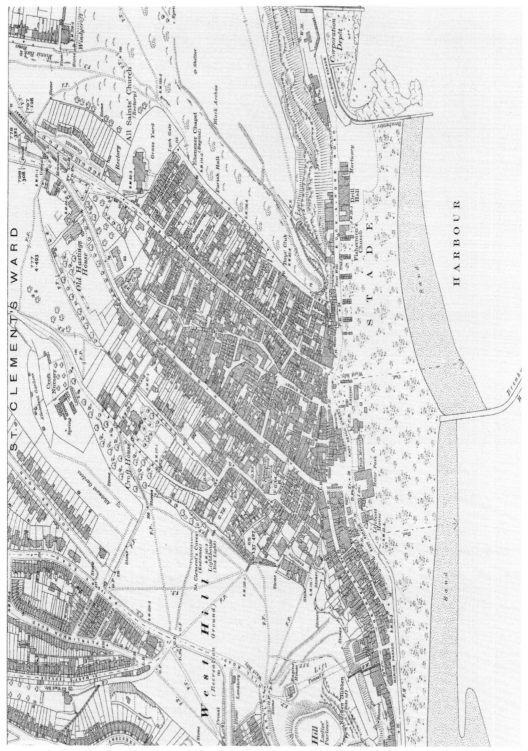

The highly populated Old Town. 1929

portions of houses are available nearby, and to live in crowded and slum conditions. The loss of the Borough on the rehousing of these people must be added to the cost of the road itself.

2. Building in the new road, the scheme makes no provision for this.

It proposes to remove the existing buildings to a width of 60 feet, thereby, opening up views of the backs of the houses on either side with their out buildings and sanitary conveniences. The scene of desolation, due to the Councils recent operations, which is now visible near Roebuck Yard, will be extended right throughout the Bourne and this will continue until private enterprise builds on each side to cover it all up.

The owners of land on either side have generally neither the capitol nor the enterprise to build, and any building which speculators may gradually put up may be totally out of harmony with the Eighteenth and Nineteenth Century houses of the Old Town. The aspect of the Old Town, like the aspect of the neighbouring and similar town of Rye, is a asset of considerable value to the Borough and should therefore be preserved. The proposed reservation by the Council of a strip of just one foot in depth on either side of the road, which owners wishing to build must buy at such prices as the Council chooses to exact will diminish the incentive of substantial profit without which, owners and speculators will not venture to build. It will have the same effect as the disastrous land values legislation of 1910.

3. Position of the road. The Corporation garden at the top of the High Street, and the beautiful wooded grounds of the Wilderness adjoining with the stately tower of All Saints Church standing boldly up to the eastwards form probably the most charming piece of landscape in the Borough. The Town Planners mentioned in their report of March 1924, sketched their suggestions for the Bourne road, and provided for the retention of the Wilderness grounds. The present scheme provides for the complete destruction both of the gardens and the grounds.

4. Width of road. The Town Planners provided for a 50 foot wide road. The scheme now however for a road width of 60 feet. Such a road would become (like even Old London Road) a sort of racing track and a death trap for the many children and adults alike who would have to cross it. The southern end of Old London Road is only about 45 feet in width. The wider the new road the more costly it becomes, and the less space for rebuilding is left on either side, this, I believe is an important consideration. (does this new road have foot paths.)?

5. Schools and Churches. All Saints Infant School (which can accommodate 190) would be bought and pulled down, the children would probably find their way to Waterloo School, displacing the handicraft centre there, for which a new home would have to be found.

An aerial photograph of the top end of the Bourne showing the Wilderness.
c1930s

The Roman Catholic School would undoubtedly lose its playground and another would have to be found. A new site for rebuilding would have to be provided for the Wesleyan Chapel and the associated School.
The playground for Waterloo Place would be seriously curtailed.

6. The Brewery would be effected; whether this would involve acquiring the whole I cannot say, but the scheme does not contemplate this.

7. The Borough Engineer has fairly pointed out some of the difficulties. The schemes should considered side by side with that of the Town Planners referred to above.

Your Truly,
F. W. Morgan

September 1929.

A Correspondent Suggests Another Scheme.

Sir, I read with great interest the report submitted by the Borough Surveyor on the Old Town Improvement Schemes. He recommends the making of a new road through the Bourne, why does he consider this the best one? On one side you would have the Brewery buildings, and on the other, the back-ways of the houses in All Saints Street. One can see just what a back-ways looks like by taking a train journey, or, better still, visit the spot and see the ruins where the slum houses have already been removed.

What a splendid first impression our visitors would get who approach from whichever direction! There would be no room to build anything there to make it look nice after the road was made.

The only scheme which is practical is the widening of the High Street, which has got great advantages over the other one. The trams must run that way; all is needed is road wide enough to allow three large vehicles to pass each other easily. Most of the congestion is caused by lorries unloading at the shops.

Does our Borough Surveyor realise that all the houses in the High Street could be rebuilt on the land behind, without destroying cottage property. From the bottom up to Reeves Corner, all could be put back, and yet only demolish six cottages, four of them, more truthfully described as hovels. Three are in John Street, two in Winding Street, the other in Post Office Passage.

Then there is the Tallow Factory, the stench from which is vile. All the folks in the neighbourhood would welcome its removal. The rest of the area is composed of old store buildings, accommodation for which could be found. Then, higher up the street, there is a redundant public house, which is to be closed. Why not pull that down and rebuild a shop to suit the furniture store next door. Then pull down the next two and rebuild for the next lower down. Mr. Beney's shop, over which there has been so much controversy, could easily be built in the space behind, as can be seen from the road.

Then no doubt ex-Councillor Whicker would like an up to date shop instead of his old fashioned premises, and this would give another site for another occupant. This idea is currently being carried out in Western Road, Brighton, a road which ranks with our own Robertson Street, and if it can be done in Brighton, why not here in Hastings?

Whose are the vested interest in which obstructs this scheme? I have no axe to grind; I possess no property; I have not even a vote!

Sooner or later High Street will have to be widened, why not do it now? Why waste money on a scheme that will be very costly, and yet not remedy the terrible congestion in the High Street? The High Street Scheme, if carried out as suggested, would not be more expensive (perhaps less in the long run), and it would then be a fine thoroughfare.

I am afraid this has encroached on your space, but it is useless to say a thing should be done, or ought to be done, without explaining how.

Signed: Mr. Anonymous.   An Old Town Resident.

There were many letters suggesting different schemes, all to try and avoid clearing so much property as the Council did.

Most of the time, the Council didn't even bother to read, or even look at some of the ideas passed on, whereby, many would have saved the Old Town from the total destruction it suffered. I for one could see that some of the alternative schemes offered would work out better than a road straight through the heart of the Old Town, but there you are, the Council knew better than anyone else and got their way finally; as it always does!

Looking across the valley towards the Catholic Church
at the top end of High Street, as seen from Tackleway.

Concentrating on the Bourne

£96,000 Scheme referred back for new report.

Borough Accountant on the financial aspect.
1929.

A further delay in connection with the £96,000 scheme for a 60 foot roadway through the Bourne was the only result of a two hours discussion at a special meeting of the Council in Committee, held recently at the Town Hall.

After the scheme had been thoroughly dissected, criticised, praised, and debated in general from every angle possible, it was referred to the Highways and Improvement Committee and to the Finance Committee for further consideration. The only definite step taken was a decision to proceed entirely with the Bourne scheme, and to dispense altogether with the alternative proposal of widening the east side of the High Street.

Councillors then visited the Bourne with the Borough Engineer Mr. Sidney Little, and the proposed cut to be made through the heart of the Old Town was explained to them step by step, together with the properties to be demolished.

The Rehousing Problem.

The Borough Engineer submitted the following supplementary report:-

The line of the road shown on the plans submitted last month might with advantage be altered at the two ends; at the south extreme it would be moved eastward, thereby avoiding the demolition of the public baths, and Watney's bottling stores, and also reducing the number of houses to be demolished by eleven. This altered line would have the added advantage that traffic moving from the north end would get a good view of the sea, providing any obstructing buildings on the foreshore were removed. At the northerly end, I suggest that the line be diverted from the original intention in a westerly direction, thereby considerably reducing the area taken from the 'Wilderness', and the land of a neighbouring house of that name.

In any plans submitted they would of course, include for securing powers to acquire land and property, and construct works outside the area shown on the plan, such limits being marked by 'a limit of deviation.' This is the usual procedure, and allows reasonable latitude to make alterations at a later date.

In my previous report, I drew attention to the fact that this road would open up a view of the backs of the property, but the length opened out is reduced by the alteration in line, whereby, the road for part of its length is made to follow Bourne Street.

These objections are inseparable from a scheme of this character, and in order to meet them, I again suggest that powers be obtained to acquire land and property for a width of 80 feet, instead of 60 feet, and that margins of 10 feet wide be planted on both sides. The additional cost would be comparatively small, apart from the extra cost of the property to be acquired, and on which, the Borough Accountant is reporting; and this would meet the criticism made by some members of the Council at the last meeting, that the width of the road was insufficient, as it would enable an 80 foot road to be constructed at a later date should it be found desirable to do so. The width of construction would, of course, be 60 foot.

West Hill Housing Scheme.

With regard to housing, there is suitable building land to the west of Torfield, and on either side of Croft Road, there is an area of between five and six acres capable of providing sites for about 120 to 150 houses.

This site is within a quarter of a mile of the centre of the proposed road, measured as the crow flies, and presents no insuperable difficulties as regards levels. Incidentally, the acquirement of this land would provide sites for additional houses, which the Housing Committee are very anxious to obtain.

The Borough Accountant submitted the following report dealing with the financial aspect of the scheme:-

I have prepared an estimate showing that the cost of acquiring the property for the purpose of constructing a 60 foot road would be approximately £60,000; this figure allows for payment on the basis of a valuation including, in the case of business premises, compensation for disturbance, etc.

I understand that it is now proposed to purchase land to the extent of an additional width of 20 feet to permit, for the present, of tree planting, and the resale of one foot on either side for frontages.

I estimate that the cost of this part of the scheme will work out as under:-

	£
Original cost of scheme	60,000
Additional land	10,000
	70,000
Less	
Resale of frontages	5,000
Nett cost	£65,000

The Borough Engineer estimated the original cost of constructing the new road at £33,000; to this must be added £500 for tree planting, making the total cost £33,500. it is estimated that 85 houses will be required for the purpose of providing accommodation for the dispossessed tenants, and that the construction of roads and sewers will be approximately £550 per house, or a total figure of £46,750. the question is to what assistance can be obtained from the Government in connection with the scheme will depend on the attitude adopted by the Ministry of Transport.

Looking 10 Years Ahead.

Certain Councillors were in favour of the High Street scheme. It is quite true to say that it would cost more, but there was no doubt that it was a better scheme. The whole difficulty is created, because the advocates of the Bourne scheme are frightened to go the whole hog! It was stated that there was no extreme urgency over the matter. It was necessary to look ten years hence when motor traffic would probably be double as to what it is today.

The financial aspect is one which, we are bound to bear in mind, and to consider whether the town can carry the burden. To my mind, one Councillor replied, the proposal to house these people up on the West Hill at the rentals proposed by this Council is of an unsatisfactory character. You want to house them at the bottom of the hill, not at the top. The most satisfactory way, if the Bourne scheme is adopted, would be to build in the Bourne itself, and make a road a residential one instead of a shopping thoroughfare, except for perhaps, for a limited number of sites for shops. If you take the people from 80 houses, and put them on the West Hill you are taking away about 500 people from the custom of the shops in the Old Town. You would thus be diminishing the need for shops in the Old Town, and yet you want to place more there.

One or two Councillors went on to criticise the proposed width of the road on the grounds that it would encourage speeding. The comments went on to say, that with the High Street and All Saints Street there would be a total street accommodation through the Old Town of 120 feet to carry traffic coming from roads no more than half that width. We don't want a high speed through the Old Town, motorists can get through the Old Town within a minute now, so why should they be allowed to have a 60 foot wide road to get through in half a minute, we just don't know. Another question was raised as if the dispossessed tenants were rehoused on the West Hill, what was to happen to the fishing industry if your going to send them all up there?

It was stated that it was extremely necessary that all the details of the scheme should be thoroughly thrashed out in a Committee. It was an urgent matter, and there was no reason as to why the Committee should not go hammer and tongs at it, and present a report for the next full Committee. The traffic problems were getting more and more difficult every single day this lingered on. A unanimous decision was told when, they thought that they should not go in for a too wide a road, they were simply cutting an enormous piece out of the heart of the Old Town which, was going to upset everyone in the area. The rehousing of the people is an essential part of the scheme, but we are afraid that all we will get is 'Fried Fish and Chip' shops up the road, unless we, the Council take steps to prevent this.

One Way Traffic

It was suggested that a one way traffic system in the High Street and All Saints Street be adopted as an experiment be brought into force with immediate effect. In reply, it was said that the matter would be settled as soon as the Committee appointed to consider the scheme would get on with it as soon as possible, and that their decision was wholly justified. The main difficulty at present was the question of rehousing, and until that was settled nothing could be done, basically road construction, or anything else for that fact was at a halt. It had been mentioned before at previous meetings that they, the Council, thought there was ample room in the Old Town to provide building sites for the accommodation of the dispossessed people.

The Borough debt currently stood at close on £2,000,000, and as schemes which were sanctioned or pending would involve yet another large sum of £836,000 it would bring the debt within a measurable distance of £3,000,000.

After the motions were passed on and closed, a single voice spoke out declaring that the decision to postpone the scheme had definitely been engineered. I honestly think he said, that the matter has been shelved for another generation. There was no reply, and the meeting closed.

An Independent Readers View.

Sir. As one of the earliest advocates in your columns of the extension of the Parade and Highway from the eastern end of the Baths - not to the Cinema, but to the Fishmarket, might I be allowed to ask a simple question?

Are three avenues really necessary for the traffic from the beautiful top of the High Street to the Front? Surely it would be wiser as well as economical to widen one or the other or both the High Street and All Saints Street, meantime leaving each of these narrow streets for one way traffic only, up one street and down the other. London has many one way streets as well as roundabouts, and it is very wisely proposed for the narrow end of the Old London Road.

Councillor Morgan gave a very full and clear account of the objections to the Bourne scheme in addition to those frankly admitted by the Borough Surveyor, but he did not exhaust the list. He gave his case away by admitting that at some indefinite date, a new road would be necessary without neither fact of argument. What signs are there of the wonderful development in this quarter to justify the construction of a 60 foot road? I have been a frequent visitor to Hastings since the late 1800s, and have been a permanent resident for the past 12 years; I have been up and down the High Street hundreds of times, and excepted the workmen's dwellings, so many of which are occupied by those for whom they were never intended, a new house is rarely to be seen.

The poets and novelists and actors which live in Winchelsea and Rye are after old houses and would not look at a new one. Then what sort of houses do you expect to be erected in this spacious road, and what sort of tenants are likely to occupy them, without gardens, with slums to right of them, and slums to left of them also. Mr. Morgan's prophecy is quite likely to be fulfilled, and it will for years be unoccupied, and become a racing track for motor cycles in a town with so many narrow streets, and without a speed limit. To make a good road with footpaths on both sides, with sewers, kerbs and channelling is a very expensive affair, and if ever the houses go up, the road has to be dug up to make the connections with the mains, gas, water and electricity every time so that when the buildings are finished, the road will be so full of potholes as to practically require remaking at the ratepayers' expense. No 50 per cent Government grant this time. By all means let every practical suggestion be carefully examined in detail, and published for the judgement of all the ratepayers. I believe that this 60 foot road will eventually accompany the bridge, and the tunnel to the limbo of forgotten things. Let the Council give all its attention this year to the construction of the new parade and highway to the Fishmarket, which will supply a good deal of employment during the forth coming winter months.

B. D. Mackenzie.
St Leonards

Sir, May I ask why the original simple and economic scheme for overcoming the traffic problem in the Old Town has apparently been dropped in favour of an unnecessary and widely extravagant enterprise?

The simple scheme to which I refer was the widening of the south end of All Saints Street only, and then running all south going traffic (including the trolley buses) down that thoroughfare, only north bound traffic would be using the High Street. Such a scheme would cost only hundreds in proportion to thousands of pounds for the Bourne enterprise.

That such a thing is possible was shown when (even without widening at its southern extremity) All Saints Street accommodated all the High Street traffic when the later thoroughfare was closed for repair. It is also shown that this scheme was though feasible from the fact that the Tramways Company have anticipated this, by only fixing single wires in the High Street, and stating in their public notices that only a one way service through the Old Town was possible, until the widening of All Saints Street. Since then, this commonsense and cheap scheme of surmounting the difficulty has been relinquished. Why?

Quid Nunc.

The narrow High Street.

A bus trying to negotiate All Saints Street. April 1928.

All Saints Street.

The bottom of All Saints Street below Crown Lane.

Widening of Croft Road.
Feb 1930.

The Highways and Works Committee had before them a report from the Borough Engineer on an offer received from Mr. J. Whicker, to give up a strip of land on the east side of Croft Road for the purpose of widening the road, subject to the Corporation erecting a supporting wall. By a deed of covenant dated May 3rd 1901, the owners of the Croft Meadow Estate covenanted to give up at any time thereafter, upon being requested by the Corporation to do so, a strip of land for the widening of so much of Croft Road as abuts on the estate; and since the date of the deed part of the estate has already been built on, and the roadway widened in front of the houses, and the necessary retaining walls have been erected by the building owners.

Mr. Whicker has acquired the balance of the land to which the covenant attaches (about 68 foot frontage), and does not propose to build further houses at present, but he is erecting a house on land adjoining that before referred to, but in respect of which no arrangement has been entered into for the widening of the road. The Borough Engineer estimates the cost of widening the roadway and erecting a retaining wall along the whole frontage of Mr. Whicker's land at £217. 10s., and Mr. Whicker is prepared to contribute the sum of £10 towards the cost of erecting the wall along the frontage of his house. The Committee recommended that the work be carried out as suggested by the Borough Engineer.

Roadway through the Bourne
July 1930

The Joint Sub Housing and Finance Committee reported that the Housing and Improvements and Finance Committees had referred to them steps to be taken in connection with the preparation of a detailed scheme for a roadway through the Old Town. The Joint Sub Committee instructed the Town Clerk to report upon obtaining the services of an expert, who would be prepared to give a report upon the scheme, including the most suitable utilisation of the frontages to the roadway, the preservation of historic buildings, and the method of dealing with the areas from the frontage to the road to High Street and All Saints Street. The Town Clerk has been in negotiations with Messrs. T. H. Johnson and Son, architects, surveyors, and town planners of Doncaster, who have recently carried out work of a somewhat similar nature at York and other places. Mr. Johnson has viewed the site in question, and reported that the scheme would appear to involve a most searching investigation, which of necessity would occupy a certain amount of time, apart from the preparation of the written matter and diagrammatic plans, and that although it was difficult to

suggest a fee, they would undertake to prepare a plan and report for a sum of one hundred guineas along with all outgoing expenses.
The Joint Sub Committee recommended that the services of Messrs. T. H. Johnson and Son be engaged for the purpose at the fee and expenses above named. The Borough Engineer said that, he would agree to this, as he had not had sufficient experience of architectural work to lay out such a site as this.
The Old Town was a goose that laid the golden eggs, and it was in the interest of the town that its medieval character should be retained at all cost.

But, where did that phrase go wrong, perhaps the egg broke!!

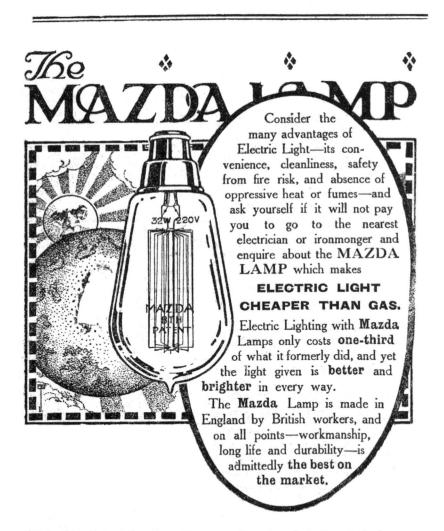

Old Town Traffic Problem.
Chief Constable suggests "One way" system
Possible reconstruction of all Saints Street.
July 1930.

A suggestion from the Chief Constable, Mr. F. James, that one-way traffic should be instituted in High Street and All Saints Street to alleviate the Old Town traffic problem was considered by the Council in Committee at their recent meeting.

The Watch Committee reported they had before them a report from the Chief Constable recommending that in view of the volume of traffic through the Old Town, and the fact that trolley buses were about to run in both directions in High Street, one-way traffic should be instituted in High Street and All Saints Street as soon as possible. The Committee approved of this recommendation and instructed the Town clerk to take the necessary steps for carrying the same into effect. The Committee were later informed by the Town Clerk that the Highways and Works Committee had received a report from the Borough Engineer that All Saints Street was not suitable for carrying heavy traffic, and that if one-way traffic were instituted it would necessitate the entire reconstruction of All Saints Street, and that the Highways and Works Committee has passed a resolution that in their opinion the question of the utilisation of All Saints Street for one-way traffic should be deferred until a report is received on the question of the new road through the Old Town.

The Watch Committee were of the opinion that the traffic problem in the Old Town required the urgent consideration of the Council, and in view of the fact that a new road through the Old Town could not be made for some considerable time, referred the matter to the Council in Committee for their instructions. Councillor Morgan said that the report be referred to the Highways Committee for information as to how soon All Saints Street would be available for traffic and the cost of making up the road. The Bourne Scheme would probably not be completed for another five years, and he thought the Chief Constable's suggestion should be followed.

Councillor Beck said the report emphasised the necessity of getting on with the work of making the new road through the Old Town. He hoped they would not have to wait five years. In the meantime, however, they would have to adopt temporary measures.

Alderman Smith recalled that two-way traffic in All Saints Street had worked well during the reconstruction of High Street, and moved an amendment that the Chief Constables' suggestion should be carried out. Alderman Shoesmith seconded. Councillor Hollaway anticipated an increase in road accidents in one-way traffic. He said that he would like to see High Street and All Saints Street left alone, and a 60 foot wide road driven through the Old Town.

He opposed the amendment.

The Deputy Mayor submitted that the Bourne Scheme had no bearing on the matter under discussion. He suggested as a compromise one-way traffic should be allowed for a trial period of three months only.

Councillor Breeds believed that the by-pass at the Roebuck Inn would solve the traffic problem in High Street. Traffic through All Saints Street would be a serious peril for the children who played there.

Councillor Dymond said the Borough Engineer had definitely stated that All Saints Street must be reconstructed if it were to be used for one-way traffic, or the houses would be shaken down.

Councillor Tingle opposed the one-way traffic suggestion. High Street, he said, was one of the safest streets in the borough, because it was narrow and more care was taken by motorists.

Alderman Chesterfield thought half the traffic that went up High Street might be turned up Queens Road and Mount Pleasant Road.

The amendment was lost and Councillor Morgan's resolution was carried.

No One-Way Traffic
All Saints Street deemed too narrow.
Council decide against its reconstruction.
August 1930.

All Saints Street is not to be used for one-way traffic.

The Hastings Town Council in Committee on Tuesday reached this decision after consideration of a report from the Borough Engineer Mr. S. Little setting out the cost of making up All Saints Street for heavy traffic, and stating that the existing traffic using this road would necessitate only slight repairs to the highway for many years.

The Committee called attention to the width of All Saints Street at various points, and were of opinion that owing to the extreme narrowness of the roadway it should not be used for one-way traffic, which would include omnibuses and trolley vehicles.

In this report the Borough Engineer stated that the minimum width of carriageway was 7ft. 11ins., between the lower end and Union Street, a distance of about 220ft., the carriageway width varied from 7ft. 11ins. to 10ft. 6ins.

In advising the Committee on this question, continued Mr. Little, "it is necessary for me to have some idea of the period the road would have to carry the heavy traffic, as the narrowness of the carriageway would result in vehicles being confined to more or less fixed tracks, increasing the wear and tear to an enormous extent as compared with a road of greater area."

"A concrete foundation would be necessary in any event, and for a period not exceeding four years a cold asphalt surface might withstand the traffic, providing it received regular attention, but if this period is greatly exceeded, the extra cost of wood paving would probably be justified, at least at the lower end." He estimated the cost as follows: Cold asphalt road, £5,571; wood paved road, £7,321: part cold asphalt, part wood paved road, £6,171. In view of the small amount of traffic using this road at the present time, it was probable that it would go for many years with only very slight repairs, and the cost of these would be negligible.

"I purposely refrain from passing any opinion on the safety of the lower part of this street when used for main traffic," concluded Mr. Little.

Alderman W. J. Fellows, J.P., who moved the adoption of the Committee's recommendation said if one-way traffic were introduced it was thought its direction would have to be down High Street and up All Saints Street, and the resulting chaos at the bottom of High Street could be imagined.

The recommendation was adopted.

Replanning the Old Town
Comprehensive report to be considered by the
Council preserving existing amenities.
December 1930

The most comprehensive scheme yet suggested for the replanning of the Old Town will probably come before the Town Council for consideration in February 1931. The report of Mr. T. H. Johnson, the Doncaster town planning expert, has already been revealed in Committee, and a further report on the question of cost will be drafted.

The Scheme provides for the construction of an arterial road through the heart of the Old Town and the erection of approximately 112 houses, accommodating 450 people. Steps would be taken to preserve existing houses of historical and artistic interest.

Before coming to any conclusion as to the best method of approaching the present problem, it is proposed to review briefly the existing conditions with a view to determining the future needs and necessities of the Old Town and out lying district.

The modern town of Hastings is really composed of three separate entities, namely St Leonards, the 19th Century Town of Hastings, and the Old Town of Hastings. The first two of the above have now coalesced into practically one continuous urban mass, but the latter still preserves certain independence, mainly due to its topographical position. This factor is not so evident to the casual visitor, who sees only an extension of Regency Facades leading him along the sea front to a further centre of obvious earlier age, connected with the fishing and other maritime pursuits. It is, however, the extremely steep East and West Hills that rise on either side of the long sloping valley, containing the Old Town, that are responsible for its delimitation between these well-defined boundaries. At the northern end of this valley the Old London Road leads out through Ore towards Winchelsea and Rye and in earlier times the main route to and fro London. At the valley foot stands the harbour ruin and sea. An ideal site for a small self-contained community. Thus, at the time of the growth of Hastings as a seaside resort, a start was made by an extension towards the west at the foot of Castle Rock, any attempted development in an easterly direction being limited by the East Hill, which rises in a sheer cliff from the sea. The Old Town has then, but for the changes in its architectural dress through the various vagaries of fashion, remained unaltered in general plan since medieval times.

THE BOURNE WALK

Its two streets, High Street and All Saints Street, run up the valley; separated by the Bourne Walk on the site of the now vanishing brook that bore this name, uniting at the top. Less than a hundred yards separate these thoroughfares, and the intervening space is a mass of small old houses, sloping terraces, passageways, etc., with unexpected turnings revealing a richness of interest and variety of view, that one usually associates with the lakeside towns of Italy. And yet there is that intimacy of homely scale apparent throughout that appertains solely to English tradition, and reminds one subconsciously of the connection of Hastings with the past, and its importance in days gone by. The value of the Old Town as it stands in relation to its attraction and interest to the visitor is impossible to define in any exact monetary sense, but that a commercial element exists in this old-world charm, and must grow year by year in this mechanical age, is certain. Unfortunately, modern conditions impose somewhat more exacting demands for transport facilities than those existing, and it is here that the difficulty arises.

The tremendous increase in motor traction has placed impossible burdens on the carriageways of High Street and All Saints Street. The former, which carries the heaviest traffic, is some nineteen feet in width at its widest part, the latter but sixteen feet, and minor accidents are of almost daily occurrence in both these streets, frequent obstructions and blockages taking place hourly especially in High Street, which is further obstructed by a trackless train service operating through its length. Any improvement scheme involving the destruction or demolition of any of the fine old houses fronting either of these thoroughfares is in our opinion quite out of the question.

It would be impossible to design any new buildings to take the place of the old without losing that asymmetry of form and character of long use at present associated with them. Some alternative means of finding a north-eastern exit to the town must therefore be found.

Proposed Route of the New Road

At first sight one of the most obvious solutions would appear to lie in the extension of the sea front, in the form of a marine drive, in an easterly direction; turning this route inland up one of the valleys running from the sea, to eventually join the existing Winchelsea Road, a few miles outside the town. Against this, however, the varying differences of level raise engineering problems of considerable difficulty, unless the proposal is carried far enough east, where more satisfactory gradients can be obtained; but even here access and connection back again to the existing road must necessarily be lone and circuitous. It is unnecessary to stress the attraction and desirability of a marine drive to a seaside resort of the rank that Hastings enjoys, and we are of opinion that although this cannot be designed to serve the dual purpose of a coastal road and eastern exit, it should be carried eastwards as far as Pett Level, and then return along the route of existing roads to rejoin the Winchelsea Road near Guestling Green. It should be stated that we fully realise the constructional difficulties and cost that would be involved in any extension of the marine drive, but this should be considered in its relation to the development of the surrounding parts, and the future extension of the borough boundary. This latter expedient would logically infer a readjustment of the existing boundaries on the north and east sides and in our opinion is essential to secure the preservation of the great expanse of open country along the cliff top from East Hill including the famous Glens of Ecclesbourne and Fairlight. In addition to this, it would further be possible to control the development of the foothills round Pett Level, and prevent the spreading of spasmodic building, which at present tends to spoilage this countryside.

To Pett Level

This suggested marine drive extension would then form a circumferential road round the new boundary and be invaluable for communication and development purposes, apart from its scenic attraction for the visitor. As to the possibility of continuing this route across Pett Level into Winchelsea as a coastal road, there would appear to be many difficulties involved, and it hardly comes within the scope of the present report but it would seem at least worthy of consideration by the county authorities.

We have also examined the possibility for a tunnelled route under the East Cliff emerging at the top to join the existing road system at either Belmont or Clive Vale and are of opinion that this is not a very practicable solution; unsuitable on both economic grounds and foreignness to English tradition. road tunnels have been very successfully employed on the Continent where the same problem has been encountered, as witness the well-designed approach from the Danube up to Old Buda; and whereas the very artificiality of the treatment appears in keeping with the Baroque background in this case, it would be another matter if transferred to the Old Town at Hastings.

Other routes impossible

We may add that we have also fully considered the possibility of any route from either Queens Road or Wellington Square, but the differences of surrounding level render any solution unfeasible except the most circuitous.

We are therefore of considered opinion that having regard to all the points involved, the proposed new road through the middle of the Old Town on the lines formulated by the Borough Surveyor, Mr. Little, offers by far the most satisfactory solution to the problem. The proposal of necessity involves the destruction of a certain amount of property, but offers by far the best gradient and is easily the most economical suggestion from the consideration of constructional cost. As to the method of treating the frontages, so as to work the old in with the new, forming its entrances and junctions, etc., but before discussing this we think it advisable to look a little more closely into the existing housing found off the Bourne Walk.

Present Housing conditions

The Bourne Walk starting from Bourne Street pursues a winding path up the valley and affords one of the principal means of access to the housing.

The latter is situated for the most part at right angles to this footway the further pathways through the courts formed by the houses, giving additional access to High Street and All Saints Street. The whole area is very dense and with no pretence at any formal plan, but it contains some very interesting examples of smaller domestic architecture, that it is proposed to preserve if possible.

The authors would like to add that they have inspected practically every house existing in this district, but for obvious reasons will give their views on this matter in as collected form as soon as possible. Between Courthouse Street and Bourne Passage has an area that is not very interesting, consisting on the one side of Messrs. Breeds Brewery, and the cottages belonging to them in moderate condition, but of unattractive appearance, (mid-19th century), and on the other side for the most part a condemned and partly cleared area.

Very nearly the same conditions prevail up to Waterloo Place, but here there is some very interesting architecture. These houses with the very fine tile hung fronts and curious almost Mansard forms and yet with two ridges, are certainly amongst the finest in Hastings and should give a certain flavour of form to any rehousing work necessitated.

Damp and Insanitary

Examples eliciting special admiration are found in Woods Row, the very fine tiled overhanging gable to Union Row, and the black weather-boarded cottages forming Providence Row. There are many others too numerous to mention, but equally deserving of praise. As to the condition of the property, much of it is dark and unhealthy, with insufficiency of air space and a great deal of it is damp and insanitary. The most satisfactory structural examples are those of unfortunately the least attractive appearance, and it is very difficult to determine as to what should stay or disappear. The principal factor exacting the greatest influence on this account is the actual line of the proposed road, and after that the consideration of the retention of certain parts to form some balanced treatment, or preconceived plan.

Bourne Walk.

The High Street.

Replanning Old Hastings
Expert Explains scheme at crowded ratepayers meeting
Preservation of Old-world streets.
January 1931.

The important scheme for the re-planning of the Old Town, recently published in the "Observer," which includes proposals for an arterial road through the Bourne area and the building of 112 new houses to replace existing slums, was explained at a crowded meeting of ratepayers at the Town Hall on Monday evening by Mr. T. H. Johnson, the Doncaster town planning expert who prepared it.

Mr. Johnson's visit was arranged by the Hastings & St Leonards Ratepayers Association, who organised the meeting. The keen interest taken by the towns people in the Old Town problem was shown in the questions with which the speaker was assailed after his address.

Mr. Johnson strongly deprecated any interference with High Street and All Saints Street and suggested that these two picturesque thoroughfares might be acquired for the town and preserved for all time.

Marine Drive Possibilities.

The Mayor, Councillor G. H. Ormerod, presided at the meeting, and in introducing Mr. Johnson, congratulated the Association on its enterprise in securing his visit.

Mr. Johnson said – "It is unnecessary for me to reiterate how considerable has been the growth in road traffic during the last few years, with the consequent increased burden on the carriageways. By plotting the loads carried against the width of the street, High Street would have been by comparison probably four of five times as wide as any of the other main roads. There are still further factors to take into account in relation to High Street in that it is a shopping street with a great deal of stationary and stopping traffic in it and a bus thoroughfare with passenger traffic alighting."

High Street Dangers.

"If you attempt to measure this amount of obstruction you would find that the congestion in this street is positively dangerous. I personally had the unfortunate experience of being pinned against the raised footpath on my first visit here. However, the bus drivers seemed well versed in the quickest methods of extrication and I escaped with little damage to my car."

The problem arose of finding some alternative route for this traffic, which should at the same time be strictly economical and not a too circuitous solution to this problem.

The plan of the Old Town is of the simplest type, consisting of its two main streets running up the long valley contained by the very steep East and West Hills, and uniting at the top to form the Old London Road and present connection to Winchelsea and Rye. Through the middle of this valley once ran the Bourne Brook, now the site of the present Bourne Walk, more or less equidistant from the two streets. The intervening spaces are a mass of small old houses, sloping terraces, passageways, etc., which have, apart from minor changes, maintained the same plan since medieval times. High Street has, of course, been a little more progressive, and its appearance has changed more with architectural fashion, more so than All Saints Street, where again the plan has remained untouched. I should imagine very little widening has ever been done to either of the carriageways.

"In my opinion, both these streets are unique, and I can assure you that as a stranger to Hastings, it has been a positive delight to me to find these thoroughfares in their present preservation, with their raised walks surmounted by a remarkably fine collection of 18th century and in many cases earlier buildings. One is impressed at once by the feeling of antiquity and the character of long use which these streets convey and I say again that any improvement scheme involving the demolition of these allude groups of buildings is quite out of the question, and would be nothing short of an act of vandalism."

Purchased for the town.

We made a suggestion that these two streets should be purchased for the town. This has been done in Brussels in respect of old streets and buildings, and if you did so here you would be preserving something that every tourist in the future would be grateful for.

We determined, therefore, to find some other means for the relief of the present traffic, and I should like to say here that, one of the first solutions, which would appear to suggest itself is that of utilising a one-way traffic system, which we did not mention in our report because of its many obvious disadvantages. High Street is some 19ft. in width at its widest part, and All Saints Street but 16ft., and both are shopping and residential streets.

These widths are insufficient to contain any mixture of moving and stationary traffic at all and, indeed, would be unsuitable anywhere except in a lesser residential area. A one-way traffic system would further give no alleviation to this problem, if any consideration at all is to be given to the safety of the inhabitants and pedestrians. It has been a marvel to me that no really serious accident has not already occurred in these streets, and it ought to be remedied without delay that an accident does not occur in the near future either.

Another proposal to which we gave a great deal of consideration was in the possible use of tunnelled routes going under the East Cliff and emerging at the top to join the existing road system at Clive Vale or some other suitable point. This, at first sight, appears to be a very interesting suggestion, and has been successfully employed on the Continent, where the same problem has been encountered. The application is not relevant; we are dealing here with a typical small English town and not with a capital city. Again, it is not a practical solution; the cost would be very heavy indeed.

The whole question of the use of tunnels in England, except under very exceptional cases, seems to me to be very foreign to our traditions and to use this method for entering a seaside town is altogether wrong. In Hastings, at any rate, those who prefer this method are very well catered for by the Southern Railway.

Marine Drive Profits.

At first sight, one of the most obvious solutions would appear to lie in the extension of the sea front in the form of a Marine Drive in an easterly direction, turning this route inland up one of the valleys running from the sea, eventually to join the Winchelsea Road a few miles outside the town.

This suggestion raises engineering problems of a very considerable magnitude, unless the proposal is carried far enough east, where more satisfactory gradients can be obtained, but this does not obviate the very difficult construction along the sea front, which would be doubly hampered by the doubtful nature of the overhanging rock, and again, its connection back to the existing road would be long and roundabout. Fairlight Glen, for instance, would not be too good apart from the inadvisability of putting a road of this character through such a fine piece of open country.

We should like to stress the desirability and attraction of a Marine Drive for a seaside resort of the rank that Hastings enjoys. This, we feel, should be considered in relation to the development of the surrounding district and the future extension of the borough boundary. This latter expedient would logically infer a readjustment of the boundaries on the north and east sides, and would at the same time secure the preservation of a fine expense of open country along the cliff top from East Hill, and also the control of the development of the foothills round Pett Level and the spreading of any harmful sporadic building. As to the possibility of continuing this route across Pett Level into Winchelsea as a costal road, this, we think, might be ultimately considered by the County Authorities. Mr. Johnson quoted figures in relation

Looking up All Saints Street.

Top end of All Saints Street by Ebenezer Road.

The High Street opposite Sinnock Square and passage.

to two English Marine Drives. In one case a profit was shown of £2,000 a year, and in the other case, where all capital expenditure had been paid off the net profits amounted to very nearly the same sum.

Mr. Johnson, continuing, said, the possibility of any route from either Queens Road or Wellington Square leading out towards the Old London Road had been carefully examined, but here again differences of surrounding level rendered any solution unfeasible.

Mr. Little's Scheme.

We therefore, he said, come back to the design of a proposed new road through the middle of the Old Town as originally formatted by Mr. Little, the Borough Surveyor, which in our opinion offers the most satisfactory solution to the problem. This route gives by far the most evenly graded incline consisting for the most part of not more that one in 51, it preserves All Saints Street and High Street, in their initial state and is easily the most economical suggestion from the consideration of constructional cost. A further advantage of this route is that it would take all the heavy through traffic and give a much greater freedom to the lighter traffic in the narrower streets of the town with additional facilities for shopping and local users. The provision of a more easily graded route in place of the existing roads means that this would make a considerable saving to the Corporation in upkeep, and also to owners of motor vehicles in running costs.

A proposal of this magnitude cannot of course be carried out without the destruction of a certain amount of existing property. I should like to say what has been the determining factor for retaining certain buildings in the scheme, and, which of necessity have had to be scrapped. The existing housing in the Old Town lies for the most part at right angles to Bourne Walk, in no particular plan formation beyond a series of parallel terraces and courts, with their connecting passages through All Saints Street and High Street.

The unexpected turnings and twists reveal most attractive groups of houses, many of which date from the 16th and 17th century with very fine mellowed roofs and tile hanging. In fact the whole area is full of colour and charm, and at first this romantic interest is inclined to mislead one's better judgement as to the exact condition of so much of the property. To mention but a few of the outstanding examples, there is a very fine group of houses in Waterloo Place, other in Woods Row and Union Row. I can think of so many little bits and remember for the most part how disappointing their general conditions proved on closer inspection.

Waterloo Place.

Beyond Repair.

We visited practically every house in this district and found it impossible to retain much of the existing housing in our scheme; most of it is in such a poor state as to be beyond structural repair and the general condition of health and amenity are very bad indeed. The insufficiency of air space renders it dark, and a great deal of it is damp and insanitary with slum conditions prevalent to a large extent, and as is usual in these areas the most satisfactory structural examples are unfortunately those which have the least attractive appearance. It is very difficult to determine as to what should stay or disappear, but the principal factor exerting the greatest influence on this account is the actual line of the proposed road itself, followed by the retention of certain parts to form some balanced treatment to the frontages or again the preservation of the building or group of particular architectural interest that it is proposed to work into the scheme. In the suggested planning of the blocks of the frontages we have got a certain formality running through the whole plan; it would be impossible and inadvisable to reproduce the Old Town again on the sides of the new roads. Generally speaking the most attractive of the old houses have been retained and worked in with the new to form cottage squares and quadrangles grouped round grass and garden spaces.

It is suggested to retain All Saints Square and parts of Woods Row and Waterloo Place have been worked into the scheme. We then come to the biggest of the new housing blocks, which is grouped in a series of quadrangles and has a through footway on a main cross axis connecting it to the two side streets. On the other side of the road the narrowness of the remaining plots forbids the erection of any buildings to balance the composition, but these spaces are taken up, in the top one by a children's playground, which would be entered from All Saints Street only, and in the lower one by a proposed garden, which would also have the effect of opening up a vista of some excellent 15th century cottages on the far side of All Saints Street.

Greater Formality.

Continuing the route from Courthouse Street a still greater formality is introduced into the plan and would be reflected first of all in the housing, which would be so designed to work in with a rather nice old group retained here, and would form an introductory feature for the shopping centre proposed to front on to the open place at the bottom. We have allowed for the passing through of the Marine Drive and also for the site of a bathing pool; this very controversial building development has nothing to do with this scheme.

As a terminal object for the road a well designed garden, with possibly an underground parking space beneath it, would serve equally as well on this site, and would close this side of the square. The buildings at this end of the road, consisting for the main part of shops, should be quite a modern character. Simplicity of form and the correct use of colour and materials employed should ensure the harmonious blending of the old work with the new.

There is no reason why a great deal of the existing tiling, which lends such a fine colour to the Old Town, should not be used on the more noticeable part of the new buildings.

Although this scheme would provide for approximately 112 houses, not all of the dispossessed tenants could be rehoused on this site, and we suggest that preference should be given in the allocation of new houses to those whose employment is nearby, the others being accommodated on a further site elsewhere. A similar difficulty of rehousing fishermen dispossessed by a slum clearance scheme in the centre of Amsterdam just after the war was overcome by the Dutch government building a fishermen's colony as an entirely separate entity adjacent to the sea. This scheme has worked well and the provision of a house at a low rent for the poorer paid seafaring man would, in our opinion, be a good investment.

A guaranteed supply of fresh fish to a town at a reasonable price is a decided asset. You have also another local industry close at hand in the net making and repairing sheds. This is probably of minor importance at the moment, but that is no reason why it should not be fostered. The local colour lent by the fishermen and the fishing fleet is an attraction of very considerable value to a seaside resort, and might be made more use of at Hastings, as an advertising medium than at present.

Health Inhabitants.

Despite the bad condition prevalent in the Old Town we were most forcibly impressed by the exceptionally fine physique of the women and children living there. The houses were well kept in nearly every case and entirely different from similar areas in the large industrial towns with which we are conversant. Outlining the suggested method of carrying out the scheme Mr. Johnson said, it was proposed that a start should be made on the cleared site in the middle, and then the first rehousing work commenced to the north of this, the dispossessed people coming into the first mentioned group of cottages.

This system would obtain for the rest of the scheme, which could be carried out in convenient stages. We have not prepared any figures as to the cost of this work yet, he said, but I know the most of you will be thinking what are we likely to get in exchange for the expenditure of this money?

This may be summarised as follows:

(1) a relief to the present traffic congestion in the Old Town and the preservation of High Street and All Saints Street in their existing state, and

(2) the removal of the stigma of an unhealthy housing area from the district and the provision of more satisfactory conditions.

Replying to questions Mr Johnson said the width of the proposed roadway was 60 feet, with 40 feet carriageway and two 10 foot footpaths. As far as possible houses, which were worth keeping would be retained.

Referring to a question by Mr. J. E. Ray who asked what provision the scheme made for dealing with the Old Town wall, which lay behind the house fronting the parade, Mr. Johnson said he had only been able to discover three or four feet of the wall remaining. He went on to state that, no provision for sites of schools had been made in his scheme. It was a question whether the best site for the whole of the Old Town schools would not be more in the centre of the population using them.

Speaking of the suggested Marine Drive, he declared that when the country was in a better financial position it would be a great asset to the town. Should such a drive be made this could become a profit making concern by charging a small toll.

All Saints Street left intact.

He stated that the only houses it was proposed to remove from All Saints Street were three that were in very bad condition and had been condemned.

I should not like to see a single house taken from All Saints Street or High Street, he said. If I were your Town Clerk, when the next Town's bill is before Parliament I should try to get hold of those streets, or at any rate do nothing to them without the town's people permission.

Speaking of the proposed bend in the new road, by the old brewery site, Mr. Johnson said, this had been introduced to avoid monotony and as a measure of steadying traffic. It would be impossible, he said, to get a satisfactory road from Wellington Square to the West Hill. Not only was the gradient too heavy, but it would lead through traffic into the town's shopping centre.

Mr. Johnson was thanked by the Mayor for his lucid explanation of his scheme, and Mr. Godfrey West endorsed the expression of thanks on behalf of the Association.

All Saints Street.

OLD TOWN IMPROVEMENTS

Councillor Dr. Newell's Criticism to a scheme
put forward by a Mr. Johnson.

All citizens should be interested in the future development of the Old Town, and should bring to bear in their judgement an unbiased frame of mind on any proposals for its betterment. Broadly speaking, we are dealing with an area of the shape of an isosceles triangle, with its base to the south lying in a valley with hills on the east and west. There is a gradient up to the north, with two roads forming its sides being much raised above the centre of the area. Both these roads contain, with the lower part of the area, houses of intense architectural interest. Interiorly the large majority of the properties must be regarded as insanitary, and the houses unfit for human habitation. Not far from the apex is a church, and to the south of this, very near the centre of the triangle, is a school. Near the centre of the lower half (about the junction of the lower and middle third) is an old brewery, and whose smoke hangs as a cloud to spoil the atmosphere breathed therein. The High Street, on the right, is 19ft. at its widest, and All Saints Street, on the east, is only 16ft. at its greatest breadth. It is estimated that there are no fewer than between 10 and 12 thousand persons living in the whole area, including both these streets, so no one can deny the existence of density of population and overcrowding of the houses. The existence of many narrow passages prevent sufficient light and ventilation ever reaching the inhabitants, and were it not for the fact that their livelihoods takes them mostly out of their houses, and they have the benefit of sea breezes, the sickness and mortality rate would be much heavier. Obviously, then, for reasons involved from the above factors, the time has come for a definite attack on this insanitary area as a public health duty to our fellow creatures, to lift them up by giving them better houses, throwing into the structures of these poetry of architecture, as well as permitting future dwellers to have more of the free gifts of nature - sunshine and natural light. Incidentally, the improvement of this area will mean less risk of epidemic diseases to the other inhabitants of the town. Thus, I look upon the attack of this triangle primarily from a sanitary point of view, and secondarily, epidemiologically. Thirdly, considerations for traffic have been pushed forth into prominence as the prime motive for attack. I put the motives in order stated. Whatever point of view you take for this attack, so will your plan of action be influenced. But from whatever point of view of attack you make, it is a *sine qua non* that the historic houses in the lower half and in the two side streets shall remain. Consequently, the town planner is making his incision into the area must constantly have before his mind the question *quo vadis?*
The essential thing for citizens is to recognise that the area must be attacked.

Waterloo Place.

The question is how best? The proposals so far put forth have all primarily from the point of view of a one way traffic or a wide road through the area. The layout or real improvement is fitted onto this. Since any layout must have roads, apart from my point of view it is more important to concentrate first on how you can best lay out, and your roads will necessarily be easier to place.

THE JOHNSON SCHEME.

This scheme primarily starts with the demand for transport facilities.

The report says, "Unfortunately, modern conditions impose somewhat more exacting demands for transport facilities than those existing." Mr. Johnson has found "it very difficult to determine as to what should disappear." He proposes a wide road from the apex (where, mind you, a lot of traffic will meet) down through the area, keeping mainly to the east side and giving a sharp bend round the greatest eyesore to the area - the brewery! He has found "the principle factor exerting the greatest influence" with him to be "the actual line of the proposed road," and (please note) "AFTER THAT the consideration of the retention of certain parts." He says there is bound to be a certain "formality" in the planning. Why? Further, we are informed "any new buildings should be expressive of modern conditions." "Masked by a screen wall treatment" will hardly be "in accord" with the old, the "shopping centre" is quite unnecessary. The buildings proposed for this are to be three or four storeys high, to become shops with a hotel over them, and other shops with flats above; a picturesque sight, indeed! The type of plan for the houses will have a living room and kitchen (with larder) and bathroom downstairs, and three bedrooms on the first floor. That means on a average of four persons per house. Owing to the wide road and the layout, we will be lucky if we even get half the dehoused people into the area at its likely high cost. With the loss of the school, there will be further cost of a new school (land, etc.) and the distance for the children to travel. The number of houses to be erected will be 112, which means 448 persons rehoused. Even taking his estimate of £340 as sufficient (and probably it is, considering the type), the houses alone will cost £38,080, to which must be added to the cost of the road, sewerage, compensation, legal expenses, architects' fees, etc., etc. It has been impossible for me to get the actual population of the Old Town, and in view of the improvement scheme, I am surprised that actual figures have not been calculated. Working on guess figures for a scheme of this sort and for the calculations of rehousing of the people is very unsatisfactory. I think that the true population should be investigated. I read that 12,000 persons has been put as the population of the Old Town, and presume this includes both sides of the two streets and parts immediately behind them. Even if you put the number of person affected by his plan as low as 1,000, this leaves at the very least 500 persons for the Council to find houses, and which the Council will not do for another £38,000. adding £50,000 for a new school, the scheme would on this basis, cost £126,000, without any of the amenities, such as a Bathing Pool, Marine Drive, Car Park, removal of the old and the erection of a new Fishmarket, removal of present unsightly garage, etc. So many other things make me sure I am very short of the likely bill at costs. It may be a second rival to our debt settlement to America! As I am not prepared to accept the scheme at all, one would ask of me an alternative solution. It is a ....

Y PLAN

I enclose a rough sketch of my plan of attack on the area as a whole, and how it looks apart from the area. Briefly, it is to make a sufficiently wide road from the south (the Johnson plan entrance here may do) and to carry it up straight to the brewery (which must go). At this the bifurcation of the Y takes place. From here the two limbs of the Y will be taken up, either to the crossroads above the County School, or if desired, higher, to end respectively into the upper part of the High Street and All Saints Street. This will give, roughly, a diamond shaped area between the apex of the area and the bifurcation of the Y. I would have a crossroads (above the school) at the W. and E. points of the diamond. On the north side of this would be cottages of two storeys (or three) of artistic design, with gardens in front and behind the cottages facing south, and looking on an open space (for the children) to the north of the school, which thus has an open space all round. On each side of the inverted pyramidal area (of which the school is the centre) I would have three storied terraced flats, after the London County Council plan, with gardens in front. These are cheaper to build than single cottages and are attractive. At the apex of the pyramidal area I propose a Fisherman's Reading Room divided into two parts (men and women). At the back there could be a covered veranda, so that mothers could sit there and see their children play in the open space, where they are safe from all traffic. I think the Council should give this Reading Room as a gift to the fishing community, conditional to them in keeping it in good repair. The treatment for the east and west sides of the limbs of the Y and down to the south entrance is the most difficult part of my scheme, because it depends upon how high you are going to take the limbs into the two side streets, and whether from your decision to preserve certain parts, the limbs are going to be straight or slightly deflected; also whether you adopt the three storied flats for greater numbers to be rehoused. Having decided that, it should not be difficult to harmonise an artistic form of dwellings along these sides. I do not think however, they should be high.
I would prefer really artistic double bungalows on raised plinths, with a veranda, and relegate the whole of the lower sets (or as many as required) to the fishing community. I believe the whole of your displaced population will thus be comfortably and satisfactorily rehoused in the area. If the number can be rehoused in the flats and cottages above, the sides could be garden plots.

Where Mr. Johnson puts his shopping centre, I would put a Municipal Central Fire Brigade Station (centralisation scheme) with rooms above for the officers and staff. On the corresponding opposite side I should put the Ambulance Headquarters. The plan shows adequate one way traffic through the limbs. My objection to Mr. Johnson's layout is that you are going to retain density of population between High Street and the western side of his wide road.

My plan distributes the housing with open space around all. His plan is lop-sided. Mr. Johnson retains the old brewery. I insist that this should undoubtedly go for good, and the citizens of this town should boldly face this proposal as one worthy of the best that can be done for this area. Its continued existence would be an incongruous anomaly to any respectable town improvement, let alone the dirt it causes in the atmosphere and houses.

Mr. Johnson's excuse for making a bend in this wide road in the cause for safety is not altogether on safe grounds. Anyone can stand at certain bends of any road and see if there is very much lessening of speed; and when it becomes well known to drivers down this road you will find that the bend will make little difference.

There may be more safety, both to motorists and pedestrians, in a straight road nowadays when people are educated about crossing. "Slow" indications are effective.

I have lessened the width of the entrance road, and of course, the two limbs will be much less for a one way traffic.

The advantages of my scheme are:-

1. Density of population dealt with.
2. Adequate open space ensured.
3. School retained.
4. Children's playground given.
5. Safe one way traffic ensured.
6. Easier Police control of traffic (three men at most).
7. A more artistic layout possible.
8. A Central Fire Brigade Station with less cost to the Council to provide one elsewhere.
9. An Ambulance Headquarters near to the most required spots.
10. No destruction of the architectural buildings in the lower two-thirds of the area, and by treatment of limbs of the Y avoiding others.
11. Possible preservation of any architectural buildings in the upper parts according to decision by possibility of carrying the limbs of the Y as thought best.
12. Rehousing in the area a greater number (or all) of the dehoused people, and therefore, a very great saving to the Council. (I make the road frontage for building as 10 to 15 in my plan, i.e., half more than Mr. Johnson's).

13. Houses could be provided straightaway in the area ready for dehoused persons (the cottages to the north of the school could be done before any were dehoused).
14. It will allow only one way traffic up High Street and down All Saints street, and thus ensuring further safety.
15. The saving in cost to the Council in saved in building a school, finding land for a Fire Brigade Station, finding land and building houses elsewhere for dehoused persons, finding land and building houses for 500 persons not provided for all these savings and their concomitants (interest, etc.) will justify the demolition and compensation for the old brewery.
16. The Johnson scheme must be accepted as a whole or not at all. It is not easy to modify it. The 'Y' plan is capable of modification according to the height to which you carry the limbs.
17. The Johnson scheme will give posterity no alterative when the houses in the High Street and All Saints Street become inhabitable to have complete demolition of these at great cost as they are hardly likely to continue these narrow streets. My 'Y' plan gives posterity a chance of having a complete open space to the south, and then there would be little objection to continue houses in the upper half of these streets.
18. My scheme is amenable to alterations according to what is decided on to retain - his must be accepted as a whole.

As one of the amenities which the Council could afford in the houses is the provision of gas stoves, and thus lessen the smoke accumulation in this area, it would pay the Council to provide a women domestic social worker to teach any the art of cooking by gas. Those who used gas stoves could be given a special rebate in this area. It would certainly lessen the risk of fire from the use of coal when hot embers are carried from an open fire in one room to a grate in the scullery to cook by, thus this would be an added insurance for Council owned property. On the same principle, I should equip each and every dwelling with electric light. All refuse should be removed between the hours of 6 a.m. and 7 a.m. (an hour later in winter). L.C.C. provides gas by arrangement with the Gas Company for lighting, heating and cooking and one gas fire, and they lay the mains, pipes and supply the meters and cookers.

The water for baths is heated in coppers in the kitchen, and by a simple syphonic device enables the tenants to transfer the hot water from the copper to the bath.

Extra's to the scheme.

Motor Park. - This I consider absolutely essential. You can't have a stream of people coming in without adequate provisions for such. The present unsightly garage must go.

Marine Drive. - I do not know why it has been given this ridiculous name, but an extension of the road here is necessary to say the least.

Bathing Pool. - I am glad to see that Mr. Johnson agrees with me here, as also do the town planners for the Borough. You are advertising for people to come to Hastings and yet you have now reduced their beach accommodation by the Parade Extension and by doing so access to the beach is now very much restricted. The provision of a Bathing Pool will provide a present demand, and at this spot will be a very paying concern. I do not agree with the shape nor with the actual location he has placed it upon.

My idea is that it should be on the western side of the upper half of the shore portion of the Harbour Arm. It should be brought along the beach for a certain distance and carried up the beach to provide ranging depths for children, with a toddler's pool at the top. The effect of this bathing pool will be to act as a large groyne, and in years to come there will be great accumulations of the beach. Now, as you have taken away a good expanse of beach at the Parade Extension, here is a good opportunity of compensating yourselves and at the same time not only providing an additional amenity, namely a Bathing Pool, but, not likely, saving further expense by not having to touch the Harbour Arm. The beach accumulation and the bathing pool may prevent any money being spent thereon for many years from the protection afforded. All that would be required would be to repair the gap in the Harbour and carry the arm up the existing beach by piling. Charabancs full of day trippers arrive for the day there, with limited time and purses, will not go to Bopeep and pay 4d. for the bus and, say 2d. for the pool bathing. Further, you have the natural platform of the beach from which the people can see the bathers in the pool.

People come down to enjoy the beach and sand, and at the same time have near at hand some of the Pier side shows. A £62,000 Bathing Pool at Bopeep requires deep consideration. Five per cent of the trippers of Hastings will not go there, and I feel sure nor five per cent of the residents of Bulverhythe or Bexhill Road area. You are then left mainly with the residents of St Leonards and a portion from Hastings. Will that suffice to make the scheme pay?

If you want to do something to help the smaller hotels and boarding houses of St Leonards, as well as St Leonards Pier, then by all means have a second bathing pool (of lesser cost) on either side (preferably to the west) of St Leonards Pier. This is more likely to be a greater success than one at Bopeep. I do feel strongly that the Council should not turn down the Bathing Pool at the Harbour Arm, as, apart from its paying proposition, the influence it will have in giving more beach and saving a costly expenditure on the Harbour Arm in the very near future when so many other important and costly schemes area launched. I think it better to pass one estimate for the scheme, parking, drive and pool. In putting these views before Council and the interested citizens, I do so from a sense of true citizenship, trusting they will receive fair consideration for the best interests of the Old Town as well as the public purse The 1930 Housing Act gives adequate powers to the Council, and surely will save the ratepayers a costly Bill in Parliament. The Old Town Scheme deserves the higher opinion of an expert from London.   A. G. NEWELL.

Mr. THERM

sends greetings to all his friends for

THE NEW YEAR

He hopes that during the Festive Season his Constant Service has been of assistance and appreciated.

GAS SERVICE

PROVIDES FOR

LIGHTING

COOKING

WATER HEATING

SPACE HEATING

REFRIGERATION

and many other purposes.

Up-to-Date Appliances

are Exceedingly Economical and Satisfactory.

Hastings & St. Leonards GAS COMPANY

TO PROTECT YOUR EYES

INSTALL

MODERN

GAS

LIGHTING

RELIABLE — ECONOMICAL — COMFORTABLE.

The Best Quality Incandescent Mantles, which maintain their original Luminosity, cost only 6d. or 7d. each.

New Incandescent Burners fixed to approved fittings free of charge. Modern fittings purchased are also fixed free of charge where suitable connections exist.

Call at our Showroom and see our latest patterns in British Made ARTISTIC FIREPROOF GLASS AND FANCY SHADES.

SEE THE SWITCH CONTROL IN ACTION.

All details from

The Hastings & St. Leonards GAS COMPANY

Queen's Road

HASTINGS

(Tel. 2400).

Branch Showrooms:

61, Robertson Street,

HASTINGS

18, London Road,

ST. LEONARDS.

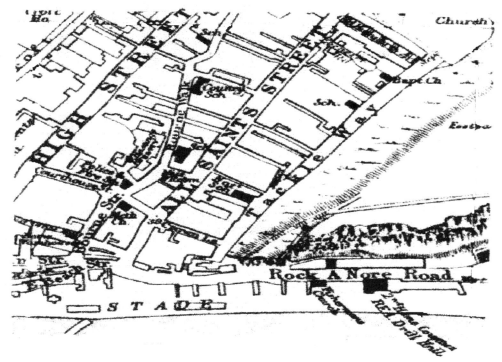

The 'Y' plan as proposed by Mr. Johnson and altered by Dr. Newell.

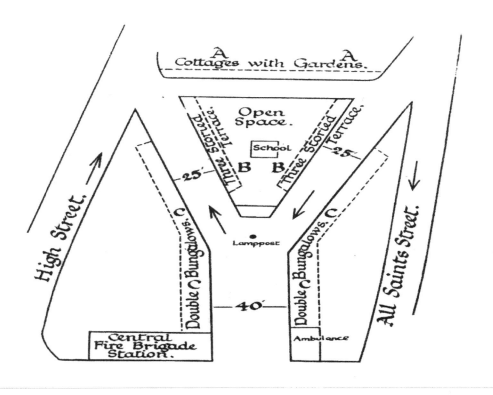

J. HOLLINGSWORTH LTD.

MAIN FORD DEALERS

HAVELOCK ROAD and BRAYBROOKE ROAD HASTINGS

have the following used cars and commercial vehicles for sale

PRIVATE CARS

1954 ZEPHYR 6 (Green). Leather upholstery and heater. Licensed. Low mileage. Perfect condition. 3 months' guarantee **£675**

1954 CONSUL (Black). Leather upholstery. Heater. Licensed. Excellent condition. Three months' guarantee **£625**

1952 PREFECT (Beige). Leather upholstery. Extremely good condition. Licensed. Three months' guarantee **£425**

1949 ANGLIA (Black). Reconditioned engine. Licensed. Very good condition. Three months' guarantee **£285**

1937 HUMBER 18 SALOON. Licensed. Good condition **£85**

COMMERCIAL VEHICLES

1953 FORD 5cwt. Van. Three months' guarantee ... **£250**

1949 FORDSON 2-ton Van **£75**

1948 AUSTIN 2-ton Van. Very good **£150**

1947 BEDFORD 5-ton l.w.b. Truck **£250**

1946 BEDFORD 10/12cwt. Van **£85**

1945 BEDFORD 5-ton l.w.b. Truck **£195**

1937 FORDSON 2-ton s.w.b. Truck **£75**

1936 BEDFORD 30cwt. Van **£50**

ALL IN GOOD CONDITION AND OPEN TO ANY TRIAL

PHONE HASTINGS 2727 (3 lines)

The Hastings of the Future.
First steps already taken.
Oct 1932.

What will Hastings be like in say 50 years time? The fascinating possibilities conjured up by the questions that were put before the Town Planners Institute annual meeting, held in Hastings this year. There were experts from all over the country attending the conference, with many members of the Council from Hastings, Bexhill, Eastbourne, Rye etc.,

In an opening speech led by Dr. Adams of the Institution, he said that, One interesting fact known to me was that Winchelsea is one of the earliest towns to be planned on idea lines, a result of a vision shown by Edward I.

Hastings was warmly praised for having made such a satisfactory start to the towns general development plan, whereby, the front line had been pushed out seawards to give what they called an excellent approach to Hastings.

This new road stretched from White Rock as far Eastwards as the Old Town, but all traffic was still led up and down the High Street. Having spoken about the many suggestions made not only by the Borough Engineer Mr. S. Little, but also from private individuals, that there were many suggestions of a new road that should now be pushed through the centre of the Bourne, despite the fact that many people would be made homeless by the demolition of their houses, this was to be looked at as a vision to the future.

The Town Planners Institution gave their approval to the scheme, as they knew that several professional bodies had been involved in the decision making, whereby, each and ever one had come to the same conclusion, that a road through the heart of the Bourne was really the only practical answer.

Tunnels, viaducts, and alternative routes were discussed, but it all led to the same answer, The Bourne!

At this period in time it was still thought that perhaps a Bathing Pool was to be built on the beach opposite, what was to be the entrance to the Old Town through a new arterial road. The planners suggested that, if this was the case, an amusement park should also be constructed nearby, but away from the fishing quarters, this, in their opinion would entice visitors to move further eastwards away from the town centre towards the Old Town and venture into the area.

It was envisaged that a coastal traffic road would be constructed along the front line of all the coastal towns situated between Hastings and Brighton.

The Mayor of Bexhill stated that they certainly didn't want the main road driving through their town, as everybody could see this ultimately as becoming a race track between towns.

Dr. Adams thanked everyone for listening to what he had to say, and was followed by general discussions from the floor.

Suggested Improvements.

The proposed plan for future improvements to the town were discussed at depth, these indicated that there were proposals for zoning, road widening, new roads, building lines and open spaces. There were suggestions made for further water front improvements, including the extension to the parade, which had been achieved and admirably executed and planned by the Borough Engineer. Other planned ideas were to build a new civic centre at Bohemia, a design that had been put forward, but awaited decision. This design would have incorporated a new road layout, whereby, a viaduct constructed over Alexandra Park would have taken all through traffic away from the town centre, out onto the coastal road in either a westerly or easterly direction, and ultimately through the new road proposed to be built in the Bourne if travelling towards the eastern outskirts.

The Council had already acquired land in several parts of the town, but were running out of money, even though Government grants were still readily available, there was no sense in borrowing more money if the project didn't actually benefit the town to prosper for the future.

The new Parade extension cost £180,000, whilst the road widening of Sedlescome Road North, connecting with the new A21 set the Council back a further £50,000, but these were a necessity in getting people from London and alike into Hastings easily. With the new road through the Bourne and all the compensation to be paid for those that would be dispossessed, and the building of new houses to put all these people in amounted to many thousands of pounds; the general debt was now in the region of £2,000,000., and who had to find all this money, yes, the ratepayers!

One comment was made from the floor as regard the 50 years ahead, that as the Council couldn't see between 2 and 3 years ahead, what chance was there of looking 50 years ahead, who out of us lot will be here to see 10 years ahead let alone 50! With that, the Conference was closed, everybody then attended a civic reception held at the Queens Hotel, the party consisted of about 80 guests, the next day the party went for a motor coach tour of East Sussex resorts. (How much did this cost the towns ratepayers we wonder?)

During the two years that are missing 1932 and 1933, the arguments still raged as to what scheme was to be adopted, as the Council now realised time was running out, so was that of the residents too. In the meantime, proposals were submitted time and time again, all in different forms, until finally in 1934 the Housing and Improvements Committee made a definite decision as to what action was to be taken in trying to sort out the good from the bad in property that was scheduled to be demolished under the only scheme that was to be finally adopted, and that was the roadway through the heart of the Bourne.

£100,000 Slum Clearance Scheme.
Jan 1934.

Hastings Town Council approved at their meeting this month that a £100,000 slum clearance and rehousing scheme for the Old Town was to go ahead.

The Housing and Improvements Committee reported that, in connection with the letter received from the Ministry of Health, urging the Council to now take immediate action for carrying out the slum clearance and improvement schemes, they had been informed that the Medical Officer of Health had completed his investigations into the housing conditions in certain areas of the Old Town, and as a result he had presented official representations to the Council in respect of each area set out in an accompanying schedule, declaring that the houses were unhealthy, and that the most satisfactory method of dealing with the conditions in the areas was the immediate demolition of all the houses. Seventeen areas were affected, comprising:

Zion Cottages, Ebeneezer Road, Hope Cottages, Union Row, Woods Row, Waterloo Place, Fishers Cottages, Bourne Passage, north of All Saints Infant School, The Creek, Bossom Square, Winding Street, Wellington Court and Gibbons Square. The Council had agreed in principle with the proposition and with the compulsory rehousing programme of the dispossessed tenants.

The report involved demolition in every case, and it meant that the Council undertook to rehouse the people within a period fixed by the Ministry of Health. This action now legally bound the Council, and the Chairman said that, he did not want members to say afterwards that they did not do it with their eyes open. The Ministry of Health added to the letter that, the Corporation had not progressed in speed in this matter as they should over the past few years, as this insanitary condition had been raised on more than one occasion during this time, time for action in now upon you.

Members of the Council had inspected the areas concerned, and found for themselves what terrible places they were. They commented that one particular property visited one water tap was shared by four properties, and beneath the tap was filth of the worst description.

It had to be noted that, most of the tenants tried to keep their houses in a very clean condition. The delegated party said that, some of the properties scheduled for demolition were not in a condition that justified it. It was not justice to the owners that they should be robbed of their property. A good deal of the cleaning up of the Old Town could be done in other ways than a wholesale clearance by demolition.

If, property was to be acquired, then adequate compensation must be given to those that are to be dispossessed, although the Ministry had said that, for those properties to be acquired for the purpose of Improvements, the Council can only offer site value only; which only amounted to a few pounds in most cases, this was truly scandalous, and the Council knew it as well.

There were cases in which this practice was absolutely iniquitous. A case was quoted to where the owner of a house in Winding Street, which had very recently been put in order at the instigation of the Health Committee, but was now asked to give up the property at site value only. It was generally wondered to what would happen if the Health Officer was let loose in the London suburbs? Were the people living there in the same conditions as those here in the Old Town, the simple answer to that is, yes, far worse, but London County Council wasn't doing the same as here in Hastings. It was a fact that the people living here in the Old Town were a healthy lot, by far better than those in London. The report failed miserably in discriminating between the houses. If decent houses are to be included in order to facilitate these so called improvements, then they should be paid for at their proper face value, and not confiscated, or paid peanuts in site value only.

The Council were adamant that the houses to be taken were not fit for human habitation. Owing to consideration of the question of justice, the matter had been deferred again and again. They were now definitely up against it, and the Government intended to go through with it. Were they to be placarded up and down the country, as the town that would not carry out its slum clearances?

It was contended that there had been inequality of treatment in dealing with this question. The complaint had been made that tenants were paying exorbitant rents, and the owners of the slum properties should not be considered. The Town Clerk presented a report from the Borough Treasurer, stating that the total estimated cost of clearance and rehousing was £100,000, and the ultimate charge on the rates would be £1,000 per annum.

If people have made a bad investment, why should they expect the community to compensate them for their errors?

The report was adopted by a vast majority in favour of the work starting immediately. Another report from the same Committee dealt with properties on the north western side of All Saints Street, and on the suggestion of the Medical Officer of Health, the Committee recommended the demolition or repair, as circumstances might require, of houses unfit for human habitation; the purchase by the Council of land for opening out the area; and the abatement of overcrowding in the area.

An undertaking was given to carry out the necessary rehousing operations with immediate effect. Comments were made to the effect that, in this case the area might contain some fit houses, some that could be repaired, and some that should be demolished, how are you going to differentiate to what is good and to what is bad? You will never shift these people in the Old Town, said one Councillor. They must be near their work. If we rehouse these people in the neighbourhood of their work, it will be a great feather in the cap of the Corporation, but if they were to be moved to the Hardwicke Road site, or even further afield, how are they going to tend their boats and sell their wares.

The travelling distance between shore and the houses you intend to put them in will be the end of an industry that has been here for centuries, do you want blood on your hands?

With that, the meeting was closed and wheels set in motion to demolish the first set of houses that stood in the way of progress and a ROAD, that once constructed would be the end of ends for the close knit community of the Old Town of Hastings and especially the people to whom worked and lived in the area of the Bourne.

Those that were moved out in the first phase of the Old Town Clearance Scheme had all their belongings from their houses taken to the disinfector house at Rock-a-Nore to be fumigated before it was transported into their new abode. Furnishings, bedding, clothes everything was steamed to try and get rid of any infestation that might have been hiding in their goods.

Bed mattresses were the worst offenders, in some cases they were riddled with small insects, all because they survived on the damp conditions in which it was housed. There were instances as to the goods having to go through the disinfector twice before the Health Officers were satisfied they were free of all bugs etc.

There was one person who wished to remain nameless, who spoke out very frankly about living in the cramped conditions of the Old Town and how she wished she could move out, here is her letter:-

I live in the Old Town with three children. The place where I live is dreadful. I have to stay up half the night looking for bugs. The property is in a dreadful state of repair, and the landlord won't do anything about it. The cistern is outside and no lid to cover the water. I go and get my drinking water from the place at the Fishmarket. Oh to have a nice house to go to. I cannot afford much as my husband has been on the dole all winter. So please, as a man of God, hurry the scheme through. I won't sign my name as I don't want my landlord to know.

Plummers
PLUMMER RODDIS LD

The best equipped Removal and Storage Depot in the District.

Estimates Free.   Phone 618.

Robertson Street, Hastings.

NOW IS YOUR OPPORTUNITY
to get your House Decorations and Repairs at Cost Price.   Call, 'Phone 1550, or Write.

F. G. BARGH
Builder and Decorator
4, CROSS ST., LONDON RD., ST. LEONARDS
ELECTRICAL INSTALLATIONS AND REPAIRS
::   JOBBING WORK OF ALL KINDS   ::

'PHONE 568

GOODWIN
WM. GOODWIN LTD.
BUILDERS   DECORATORS

36, MIDDLE ST., HASTINGS

PUT YOUR JOBS IN COMPETENT HANDS

MANN & PAINE
Electrical Contractors' Association

75, HIGH STREET, HASTINGS

ELECTRICAL ENGINEERS

'PHONE 775   WIRE FOR US
              and   'PHONE 775
              WE'LL WIRE FOR YOU

Where are all the dispossessed people going to go?
March 1934.

Dealing with the report of the Housing Committee recommending the purchase of Bembrook Farm and all the adjoining land, for the erection of houses to accommodate all the people who will be displaced by the clearance of the slums from the Old Town. This problem of finding land to build houses upon for the people who will shortly be dispossessed of their houses has lingered on for the past 10 years or so; it seems almost impossible to find anybody with a plan, which meets all the difficulties of the problem. It is only natural, that the residents that live in Collier Road and the West Hill areas are protesting against the Councils scheme, seeing that it will bring about the erection of many small houses on the site all under the Councils control.

The people currently living on the West Hill who are writing to the press weekly on this subject, forget that the alternative scheme (if the problem is to be solved by the erection of small houses) is to build the houses on land behind Collier Road. This would certainly open up a further flood of questions from residents on all parts of the West Hill in relation to this matter.

The erection of buildings, say, standing some 50 feet tall in the Old Town without interfering with the view, or making the advocates of the City Beautiful shudder more than once a day could be achieved with care. And in such buildings as these, sufficient numbers of people who had been displaced could be rehoused under one roof. Of course, there is the all important question, will these people ever consent to residing in blocks of flats?

We realise that these people when dispossessed of their property have to go somewhere, and if they object to moving to a small house anywhere out of the area away from the Old Town, and having to be placed in flats erected for their convenience, and rents to suit their pockets, we cannot imagine to where they will live. Many Councillors were still in the opinion that, a wide road through the heart of the Bourne must be made, and blocks of flats erected on the front. If this was the case, then Bembrook Farm site should be left as an open space for all to enjoy, and, if houses were ever to be built there, then they should be of a more desirable house for the private enterprise market, and not built specifically for Council people.

Slums of the future.
August 1934.

Attention to working class property in the town that is 'slowly but surely deteriorating' in yet another report from Dr. Bruce the towns Medical Officer of Health, to the Public Health Department.

Dr. Bruce refers to this problem in a review of the Town Councils slum clearance proposals contained in a five year programme.

The nature and extent of the housing problems of this town have been fully indicated in previous reports. 550 houses over the past 10 years or so have been built on various estates such as, Barley Lane, Silverhill, Hollington, etc,.

These have dealt with mainly the overcrowding, and sub letting tenancies, but only to a very minor degree with the rehousing of tenants from houses that had been demolished as part of the clearance areas, or as individual unfit for human habitation properties. In 1924, an improvement scheme involving some 62 houses, and dealing with the central part of the Bourne Valley of the Old Town, was confirmed by the Ministry, but owing to certain technical and legal difficulties, the area has not been completely cleared. For dispossessed tenants the Hardwicke Road flats, 48 in number, were provided, although eventually they had to be used for tenants from other areas.

Final Notice to Clear slums from Hastings Old Town. November 1934.

Notice to objectors under section 2 of the Housing Act, 1930, of Compulsory Purchase Orders, confirmed by the Ministry of Health, in respect of land comprised in clearance areas, and land surrounded by, or adjoining the area.

Hastings (Old Town Nos. 1 to 10 inclusive, and 12, 14, 16 and 17) Housing confirmation Orders, 1934.

Notice is hereby given, that the Minister of Health, in pursuance of the powers vested in him by Part 1 of the Housing Act, 1930, on this day of November 1934, confirmed, (with some modifications) Orders submitted to him by the County Borough of Hastings, authorising the Council to purchase compulsory for the purpose of the Housing Act, 1930, the lands described in the schedule hereto, which lands and lands in areas declared to be clearance areas by a resolution of the Council, dated January, 1934, and also lands outside the said clearance areas, but surrounded by, or adjoining the said areas.

Reference to the Orders and maps showing the said clearance areas, will be on show in the Town Hall for public viewing at all reasonable hours.

The Orders will become operative at the expiration of six weeks from the date of this publication, but if proceedings in the High Court are instituted within that period by an aggrieved person desirous of questioning the validity of the Orders, or any of them, the Court may, if satisfied that such Order of Orders are not within the powers of the Act, or that the interests of the applicant have been substantially prejudiced by any requirement of the Act, not have been complied with, quash such Order of Orders either generally, or in so far as it, or they affect any property of the applicant.

Schedule.

Hastings Old Town No. 1.
(Zion Cottages) Housing confirmation Order, 1934.

Houses, 43, Tackleway, and 1 and 2 Zion Cottages.
House, 3, Zion Cottages.
House, 4, Zion Cottages.
Yard and outbuildings.

Hastings Old Town No. 2.
(Ebenezer Road) Housing confirmation Order, 1934.
Part 1. Lands within the clearance area.

House, 6, Ebenezer Road.
House, 4, Ebenezer Road.
House, 2, Ebenezer Road.

House, 8, Ebenezer Road.
House, 10, Ebenezer Road.
House, 12, Ebenezer Road.
Passage, yards and outbuildings, adjoining 2 to 12 Ebenezer Road.
House, 13, All Saints Street.
House, 14, All Saints Street.
House, 15, All Saints Street.
Forecourt, fronting 13, 14 and 15 All Saints Street.

Part 2. Lands outside the clearance area.

House, 12, All Saints Street.
House, Store, 12a, All Saints Street.

Hastings Old Town No. 3.
(Hope Cottages) Housing confirmation Order 1934.

Houses, yard and outbuildings, 16 and 17, All Saints Street.
Houses, (part over passage), 18 and 19, All Saints Street.
Yards, passages and outbuildings, rear of 18 and 19, All Saints Street.
House and outbuildings, 1, Hope Cottages.
House, yard and outbuildings, 2, Hope Cottages.
Houses, 3 and 4, Hope Cottages.
House, yard, outbuildings, passage and land, 20, All Saints Street.
Houses (part over passage), 21, 21a, 21b and 21c, All Saints Street.
Passage, yard and premises adjoining 21, 21a, 21b and 21c, All Saints Street.
Houses, yard, outbuildings and premises, 22, 22a, 23, and 23a, All Saints Street.
House, yard, outbuildings, garden and premises, 24, All Saints Street.
House, outbuildings, garden and premises, 25, All Saints Street.
Yard and outbuildings, rear of 25 and 26, All Saints Street.
House (part over passage), 26, All Saints Street.

Hastings Old Town No. 4
(Union Row) Housing confirmation Order, 1934.
Part 1. Lands within the clearance area.

Passage (Providence Row), yards and outbuildings adjoining 1 to 8, inclusive.
House, 1, Providence Row.
House, 2, Providence Row.
House and forecourt, 3, Providence Row.
House and forecourt, 4, Providence Row.
House and forecourt, 5, Providence Row.
House and forecourt, 6, Providence Row.
House and forecourt, 7, Providence Row.
House, 8, Providence Row.
W.c's rear of 15, Union Row.
Passage, rear of 15, 14 and 13, Union Row.
House and forecourt, 15, Union Row.

House and forecourt, 14, Union Row.
House and forecourt, 13, Union Row.
House and forecourt, 12, Union Row.
Yard and buildings rear of 12, Union Row.
House, forecourt, yard and outbuilding, 10, Union Row.
House, forecourt, yard and outbuilding, 9, Union Row.
House and forecourt, 8, Union Row.
House and forecourt, 7, Union Row.
Yard and outbuilding, rear of 8 and 7, Union Row.
Yard and outbuilding, rear of 6, Union Row.
Yard and outbuilding, rear of 5, Union Row.
Yard and outbuilding, rear of 3, Union Row.
Yard and outbuilding, rear of 2, Union Row.
Passage (Union Row).
House, 1, Stanfords Cottages.
House, 2, Stanfords Cottages.
House, 3, Stanfords Cottages.
House, 4, Stanfords Cottages.
House, 5, Stanfords Cottages.
Passage (Stanfords Cottages), yards and outbuilding adjoining 1 to 5 inclusive,
Stanford Cottages, 129, All Saints Street and Bourne Walk.

Part 2. Lands outside the clearance area.

House and forecourt, 11, Union Row.
Yard and outbuildings, rear of, 11, Union Row.
House, yard and outbuildings, 4, Union Row.
House, yard and outbuildings, 6, Union Row.
Passage, Union Row.

Hastings Old Town No. 5
(Woods Row) Housing confirmation Order, 1934.

House, yards, and outbuilding, 2, Mulberry Cottages.
House, garden, yard and outbuilding, 1, Mulberry Cottages.
Passage, rear of 1 to 7 inclusive, Woods Row.
House, 1, Woods Row.
House, 2, Woods Row.
House, 3, Woods Row.
House, 4, Woods Row.
House, 5, Woods Row.
House, 6, Woods Row.
House, 7, Woods Row.
House, 8, Woods Row.
House, 9, Woods Row.
House, 10, Woods Row.
House, 11, Woods Row.

House, 12, Woods Row.

Passage (Woods Row), yard and outbuildings.

Hastings Old Town No. 6.
(Waterloo Place) Housing confirmation Order, 1934.
Part 1. Lands within the clearance area.

Passage east side of 1, Waterloo Place, and rear of 1 to 8 inclusive, Waterloo Place.

House, forecourt, yard and outbuildings, 1, Waterloo Place.

House, forecourt, yard and outbuildings, 2, Waterloo Place.

House, forecourt, yard and outbuildings, 3, Waterloo Place.

House, forecourt, yard and outbuildings, 4, Waterloo Place.

House, forecourt, yard and outbuildings, 5, Waterloo Place.

House, forecourt, yard and outbuildings, 6, Waterloo Place.

House, forecourt, yard and outbuildings, 7, Waterloo Place.

House, forecourt, yard and outbuildings, 8, Waterloo Place.

House and forecourt, 10, Waterloo Place.

House and forecourt, 11, Waterloo Place.

House and forecourt, 12, Waterloo Place.

House and forecourt, 13, and 13a, Waterloo Place.

Yard and outbuildings, rear 10, 11, 12, 13 and 13a, Waterloo Place.

Passage (Waterloo Place).

Yard and forecourt, west side of 14, Waterloo Place.

House, forecourt, yard and outbuilding, 14, Waterloo Place.

House, forecourt, yard and outbuilding, 15, Waterloo Place.

House and forecourt, 16, Waterloo Place.

House and forecourt, 17, Waterloo Place.

Yard and outbuilding, rear of 16 and 17, Waterloo Place.

Part 2. Lands outside the clearance area.

Passage, rear and west side of 9, Waterloo Place

House, forecourt, yard and outbuildings, 8, Waterloo Place.

Passage (Waterloo Place).

Workshop, stores, w.c. and forecourt east side of 17, Waterloo Place.

Hastings Old Town No. 7.
(Fishers Cottages) Housing confirmation Order, 1934.

House, forecourt, yard and outbuildings, 50, Bourne Walk.

House (part over passage) and forecourt, 16, Bourne walk.

Yard and outbuildings, rear of 3 and 4, Fishers Cottages, and 15 and 16, Bourne Walk.

Hastings Old Town No. 8.
(Bourne Passage) Housing confirmation Order, 1934.
Part 1. Lands within the clearance area.

Passage and yard, rear of 14 and 13, Bourne Walk, and 4, 4a, and 3, Bourne Passage.

Outbuildings, north side of Bourne Passage.

House, 4a, Bourne Passage.

House, 4, Bourne Passage.

House, yard and outbuildings, 6, Bourne Passage.

House and yard, 7, Bourne Passage.

Passage between 12, Bourne Walk, and 7 and 6, Bourne Passage.

House, store, yard and outbuildings, 12, Bourne Walk.

Part 2. Lands outside the clearance area.

Store, 14, Bourne Walk.

Store, 13, Bourne Walk.

House, yard and outbuildings, 3, Bourne Passage.

Hastings Old Town No. 9.
(North of All Saints Infant School) Housing confirmation Order, 1934.

House (part over passage), yard and outbuilding, 9a, Bourne Walk.

House (part over passage), yard and outbuildings, 10, Bourne Walk.

House, 8b, Bourne walk.

Yard (between 8b and 9a, Bourne Walk), passage and outbuildings.

Hastings Old Town No. 10.
(The Creek) Housing confirmation Order, 1934.

House, yard and outbuildings, 7, The Creek.

House, yard and outbuildings, 8, The Creek.

Hastings Old Town No. 12.
(Amphion Place) Housing confirmation Order, 1934.

House and forecourt, 1, Amphion Place.

House, 2, Amphion Place.

House, 3, Amphion Place.

House, 4, Amphion Place.

House, 5, Amphion Place.

Passage, yard and outbuildings, 1 to 5 inclusive, Amphion Place, and rear of 89, All Saints Street.

Hastings Old Town No. 14.
(Bossom Square) Housing confirmation Order, 1934.
Part 1. Lands within the clearance area.

House, yard and outbuildings, 4, Bourne Street.

House, 4a and 4b, Bourne Street.

House, Yard and outbuildings, 5, Bourne Street.

House and yard, 6, Bourne Street.

House, Yard and outbuildings, 7, Bourne Street.

House and yard, 8, Bourne Street.

House, Yard and outbuildings, 9, Bourne Street.

House and yard, 10, Bourne Street.

Yard and outbuilding, rear of 9 and 10, Bourne Street.

House, 3, East Bourne Street.

House, 1, Bossom Square.

House, 2, Bossom Square.

House, 3, Bossom Square.

Yard and buildings, Bossom Square.

House, 5, Bossom Square.

House, 6, Bossom Square.

House, 7, Bossom Square.

House, 8, Bossom Square.

House and yard, 4, East Bourne Street.

House, Gem Cottage, East Bourne Street.

House, 13, Bourne Street, and 1, East Bourne Street.

House, shop, yard and outbuildings, 25, Bourne Street.

Part 2. Lands outside the clearance area.

Fish curing shed at rear of 8, Bourne Street.

Hastings Old Town No. 16.
(Wellington Court) Housing confirmation Order, 1934.

House, 1, Wellington Court.

House, 2, Wellington Court.

Yard and outbuildings, rear of 1 and 2, Wellington Court.

Hastings Old Town No. 16.
(Gibbons Square) Housing confirmation Order, 1934.

House and yard, 1, Gibbons Square.

House and yard, 2, Gibbons Square.

House and yard, 3, Gibbons Square.

House and yard, 4, Gibbons Square.

House and yard, 5, Gibbons Square.

House and yard, 6, Gibbons Square.

Road (Gibbons Square) and store between 4 and 6, and store between 3 and 5, Gibbons Square.

Dated, this sixteenth day of November, 1934.

D. W. Jackson.

Town Clerk.

As you have read there were an awful lot of people to be made virtually homeless if the Orders were ever sent out, the clearance scheme still never reached its climax, whereby, all the above listed properties were actually seized by compulsory purchase during that year (1934), the show lingered on just a little longer, until there was sufficient places to rehouse every one on the list.

Areas scheduled to be cleared during 1934 - 1937

No	Description	Area	Date	Meeting
1	Hastings Clearance Area	Zion Cottages	1934	12/01/1934
2	Hastings Clearance Area	Ebenezer Road	1934	12/01/1934
3	Hastings Clearance Area	Hope Cottages	1934	12/01/1934
4	Hastings Clearance Area	Union Row	1934	12/01/1934
5	Hastings Clearance Area	Woods Row	1934	12/01/1934
6	Hastings Clearance Area	Waterloo Place	1934	12/01/1934
7	Hastings Clearance Area	Fishers Cottages	1934	12/01/1934
8	Hastings Clearance Area	Bourne Pasage	1934	12/01/1934
9	Hastings Clearance Area	North of All Saints School	1934	12/01/1934
10	Hastings Clearance Area	The Creek	1934	12/01/1934
11	Hastings Clearance Area	No 4 & 4a Bourne Walk	1934	12/01/1934
12	Hastings Clearance Area	amphion Place	1934	12/01/1934
13	Hastings Clearance Area	Chapel Cottage	1934	12/01/1934
14	Hastings Clearance Area	Bossom Square	1934	12/01/1934
15	Hastings Clearance Area	Winding Street	1934	12/01/1934
16	Hastings Clearance Area	Wellington Court	1934	12/01/1934
17	Hastings Clearance Area	Gibbons Square	1934	12/01/1934
18	Hastings Clearance Area	Hillside Cottages	1937	12/02/1937
19	Hastings Clearance Area	Sandown Road (Area A)	1937	12/02/1937
20	Hastings Clearance Area	Sandown Road (Area B)	1937	12/02/1937
21	Hastings Clearance Area	Middle Road	1937	12/02/1937
22	Hastings Clearance Area	Lennox Street	1937	12/02/1937
23	Hastings Clearance Area	Percy Road	1937	12/02/1937
24	Hastings Clearance Area	St Leonards Central (Market Passage)	1937	12/02/1937
25	Hastings Clearance Area	Old Town (WestHill Cottages)	1937	12/02/1937
26	Hastings Clearance Area	Old Town (Kents Cottages)	1937	12/02/1937
27	Hastings Clearance Area	Old Town (Richardsons Cottages)	1937	12/02/1937
28	Hastings Clearance Area	Old Town (Tamarisk Steps)	1937	12/02/1937
29	Hastings Clearance Area	Old Town (East Hill Passage - Area A)	1937	12/02/1937
30	Hastings Clearance Area	Old Town (East Hill Passage - Area B)	1937	12/02/1937
31	Hastings Clearance Area	Old Town (Belle Vue Cottages)	1937	12/02/1937
32	Hastings Clearance Area	Old Town (Swaines Passage)	1937	12/02/1937
33	Hastings Clearance Area	Old Town (Woods Passage - Area A)	1937	12/02/1937
34	Hastings Clearance Area	Old Town (Woods Passage - Area B)	1937	12/02/1937
35	Hastings Clearance Area	Old Town (The Shaftesbury)	1937	12/02/1937
36	Hastings Clearance Area	Old Town (West Street - Area A)	1937	12/02/1937
37	Hastings Clearance Area	Old Town (West Street - Area B)	1937	12/02/1937
38	Hastings Clearance Area	Central (Castle Hill Road)	1937	12/02/1937
39	Hastings Clearance Area	St Leonards Central (Harold Mews)	1937	12/02/1937
40	Hastings Clearance Area	Central (Wellington Mews - Area A)	1937	12/02/1937
41	Hastings Clearance Area	Central (Wellington Mews - Area B)	1937	12/02/1937
42	Hastings Clearance Area	St Leonards Central (Crystal Square)	1937	12/03/1937
43	Hastings Clearance Area	St Leonards Central (Market Passage)	1937	12/03/1937
44	Hastings Clearance Area	Zuriel Cottages	1937	12/03/1937
45	Hastings Clearance Area	Waterloo Passage	1937	12/03/1937

Tackleway and Old Town viewed from East Hill c1910.

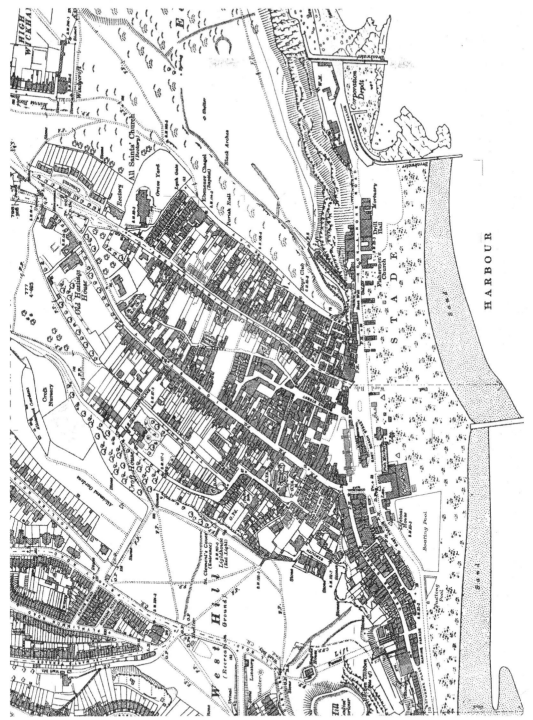

All the darker grey coloured areas
were destined for demolition.

Courthouse Street *Courthouse Street*

15   Courthouse Street
15a Courthouse Street
15b Courthouse Street

The premises as listed consists of a 3 storey block of 3 flats of brick construction, the sole access being by means of an external Cast Iron staircase from a common concreted courtyard which forms a common drying ground.

The premises as listed are approximately 100 year old and are structurally in a poor condition due to age and inadequate maintenance.

There is severe rising and penetrating dampness to the Ground Floor flat which is also affected by inadequate natural lighting by the general congestion of the area and obstructive buildings.

There is evidence of penetrating dampness to the first and second floor flat due to porosity to the brickwork.

Ventilation is adversely affected by the general congestion of the area.

All have external WC's situated at the front of the building.

Rents are 20/5d and 22/2d inclusive.

No 1 / 2 Brewery Cottages   *No 4 / 5 Brewery Cottages*

5 Brewery Cottages - Occupied by **Mr G W Collins** and Family
Rented out at 17/5d per week.
4 Brewery Cottages – Occupied by **Mr & Mrs W G Bosting**
Rented out at 17/5d per week
3 Brewery Cottages – Occupied by **Mr G B Plumbridge** and Family
Rented out at 30/- per week
Owned by **Mr L R Smith** of 33 High Street.
1 Brewery Cottages – Occupied by **Mr H J Queen** and Family
Rented out at 17/5 per week
2 Brewery Cottages – Occupied by **Mr T W Swain** & Family
Rented out at 17/5 per week

These premises as listed consist of two and three story cottages of brick construction in and around a common yard and passages surrounded by other buildings which were originally a brewery, but which for some years has been used for other commercial purposes (Warehouse and Stores, Plating Works and Engineering Factory.

Old and structurally worn out, they are generally in a condition of disrepair internally and externally.

All are affected by serious rising and/or penetrating damp. Lighting and ventilation are adversely affected by obstructive buildings.

They are overcrowded on site and there is serious congestion in the whole area.

No 43 / 44 Bourne Road *No 46 & 45 Bourne Walk*

46 Bourne Road - Owner / Occupier **Mr J H Whiting**.
(built 1852) – purchased 1957.
45 Bourne Road – Owner / Occupier **Mr G W Whatman**.
(built 1852) – purchased 1952.
44 Bourne Road – Occupied by **Mr A F Apps & Family**
Rented out at 12/- per week
43 Bourne Road – Occupied by **Mr F Holman & Family**
Rented out at 14/- per week
Owned by **Mr A B L Miller** of 22 Mount Pleasant Road

No 43 and 44 are of cement rendered brick construction with slate roofs, being back to back with the adjoining house (No 45).

The premises are structurally worn out and are affected by severe extensive rising and penetrating damp. There is no through ventilation. The sole open space within the curtilage is a common yard of 108 sq ft adjoining No 44, in which external WC's for both houses are situated. There is no secondary access to either house and the internal arrangement is bad.

No 45 & 46 are of brick construction with slate roof form a block of property with No's 43 & 44. Both are owner occupied and have been well maintained. Natural lighting is affected by obstructive buildings: access is direct to the living room via a small forecourt of 7 feet by 12 feet in depth. The only open space at the rear within the curtilage at No 45 is a small yard, in which a external WC is situated. No 46 has inadequate ventilation to the rear living room due to obstruction by roofing over a yard to form a Kitchen/Scullery. The WC – originally external – opens direct off the kitchen.
This house is affected by rising damp.

No 8 – 14 Roebuck Street   *Rear of 8 to 14 Roebuck Street*

8 Roebuck Street – Occupied by **Mr W Leonard Currie** and Family
Rented out at 30/- per week
10 Roebuck Street – Occupied by **William Currie**
Rented out at 17/- per week
12 Roebuck Street – Occupied by **Mr & Mrs Roger Griffiths**
Rented out at 17/- per week
14 Roebuck Street – Occupied by **Mrs Vera Chandler** & Child
Rented out at 17/- per week

The houses as listed comprise a terrace of small 4 roomed cottages of brick construction, the living room being entered direct from the Street.
All are effected by severe and extensive rising dampness to the ground floor rooms and penetrating dampness is present due to the defected and perished condition of the brickwork to the rear walls.
No 8 and 14 are affected by settlement at the rear.
All have external WC's situated in the rear yards.
They are overcrowded on site with small yard space at the rear, causing adverse effects on natural lighting and ventilation to the kitchens.
They are also badly ranged internally.

No 34 / 35 / 36 Bourne Walk   *No 37 / 38 Bourne Walk*

38 Bourne Walk – Owner Occupied by **Mrs Elsie May Turner.**
Purchased 1952
37 Bourne Walk - Occupied by **Mrs Marion Whyborn**
Rented out at 30/- per week
Owned by **Mrs Elsie May Turner** of No 38. Purchased 1952
36 Bourne Walk – Owned by **Mrs Emery** of 40 St Pauls Road,
St Leonards - **EMPTY**
35 Bourne Walk – Occupied by **Mr D T Spice** & Family
Rented out at 16/3d per week
34 Bourne Walk – Owner Occupied by **Mrs May Ena Veal.**
Purchased 1946

Nos. 34, 35 and 36 are a terrace of three small brick cottages with slate roofs fronting on to a common passage at right angles from Bourne Walk.
These properties are old and structurally worn out, all being affected by severe and extensive rising and penetrating dampness. Access to living rooms is direct and are otherwise badly arranged internally. The sole open space within the curtilage is a confined yard at the rear. External WC's are situated in these yards.
They are overcrowded on site, and natural lighting and ventilation is adversely affected by obstructive buildings.
A closing order dated 6th Jan 1959 is operative on No 36
Nos. 37 and 38 are a pair of semi detached cottages of brick construction with slate roofs fronting on to Bourne Walk. They are old and structurally worn out, severe and extensive rising dampness and defects of stability being present. There is no open space at the rear, the original yard spaces having been roofed over to form sculleries. WC's are situated in the covered yard space. Internally they are badly arranged and natural lighting is inadequate to rear rooms.

No 21 / 22 Bourne Walk   *Technical College Annexe*

21 Bourne Walk – Occupied by **Mrs Emma Bailey (aged person)**
Rented out at 15/- per week
22 Bourne Walk – Occupied by **Mrs Frances Baker**
Rented out at 15/- per week
Technical College Annexe – Plumbers Shop
of Hastings Corporation Education Dept

Nos. 21 and 22 are a pair of cement rendered brick cottages with slate roofs, already purchased by the local authority. They are structurally worn out and affected by severe rising and penetrating dampness.

They are badly arranged internally with direct access to living room from the Street. They are overcrowded on site with small yard spaces at the rear in which external WC's are situated, natural lighting is inadequate to the front due to obstructive buildings.

Technical College Annexe – This is an old building which by its situation causes congestion of the area and obstruction of light and ventilation to houses within the area.

Rear of 26 / 27/ 27a Bourne Walk   *26 / 27 Bourne Walk*

26 Bourne Walk – Owner Occupied by **Mr Charles Henry Britt**. Purchased 1949

27 Bourne Walk – Owner Occupied by **Mr Frank A Edmunds** & Family. Purchased 1950

27a Bourne Walk – Owner Occupied by **Mr James John Foster**. Purchased 1945

The dwellings are situated at the Northern End of Bourne Walk, which at this point is a footpath only varying in width from 10 ft at No 26 to 3ft at No 30.
Nos. 26, 27 and 27a are provided with open garden areas in the front and open space within the curtilage at the rear consisting of concrete yards only.
No 26 has an external scullery with access from the rear yard containing water supply, sink and cooking facilities and all have external WC's.
All 3 are owner occupied and well maintained properties and are included by reason of bad arrangement only, owing to the congestion of the area.

No 28 /29 Bourne Walk *No 33 Bourne Walk*

33 Bourne Walk – Occupied by **Mr W J T Holman**
Rented out at 15/2d per week
Owned by **F K Elderfield** of London W1
28 Bourne Walk – Owned by **Mrs Priscilla Phillips;** Deceased.
Unoccupied.
29 Bourne Walk – Owner Occupied by **Mrs Bodecia Florence Vidler.**
Purchased 1949
30 Bourne Walk – Owner Occupied by **Mr George White** & Family**.**
Purchased 1949

Nos. 28, 29, 30 and 33 are old and structurally worn out properties built directly abutting the public passage, causing acute congestion of the area.
All are affected by extensive rising and/or penetrating dampness.
WC's are external except No 29 which opens direct off the kitchen.
They are overcrowded on site and natural lighting and ventilation is adversely affected by obstructive buildings.

No 134   All Saints Street   *No 134   All Saints Street*

134a All Saints Street – Owner Occupied by **Mr A G Ford.**
Built 1889, Purchased 1953
135b All Saints Street – Owner Occupied by **Mr J W Fullager.**
Purchased 1956
137a All Saints Street – Owner Occupied by **Mr G R D Holland.**
Purchased 1943

These cottages as listed are situated at the rear of properties in All Saints Street, causing congestion of the area, the sole access being by passage.
All are solid backed. No 134a and 137a being actually back to back in construction with other properties creating deficiencies in ventilation and lack of air space. 135b and 137a are old and structurally worn out. No 134a is of more recent construction – 1889.
All are affected by rising and or penetrating dampness and have external WC's.

No 2 / 3 All Saints Place   *No 4 All Saints Place*

2 All Saints Place - Occupied by **Mr Hall. (Aged)**
Rented out at 8/- per week
Owned by **Miss Fry** of 4 All Saints Place
3 All Saints Place – Occupied by **Mr K Henham and Family**
Rented out at 11/- per week
Owned by **Miss Fry** of 4 All Saints Place
4 All Saints Place – Owner Occupied by **Miss Fry. (Aged person)**

These cottages as listed are constructed round an unpaved court, which constitutes a communal drying ground and which is the sole open space.
Access is by a narrow passage between 139 and 140 All Saints Street.
They are old and structurally worn out and generally in an advanced state of dilapidation externally and internally. They are solid backed with marked deficiencies in ventilation. All are affected by severe rising and penetrating dampness. There are external WC's which are mostly structurally dilapidated. They are badly arranged internally and overcrowded on site.

All Saints Place

5 All Saints Place
Occupied by **Mr G Bexhill & Family**
Rented out at 13/5d per week
Owned by **Mr G Townsend** of Sydenham, SE16

6 All Saints Place
Occupied by **Mr R V Upton**
Bequeathed by Mother 1957

7 All Saints Place
Owned by **Mr W R Adams** of Wales.
Unoccupied / Furnished.

These cottages as listed are constructed round an unpaved court, which constitutes a communal drying ground and which is the sole open space.
Access is by a narrow passage between 139 and 140 All Saints Street.
They are old and structurally worn out and generally in an advanced state of dilapidation externally and internally. They are solid backed with marked deficiencies in ventilation. All are affected by severe rising and penetrating dampness. There are external WC's which are mostly structurally dilapidated. They are badly arranged internally and overcrowded on site.

Sensational Old Town Scheme
Borough Engineer's Alternative to Bourne Highway.
Torfield Traffic Outlet.
1935.

Sensational alternative scheme to the 'road through the Bourne,' as a solution to the Old Town traffic problem, has been prepared by Hastings ever resourceful Borough Engineer, Mr. S. Little, and it was presented to a joint Highways and Housing and Improvements Committees.

The scheme, which is designed to cause the minimum upheaval in the heart of the Old Town, and at the same time provide the traffic artery, which is so urgently needed at the east end of the town.

Mr. Little, suggests a new road commencing on Marine Parade, immediately to the west of the Royal Albion Hotel, where some properties will have to be acquired to obtain the necessary width, crossing George Street, and passing to the immediate east of the entrance to the West Hill Lift. Along the back of the buildings fronting George Street, to the south east of the upper portion of Exmouth Place. It would then cross the disused graveyard, parallel with and alongside Croft Road at its lower steep portion, connecting with and absorbing Croft Road, where the gradient becomes less severe, and increasing the width of the old road to 50 feet. The new road would then continue across Torfield, where, owing to the fact of its having to be constructed on the side of a steep slope, it would be divided into two halves, to take up and down traffic in separate channels. It would join Old London Road just south of Ashburnham Road. Its maximum gradient would be 1 in 15 at the Marine Parade, which is less than Old London Road slope, and it is about the same as Cambridge Road between the Observer buildings and the Post office.

It is understood that comparatively few buildings would be affected by this scheme. This would involve just 17 houses not as listed in the clearance area of the Old Town, and to include 4 business or boarding house premises.

It does not require no great effort of the imagination to picture this in one's mind of the striking approach to the town the proposed road would afford, opening up as it would the West Hill, and providing wonderful views of the East Hill, the Old Town, and the harbour and sea to all that entered the town by this route. Incidentally, it would enormously enhance communication with the Corporation's housing site at the Bembrook Farm Estate.

The estimated cost of the construction of the new road is £60,000, which £17,000 for the acquisition and demolition of the properties, and to the gross cost a Ministry of Transport grant of £36,000 would be available, reducing the net cost to the Corporation to the figure of £41,000.

In parallel with this road, if adopted, the work of clearing up the Old Town following the Corporations clearance scheme, would have to be dealt with, and

Mr. Little, in his report, submitted a plan for carrying out this at a cost of £26,200, which includes £13,000 for acquiring property, pulling down and making good adjoining properties, £9,000 for the erection of 20 new houses and flats in place of those demolished, and £4,200 for playgrounds, recreational grounds and streets.

The scheme provides sites for 42 houses, while only 20 are demolished, and the number of houses in the Old Town would thus be increased by 22, which could be built in connection with the new slum clearance schemes, or replace any houses demolished under the road works, if any were required. If it is proved necessary to replace some of the houses on the site of the new road, the estimate would be increased by about £6,000.

This is Mr. Little's alternative to the 'road through the Bourne,' and it seems to provide a brilliant solution to the problem of providing a traffic outlet without tearing the heart out of Old Hastings, and seriously harming business interests in that area.

According to the Corporation's requirements, Mr. Little has formulated another scheme dealing with the same problem. The scheme is for a central road between High Street and All Saints Street, and at the same time he submitted the alternative route over the West Hill. He presented proposals for a central thoroughfare with an overall width of 50 feet, the greatest width feasible with the restricted space available.

The line of the road would involve the demolition of the 'Old Wesley' Methodist Church, the Bourne Street Police Station, a neighbouring public house, the Technical School, and 82 houses, and the whole of the Brewery site would be needed.

Mr. Little's scheme allows for the provision of 82 new dwellings required, in the form of eleven blocks of three storey flats, six flats to a block, and four blocks of two storied houses, four houses to each block. Sites have been allocated for a new public house, thus avoiding the extinction of the licence, a new chapel, and a new technical school, and other municipal undertakings.

The total estimated cost of this scheme, including £15,000 for the construction of the road, £70,000 for the acquisition of properties, demolition and making good adjoining premises, £36,600 for the new dwellings, and £10,000 for a new technical school, is £136,160, towards which a Ministry of Transport grant of £9,000 would be received, reducing the net cost to the Corporation to £127,160. This figure compares strikingly with the total cost of the alternative scheme of £67,200 which it will be seen is only about half as great as the Bourne Road proposal with its drastic effect on the Old Town.

No decision on either of the schemes was made at the Joint Committees at their last meeting, and will be deferred until a later date.

The top picture shows the old 'Watney's Depot' in the Bourne,
which was situated on the corner of Waterloo Passage and the Bourne,
and opposite Waterloo Place, before the road was installed,
thus cutting this building out completely.
The new car park in the Bourne (below) occupies the space this building once stood. The only two remaining cottages saved stand to the left in the picture,
Gilbert Cottages (1852).

Workmen engaged on the demolition of the
Old Wesley Methodist Chapel in the Bourne.

Adelina Cottage

Bourne Street Police and Fire Station. Early c1920s.

HASTINGS.
MR. C. J. LEWNS

MONDAY, AUGUST 12th, 1878,
SWAN HOTEL, HASTINGS
The FREEHOLD
MESSUAGE OR TENEMENT
And PREMISES.
No. 11, UNION ROW,
ALL SAINTS, HASTINGS.

Bourne Street prior to any demolition.

Bourne Walk when partial demolition took place.

The storm brews for the Bembrook Farm Estate site.
What the Old Town thinks of the scheme!
January meeting, 1935.

Further protests against rehousing the Old Town people at Bembrook Farm broke out again at the Hastings Town Council meeting held at the Town Hall last week. The Housing and Improvements Committee reported that they had considered the action taken by the Council at their meeting held last December, by which the Borough Engineer is prevented from proceeding with the construction of roads and sewers at the site to the north east of Croft Road, and west of Invalids Walk, and the Hollington housing site too.

The Committee drew the attention of the Council to the Order made at the special meeting held back in March (1934), when the question was raised on the people dispossessed by the Old Town slum clearance areas, to be rehoused on the Bembrook Farm Estate, and the new Hollington site. These matters were approved by the Council, and even the Ministry of Health also approved the moving of tenants from the area, together with the consent to borrow the amount needed. It is imperative that these roads and sewers are constructed before the erection of the houses go ahead both at Bembrook, and at Hollington, and in view of the fact that confirmation had been received from the Ministry of Health to start the compulsory purchase orders, this is now of great importance that the Council proceed forthwith with the layouts of the sites and start the erection of the houses, otherwise we will have served the compulsory order Acts, upon many of the tenants, and we shall have nowhere in which to house them.

An argument was in full swing as to the proposed Corporation carrying out the work on both sites under a direct labour scheme, comments were thrown around the floor in that, it constituted obstructionist tactics, clever, but not honest, and part of the slum landlords game. But in the Ministry's view, this is a job that should be tackled by direct labour, and was written into the agreement. The Chairman rose at this point and stated that, it would be a bad thing for us to let the Ministry see us quarrelling over such a trivial matter as to who does the manual work of laying drains, sewers, and roads, the main contract for the erection of all the houses on all sites has been put out to contract, now let us leave it here and just get on with the job in hand.

As an important thing to remember, that this would give work to many a person to whom would be doing nothing probably at this time of the year, don't forget that these next few months are the leanest of the year.

This now came to the point as to the objections raised by the people of the Old Town, as to what would happen to their businesses if moved away from the area. Tradesmen who worked in the Old Town have their workshops and stores to hand, if they are moved away this would mean that they would either have to find alternative premises to work out of, or carry all their daily needs

The Technical School in the Bourne showing the Plumbers Shop.

May we convert your
Hair Mattress into a
MODERN SPRING INTERIOR?
3ft.-£4-12-6   •   4ft. 6in. £5-12-6
HOLDINGS
(UPHOLSTERERS)
207 HAROLD ROAD, HASTINGS.   TEL. 4755

from either Bembrook, Hollington or even Red Lake site now under construction, which ever is the case, would you do this? The new houses to be erected in the Old Town would not be occupied by the Old Town people, they were destined for further away places.

The Council had heard that those people from the Old Town refused to be moved onto the Bembrook Farm Estate. Questions still remained unanswered, as to why, when an area was cleared of slum property within the listed areas of the Old Town, why couldn't the Council rehouse those that were about to be dispossessed of their properties in the clearance scheme rehoused back into the newly erected properties? The Council had appeared to of ignored the first Order of the Ministry of Health, which was that as many people as possible should be rehoused on the cleared areas. It was considered that the Corporation owned sufficient cleared spaces and old buildings, they could if they wished to do so, rehouse quite a number of Old Town people back there, and then continue the work of clearing the slums.

The Council were informed that, no more than 5 people living in the Old Town wished to be moved out of their houses, even less to be rehoused outside the area on the West Hill, Hollington or Red Lake. The Council were told on more than one occasion that they should look after the welfare of the people who grew up in the Old Town, and now you want to cast them to one side and move them as far away as you can breaking all their connections with the area they loved so much; just to make one hideous race track through the heart of their community. Several Councillors commented on the fact that, they did not consider the Bembrook Farm Estate as an ideal location, in which to rehouse the people from the Old Town, why couldn't a plan be prepared to move the people out gradually, say over a period of four to five years.

No member of the Council were in complete favour of the slum clearance programme for the Old Town, the only matter of which was to cause the most controversy, was were to site the buildings for the rehousing scheme.

Again, through one problem or another the work on the roads and sewers came to a complete stop for quite a period of time until everyone was in total agreement that this should be conducted by direct labour force only.

The Housing and Improvements Committee reported that tenders had been obtained for the erection of 18 houses at the Red Lake housing site, 32 houses on the Hollington housing site, and 76 houses on the Bembrook Farm housing site. The Committee recommended that the lowest tender at £41,022.0s.0d., be accepted. The Borough Engineer's estimate of cost for the erection of the houses included in the tenders was £51,898.0s.0d., (so what was to be left out)? The average cost per house was £325.11s.0d., one of the cheapest and best tenders for building Council houses.

Many Councillors said that the bedrooms were like boxrooms, and half the Council weren't shown the plans before the tenders went out, otherwise Mr. Little's plans would have been accepted.

Starting the Bembrook Farm Estate. Jan 1935.

OLD TOWN ROAD SCHEME

BOROUGH ENGINEER'S ALTERNATIVE ADOPTED.

TWENTY VOTES TO FOUR

July 1935

The spectacular new Old Town Road scheme, the Borough Engineer's alternative to the 'Road through the Bourne,' was adopted by a majority of 20 votes to 4 at a special meeting of the Hastings Town Council in Committee.

There were 29 members present when the meeting opened.

Details of the new road scheme, which the Borough Engineer (Mr. S. Little) prepared at the request of the Joint Housing and Highways and Works Committee's, have already been published in the 'Observer,' with a plan of the proposed road, which runs from Marine-Parade, immediately to the west of the Royal Albion Hotel, crossing George-Street, passing to the east of the entrance of the West Hill lift, to the south-east of the upper portion of Exmouth-Place, connecting with and absorbing Croft-Road, passing across Torfield, where it divides into two halves for up and down traffic, and connecting with Old London Road immediately to the south of Ashburnham Road.

Mr. Little's report to the joint committee's comprised a scheme at a net cost to the Corporation of £127,160 for a road through the Bourne and the construction of 82 new houses and flats and the alternative scheme for the road outlined above, which would involve a gross cost of £77,000, which a 60 per cent, Ministry of Transport grant would reduce to a net cost to the Corporation of £41,000.

After giving details of his Bourne road scheme, Mr. Little observed:- "I saw and felt – as members of the council must feel – that the Old Town, which has been a separate, distinct and historical community for centuries would be *'totally destroyed'* if it were given effect.

We would no longer have the delightful views from the surrounding heights of the Old Town nestling in the valley beneath, and I foresaw business interests, particularly those in the High Street, seriously effected by the upheaval in the very heart of the area, for one is forced to face the fact that once inhabitants are disturbed business connections severed may not be renewed, and therefore felt justified in spending a considerable amount of time in examining every detail of the neighbourhood to satisfy myself that there was no suitable alternative whereby we could inflict serious harm on borough generally and the inhabitants and business interests of the Old Town in particular".

FINE APPROACH

"The expenditure of time was warranted as there seemed a likelihood that the Council were about to make a decision even if they did not give it immediate effect, and I am pleased to place before you a scheme marked 'B,' which not only reduces the disturbance in the Old Town to a minimum, but increases the number of dwellings between High Street and All Saints Street by 22, besides having considerable advantages in other directions and which will cost the Corporation half that under scheme 'A'; in fact, I anticipate that it will be accepted by you without any hesitation as the proper solution to the problem."

The new Marine Parade – Torfield Road added Mr. Little, would form a particular fine approach to the town, incomparably better than any of the existing approaches, and open up the west Hill resulting in that every fine public open space receiving more recognition and appreciation than at present. The full possibilities and effects could only be addressed after the expenditure of a considerable amount of time and thought, and he had good ground for supposing that the new road traversing the fact of the West Hill, and it particular geological formation, might render practicable a development and treatment of a spectacular character of this fine property of the Corporation: indeed, it was more than likely that, taking a long view, the expenditure of the road would be justified apart altogether from the provision of traffic facilities.

If scheme 'B' were adopted, Mr. Little pointed out, the squaring up of the Old Town, consequent on the clearance schemes would still remain to be dealt with to produce the same result as scheme 'A,' and he submitted plan No. 3, showing the development in the Old Town consequent on demolitions due to the clearance schemes. It was necessary to acquire further properties to allow of a satisfactory scheme of development being evolved.

These properties included 20 cottages which would have to be demolished, and he estimated the cost as follows:-

Acquisition of properties, pulling down and making good adjoining properties.
£13,000

Erection of 20 new houses and flats in place of those demolished.
£9,000

Playgrounds, recreation grounds and streets.
£4.200

£26,200

COMPARATIVE COSTS

This scheme provided sites for 42 houses, whereby only 20 were demolished, and therefore the number of houses in the Old Town would be increased by 22, which would be built in connection with the new slum clearance schemes, or to replace any houses demolished under the road works (if any were required). If it proved necessary to replace some of the houses on the site of the new road the estimate would be increased by about £6,000.

The comparative cost for a 50-foot road were as follows:-

SCHEME "A"

	Total	Corporation	Ministry of Transport
	£	£	£
Roads	15,000	6,000	9,000
Acquisition of property, New houses and buildings.	121,160	121,160	Nil
Total........	136,160	127.160	9,000

SCHEME "B"

	£	£	£
Roads..............	60,000	24,000	36,000
Property...........	17,000	17,000	Nil
Total.....	77,000	41,000	36,000

	£	
Clearing up Old Town under scheme "B." Acquisition of property, etc., new houses etc.	26,200	Nil
If rehousing is required for houses demolished on line of new road.........................	6,000	
Total..............................	32,200	

CHIEF CONSTABLE AND TRAFFIC

1935

The Joint Committee reported that they had considered the Borough Engineer's report and had inspected the line of the proposed road shown in the alternative scheme "B," and had received a report from the Chief Constable (Mr. J. Bell) stating that if the scheme "B" roadway were constructed it was reasonable to anticipate that a proportion of the buses operating through High Street could be diverted via the new road, which, together with the diversion of the through traffic, would undoubtedly result in a very substantial measure of relief in the traffic situation in High Street, but it must be understood that by reason of the incapacity of High Street to take heavy traffic, there would always be, and particularly so long as trolley buses, etc., were there, a certain amount of congestion as in other narrow streets.

The Joint Committee had also received a report from the Borough Engineer, submitted also in accordance with their instructions, upon the density of the buildings within the Old Town upon the completion of either of the schemes now submitted, from which it appears that after the slum clearance scheme has been carried out and the new houses erected as shown in the road schemes, the density on the gross area under scheme "A" would be at the rate of 17 houses to the acre, and under scheme "B," 18.4 house to the acre.

The Joint Committee recommended the Council in Committee to move the Council to adopt the alternative scheme "B."

The Borough Engineer explained the schemes to the Council in Committee pointing out that 22 more houses would be obtained and emphasising the fine approach to the town which scheme "B" would afford. It would link up the east and West Hills, open up the very valuable land at Fairlight, and provide magnificent views.

Answering questions from members of the Council, Mr. Little said if the Ministry of Transport insisted on a 60-foot road he could get it in either scheme, but he was assuming that it would be possible to convince the Ministry that a 50-foot road was sufficient.

He believed that two houses opposite the Royal Albion Hotel and a shop would have to come down. It would be necessary to have traffic direction at this point.

Councillor W. J. Beck moved the adoption of the report.

COUNCILLOR BECK'S SPEECH

Councillor W. J. Beck, chairman of the Joint Committee, moved the adoption of the report and referred to the fact that it was a very old problem and a very controversial subject, but this appeared to be an opportunity of getting something home at long last. He pointed out to the meeting that the present chapter in the history of the matter opened with Councillor Riddle's motion of January 11th to which amendment was moved and the matter referred to the Joint Committee. The Joint Committee then instructed the Borough Engineer to prepare a scheme, and received the reports "A" and "B" which would directly affect it.

Councillor Beck then went on to describe the schemes and said the Joint Committee, after due deliberation, recommended scheme "B." Discussing scheme "A," he said that the chief point in its favour was the fact that it did solve the traffic problem and the problem of congestion, but against that they had to weigh the fact that there was between the High Street and All Saints Street a distance of about 400 feet, and they had to have a road of 50 or perhaps 60 feet width, plus four building depths. In addition to that, it entailed the maximum interference with business and interests in the area and entailed also the demolition of the Wesley Chapel, the Police Station and the Kings Head Hotel, the Technical School and 82 houses, and the purchase of the Brewery site – all this in addition to what they had already decided to do in the way of slum clearance. In order to rehouse the people in the 82 additional houses, it was proposed to erect blocks of flats, which in his opinion were undesirable. He was not in favour of flats where they could be avoided. While he was in favour of housing people, he was not in favour of warehousing them.

GIVING WINTER WORK

From the point of view of administration, of which he had some experience with housing sites, flats were exceedingly difficult to manage and control, and it was difficult, too, to keep the people who would inhabit them happy and peaceful in such close proximity. In view of the fact that they would have to rehoused these people and would only be able to charge rents to the amount that they were paying at present, it would mean that they would not be able to let them at an economic rent, and that would mean subsidising more houses where it was not absolutely essential.

Turning to scheme "B" Councillor Beck said against that was the question of the rather steep gradient and the sharp turn on entry of the road that was to lead across to Croft-Road – a gradient of 1 in 15, and what some people called the "spoliation of Torfield."

On the other hand, in favour of scheme "B" there was distinctly less interference with existing property, only 17 houses would have to be demolished against 82 in scheme "A," plus four other small properties and some slight interference with the lift at George Street.

The road would open up and make easily accessible the new housing estate at Bembrooke Farm.

They would be able to build in the place the road would occupy in scheme "A" 22 addition houses for people who desired to live in the Old Town.

They could put scheme "B" through without obtaining Parliamentary powers and would be able to start work next winter, and that would mean work for local people who would need it badly when next winter came.

As far as a suggested viaduct was concerned, that was definitely a matter for further consideration, and was not included in the present recommendations they were making.

FINAL ASPECT

Councillor Beck then turned to the financial aspect of the schemes and compared the two. Scheme "A" would cost £136,160, towards which they get a grant of £9,000 from the Ministry, leaving a net cost of £127,160.

Against that, scheme "B" was to cost £77,000, and instead of a grant of only £9,000, they would get a grant of £36,000, leaving a net amount of £41,000 to be paid by the Corporation.

But, he added, to be perfectly fair in comparing these figures scheme "A" included cleaning up and rebuilding in the Old Town, and if they adopted scheme "B" the cleaning up and rebuilding would still be desirable and necessary. That would involve a further expenditure of £26,200, bringing scheme "B" up to £67,200.

In order to replace the properties on the route of scheme "B" it would be fair to add to the cost of scheme "B" a sum amounting to £6,000, bringing the total up to £73,200. Councillor Beck went on to say that, in the opinion of a good many, if they adopted scheme "B" it could be made an even better scheme, and they could secure a much better approach from the Marine Parade if they acquired the properties to the west of the Royal Albion Hotel up to the corner, and he rounded his figures off by adding another £6,800, making a grand total for scheme "B," including all extras, of £80,000.

"Deduct that amount from the total cost of scheme 'A," said Councillor Beck, "and this will show a saving in favour of scheme "B" of £47,160. That is an aspect of the question which, in the interest of the ratepayers, cannot be over looked, and considering all the pros and cons of the question, trying fairly to weigh up and find the true balance, we strongly recommend the adoption of scheme 'B." There was, he added, another aspect of the question which, he personally could not refrain from mentioning, and that was in favour of scheme "B." It definitely gave the lie to those who had charged him and other a few months ago with only wanting slum clearance in the Old Town in order to get a cheap road through the Bourne.

Councillor E. J. Breeds seconded, and spoke of assistance the scheme "B" road would give to the High Street traffic problems.

He stressed the threat of a wide road in the Bourne to the livelihood of a hundred small traders in the Old Town.

"NOT SOLVED"

Alderman T. S. Dymond, speaking as chairman of the Town Planning Committee, said the committee had concluded there was no objection to scheme "B" – which, for nearly three quarters of its length came in a town planning area – from the town planning point of view.

He pointed out that a large portion of the cliff would have to be cut away, and feared that unless suitably treated it might mar the appearance of the West Hill. He emphasised the importance of the traffic problem, which would not be solved by the scheme. He added that any road affecting the Bourne would place their priceless Old Town in the melting pot.

Councillor Major F. O. Townsend observed that it was a simple matter to deal with the cliff face. Councillor F. J. Holdaway said he would not vote in favour of the alternative scheme unless he knew it would put scheme "A" – which he did not like – out of the way. Councillor E. M. Ford stressed the significance of the traffic congestion in relation to the scheme and deplored the waste of time involved in passing through the Old Town. He urged that they should abolish the slums, replace as far as possible the Old Town properties and preserve the charm of the area. A road would not spoil Torfield, though it would be necessary to see that no houses were built on either side. He referred to the nervous language of the committee as to the diversion of the traffic.

Councillor A. Honnor asked how the scheme would be paid for.

Councillor J. H. Tingle said that the problem of the High Street traffic would never be solved while the trolley buses ran through the street.

The Council had no jurisdiction over the trolley buses.

Councillor G. H. Payne moved an amendment that the matter should be deferred for twelve months. He had heard no concrete arguments in favour of the scheme except with reference to a concrete viaduct – linking up the West and East hills – that was in the offering. He feared a colossal blunder.

The scheme, he declared, was being precipitated by the officials and he contended that their fundamental duty – to clear the Old Town slums and find a way out of the traffic congestion problem – was not being fulfilled in the scheme. The scheme "B" road would not relieve the traffic except in a minor degree and the Council had fallen for it because it was the cheaper scheme.

NOT THE BEST

His contention was that the cheapest was not the best, and if the scheme failed its fundamentals it was dearer in the long run. There were certain things left out of the financial aspect of the scheme, notably compensation that would have to be paid for recently improved business premises at the Marine Parade end of the scheme, and he had not been able to find out from Mr. Little details of the acquisition of properties in the Croft. He suggested that they should have a proper report from the Borough Treasurer on these matters.

He charged the officials with expanding the figures on one side and contracting them on the other in order to influence opinion in favour of scheme "B," and asserted they were making the policy of the Council.

He claimed that the rents of the 82 houses in scheme "A" should be regarded as an asset that would lighten the load.

Councillor H. E. Johnson, J.P., seconded the amendment and confessed to many doubts, but a leaning towards scheme "A".

The Bourne had no historical value and the bulk of the houses there were not fit for habitation.

Alderman G. Shoesmith favoured scheme "B" which would avoid the mutilation and destruction inevitable with a road through the Bourne.

Councillor S. S. Riddle brought an accusation of personal interesting the matter and declared that the only solution to the traffic problem was to make High Street and All Saints Street the boundaries of a road through the Bourne Valley. He warmly advocated scheme "A".

Councillor A. Honnor vigorously denied an allegation by Councillor Riddle that he was interested in the potential building value of the land involved.

Councillor Riddle asserted that while the Council could do what they liked today, some day there would definitely be a road through the Bourne.

Councillor Mrs. G. M. Foxon, J.P., declared that Hastings and its history lay in the Old Town valley and all to whom she spoke said that a Bourne road would spoil the Old Town.

Councillor A. G. R. Hickes spoke in favour of scheme "B" and eulogised the new view that would be afforded from Torfield.

Councillor S. W. Thorpe described scheme "B" as one of the finest improvements the town had ever had.

Alderman A. W. Chesterfield, J.P., asked if the tramways company could obtain powers to run buses on the new road and the Town Clerk (Mr. D. W. Jackson) said it was open to the company to secure such powers if they desired.

REPLY TO CRITICISM

Replying to the discussion, Councillor Beck pointed out to Alderman Dymond that speakers against scheme "B" had in a number of cases admitted that scheme "B" must and would to some extent relieve the traffic congestion. With regards to Councillor Ford's remarks on the committees "nervous language," he pointed out that the comment was hardly justified as the quotation used by Councillor Ford was from the Chief Constable's report, and was not the language of the committee. Answering Councillors Honnor's query, Councillor Beck said the scheme would be paid for by the usual method of raising a loan and would be done in the cheapest possible way.

Regarding the assertion by Councillor Payne of expanding and contracting the figures by officials, he said that this was not the first estimate that they had

had from the Borough Engineer, and if the charge was to be admitted today it would be true to make the charge of any of his past estimates, and if it had any justification today it would be true to make it of any further estimates.

In view of the fact that the officials could not answer for themselves, Councillor Beck asserted that it was rather unfair to make criticism of this kind unless one had definite facts to bring in support of the contention.

Councillor Payne rose at this point and said he had discussed the matter with the Town Clerk and was informed that the estimates had been made en-bloc and not in detail. As to the charge the officials were making the policy of the Council, Councillor Beck said if it were so, it was the fault of the Council inasmuch as they had the power of voting and could control the officials if they so desired. Councillors Payne's charge should have been levelled not against the officials but against the rest of his colleagues, who he was trying to win to his way of thinking. Councillor Beck repudiated the suggestion that the rents of the 82 houses might be regarded as relieving the cost of scheme "A" as these houses would necessarily have to be let at uneconomical rents, which would be a charge against the scheme rather than giving an income which would relieve its cost. So far as Councillor Riddle was concerned, Councillor Beck said he was not prepared to follow him "in all his ramifications of commercial and political morality," but could probably do it better at another time and in another place.

Concluding, Councillor Beck said when Councillor Riddle's motion was brought before the Councillor in January, he strongly advised the Council that it was inopportune, and it would be better to defer the consideration of the matter till the slum houses had been demolished.

The Council were not of his way of thinking and decided to set up the joint committee and elect him to preside over it. He was now in a peculiar position of urging the Council to adopt scheme "B" where as those who were very keen for the road in January had moved the amendment that consideration should be deferred for twelve months.

In view of the very large number of years the question had been before the Council, and seeing that this was a real opportunity of getting something done, and they had got so far, he strongly urged the Council to take the opportunity of doing something here and now.

The amendment was defeated by a large majority and the recommendation for the adoption of the scheme was carried by 20 votes to 4.

Leslie Badham's, Winding Street.
Bottom: East Beach Street looking towards Rock-a-Nore.

Torfield Road Scheme Adopted.
August 1935.

After a two hour debate, during which several attempts to delay the scheme were made the Borough Engineer's Torfield Road proposal for an Old Town traffic artery road was adopted by a majority decision.

The alternative scheme for a roadway commencing at Marine Parade, and proceeding via the backs of the properties fronting George Street, Exmouth Place, Croft Road, and Torfield to Old London Road, be adopted, that application be made to the Ministry of Transport for approval of the scheme, and for a grant of 60 per cent, of the cost of construction of the road; that the borrowing of the sum of £41,000. The Committee further more asked that an additional sum of £26,200 be borrowed for the purpose of acquisition of property to be demolished, and the making good of properties adjoining those removed. The Council of course would have to find the remaining 40 per cent of the total cost. The amounts to be borrowed would cover the costs of erecting some 20 new houses, playgrounds, and recreational grounds.

It was stated in Committee that , there wasn't any hurry for either scheme, as this had been before Council for the last 30 years, and we have still got no where, and it looks as if it will be put before more Committees to the future before someone will actually make that positive move and do something rather than just talk, talk. It had been revealed that a report from the Chief Constable mentioned that the High Street was no more dangerous to traffic or pedestrians than any other road in the town.

The Council were really at a stand still, as it was asked to how many members of the Committee actually fully understood either scheme before having to vote on them? I can see this being debated for the next 30 years!

Once a decision has been made and work starts on either scheme, there is no going back, as property will have been started in the demolition process, and then what are we to do if the scheme chosen was not the right one, not only will we have spent thousands of pounds of tax payers money, which could not be replaced, but we will be in big trouble with the Ministry when they find out. There was a petition against the road over Torfield. The petition was headed by the residents of High Wickham, which the local authority in the past had allowed to be built across the top of the East Hill. Yet people living there had the audacity to put their names to the petition. Torfield was largely used by children, but where there was a road it would be easily accessible to the older people, who would make full use of it without exertion. It was pointed out that, Torfield as it was could never be built upon as this was to remain a total open space, and probably be used more after the road was built than now.

It was pointed out that, some of those that had signed the petition had done so because they were bullied into doing so, but were actually in total favour of the new road across Torfield.

Demolition starts on Winding Street.

Viewed from the top of the croft at the valley of the Old Town,
with High Wickham in the background.

The whole matter was asked to be deferred until the following February or March (1936), when a more detailed report from the Borough Treasurer was made available, it was requested that this report should be with every member of the Committee by the latest date of January 1936. a comment was made that as from July 10th this year we have not heard a single word from the Borough Treasurer on any financial aspect of any scheme. It is the first time in history of the Council that a proposal of such magnitude has had figures prepared by amateurs! The Borough Treasurer has never given his opinion on the matter. The criticisms continued in so much as the figurers presented were full of inaccuracies, and you cannot place the slightest credibility on these figures put before you, they have not received the endorsement of the Borough Treasurer. There seems to have been an intensive effort on the one hand, and deflation on the other. So far as the Bourne scheme is concerned, the suggestion has been made for a 50 foot wide road. Who wants it? No one. That is put down to show the great cost. It is grotesque that a figure of £10,000 should be put in for a new technical school. In any case a grant from the Board of Education would reduce that to £5,000. then there is the £6,000 proposed for the properties to the west of the Albion Hotel, multiply that figure by five and you will be nearer the mark. The Borough Treasurer has very carefully been ignored, and until we have seen his report as to the real cost of either of the suggested schemes, members will be voting blind.

It was suggested that, it was very unlikely they would get a Ministry's assent even for a 50 foot wide road, and would probably have to be a 60 foot road, and then where would the Bourne be? They would not get a penny piece from the Board of Education for a replacement technical school, after having demolished the present one of their own free will. These problems were thrown about meeting after meeting with no real solution as to what to do, as several Councillors voted for one scheme at one meeting and then reversed their decision at the next, they have got to make up their minds as to whether they know what they are voting for or just stand down altogether.

If the scheme to put a road over the West Hill and Croft Road we can start immediately, and start the clearing up of the mess left in the Old Town that has been far too long, ten years in fact the Bourne started a demolition programme that has gone on in dribs and drabs for all this time, the Council is not being fair to the people that live there still, let alone all those that have been moved out of their houses by force! We must make a true positive decision now, and the right one, and not leave it again to dwindle on for the next ten years. One poor Councillor who shall remain nameless, spoke about holding a public competition as to what to do to alleviate the traffic and overcrowding problems in the Old Town, he said that perhaps many good ideas would come out of this, and we could take the best and adopt some of the ideas from it, he was unfortunately shouted down and the motion was withdrawn from the minutes as an hilarious suggestion.

H. ORCHARD,
PORK BUTCHER AND POULTERER.
22, CASTLE STREET, and 5, GEORGE STREET, HASTINGS.

The Noted Shop for Cooked Ham, Beef, Home-made Polonies, German Sausage and Saveloys. Finest Pork Sausages, 8d. and 9d. lb.
Beef Sausages, 5d. lb.
ALL FRESH DAILY.
Speciality—CURED PICKLED PORK.

ESTABLISHED 100 YEARS.

ARTHUR A. HART,
WHOLESALE AND RETAIL

IRONMONGER,

Gas, Hot Water, and Sanitary Engineer,

PLUMBER, PAINTER, & DECORATOR,

Bell-hanger and Locksmith,

Heating and Ventilating Expert.

| ESTIMATES AND ADVICE FREE. | TEL. 25. | FIRST-CLASS WORK & MATERIALS GUARANTEED. |

55, HIGH STREET,
6 & 7, BANK BUILDINGS,
2, MOUNT PLEASANT ROAD,
HASTINGS.

Works: WINDING STREET.   Stores: POST OFFICE PASSAGE.

MAZDA LAMPS CAN BE BOUGHT WHEREVER ELECTRIC LAMPS ARE SOLD

An independent persons view as to the
Bourne Road improvements.
1935

The Borough Council's planning department drew up various schemes for the Bourne Road, but there was a particular version offered by a Mr. Henry Hunt, a resident of Hastings who drew up a scaled drawing of his own version to be submitted for consideration. But, yes, you all know the answer, it was just turned down, probably as this didn't come within the circles of the Town Planning Dept.
Nevertheless, the Observer did publish the full drawings for all to view.

The write up of which accompanied the scheme is as listed:-

Sir, I have for a long time interested myself in the traffic and slum clearance problems of Old Hastings. I now beg your favour to submit for you and your readers consideration a suggested scheme of mine to provide a suitable highway to meet all the requirements of the character through the Old Town.
I do not know of any scheme quite like it that has ever been previously suggested. The plan herewith will, I hope, make the scheme plain and easy to understand. If carried out in conjunction with the slum clearance scheme I believe the principal problems of Old Hastings can be solved in a highly satisfactory manner.
The course of my suggested new road will best be understood by studying my plan with the aid of an ordnance map of similar scale. The plan is to scale, and the position of the old Streets and buildings is shown, and their relative positions to the suggested new road are copied direct from a large scale Government ordnance survey map, and can therefore, I believe be relied upon.
The scheme provides for a highway with an overall width of 72 feet.
This width will probably shock some who have even considered a 50 foot road scarcely possible. Nevertheless, considering the needs of the case and the type of scheme necessary, this width is desirable, but I claim that comparatively few buildings of much importance would be destroyed by its adoption, but a host of litter would be cleared away.
Some may rue the clearing of part of the derelict brewery, but in my estimation that this has been little more than an eyesore. The passing of the Old Wesley Chapel will also probably be regretted by a goodly circle of devotees, but I think its passing has long been anticipated, and, apart from the sentimental attachments, in which I share, I have little doubt that a new chapel would be welcome.
I claim that my scheme, if treated skilfully, would lend itself to considerably beautifying the Old Town of Hastings without unduly destroying either property or historic values. It will be noted that the two schools and the public

baths remain. The scheme provides ample and safe carriageways and footways. There are two carriageways, one for up and one for down traffic, each 24 feet in width. Where crossroads cut circular turnabouts are provided. These, I claim, make for the safety of vehicles in all directions and help to prevent speeding, and to provide easy access to opposite streams of traffic and adjacent Streets. The centre gardens of the turnabouts would give pleasing and ornamental effect. In conjunction with this scheme, one way traffic can be conveniently effected in the High Street and All Saints Street, and therefore should be implemented. A study of the plan and the arrows denoting the course of traffic will show how easily and, I think, safely, this can be organised.

Two main footways are provided for, each 7 feet in width. On the kerb side I suggest that trees should be planted. In the middle of the road, between the two carriageways, is a 10 foot centre-way providing a 3 feet pathway on both sides of a 4 foot garden. Safety crossings should be provided where needed. This centre-way, which runs the whole length of the road, as shown on the plan, would, I claim, reduce the danger of Street crossing very considerably, as only one stream of traffic would have to be negotiated at a time.

This centre-way could be treated in various ways to give an artistic and pleasing effect. At the top end of the road, just above the Roman Catholic Church, the road divides and takes two distinctive routes, the up traffic merges into High Street, whilst the down traffic merges into All Saints Street. Thus is retained the old wooded grounds, known as the 'Wilderness.' This land except for that part to which the drinking fountain is annexed, has been in more or less a derelict condition for a long time, and I contend this should be taken over by the town authorities and laid out as a sunken public garden. It is an ancient feature of Old Hastings and should not be built on or destroyed, but retained and tended as a restful and delightful public retreat. In this garden I suggest that a bit of the old Bourne Stream should be brought to light in the form of a short length of waterway beautified by a waterfall and possibly a lily pond. I also believe that there is scheme to build on this land. To allow this would be nothing short of wanton destruction of what is a valuable feature of Old Hastings, and one of which is capable of being made a much greater asset to the town. Old Hastings needs this spot.

I claim that if this scheme were adopted it would solve absolutely all the Old Town traffic problems, also that it would, if treated skilfully and in conjunction with a clearance scheme, considerably beautify without desecrating. I will not further intrude on your space but beg to be allowed your favour to submit my plan, sketch and scheme for the thoughtful and unprejudiced perusal and criticism of all who have the best interests for the Old Town of Hastings at heart.

The Wilderness top end of High Street, all of which was promised to remain, but got in the way of redevelopment and the roadway.

Plan of suggested new road layout.

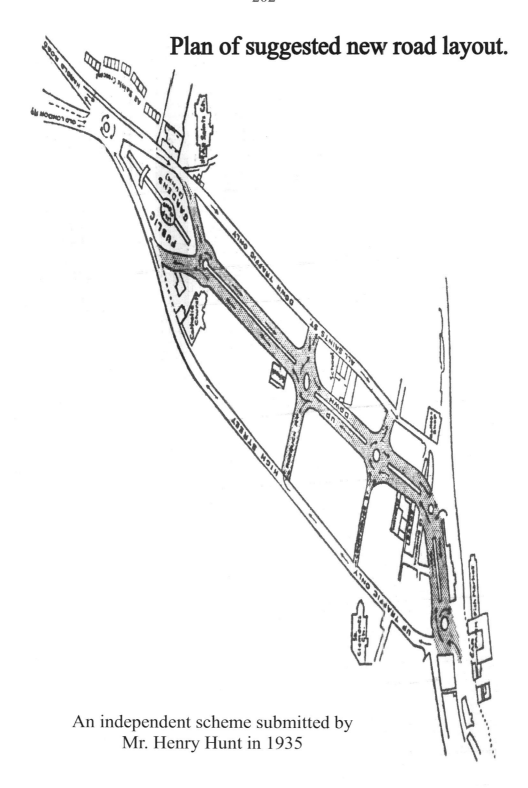

An independent scheme submitted by
Mr. Henry Hunt in 1935

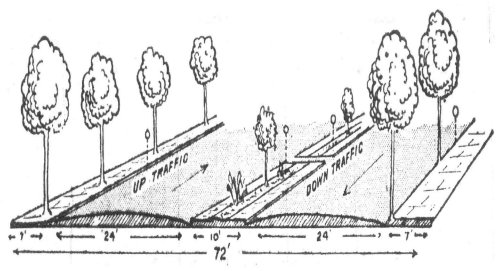

A close up view of a section through the road suggested by
Mr. Henry Hunt in 1935.

These drawings as far we can ascertain were never shown or mentioned to the council, nor did the planners ever see it apart from it being published in the local newspapers.

These plans, if adopted would have been in our opinion a far better scheme than any drawn up previously by the planning department, as they showed that someone was not only caring for the Old Town but the final appearance as well, with a centre refuge that had never been incorporated in plans before.

The inclusion of a series of roundabouts into the road plan as offered would have deterred or even alleviated the speeding, of which we suffer today.

But, alas, we have a road through the heart of the Bourne, not attractive or thoughtful by any standards, functional, yes, practical No! Again, money prevailed and dictated to what we got, and basically to what we the ratepayers of the town could afford, rubbish, as normal!

You may have already read about the alternative schemes that the Borough Engineer Mr. Sidney Little had put forward in opposition to the complete destruction of the Bourne. Unfortunately, there were a few hard and fast cases within the council who really didn't want to see anything else other than a road through the heart of the Bourne. Mr Little's other schemes would have predominately cost a lot less and caused less demolition, apart from that there are a host of reasons as to why the road should have gone elsewhere, but as I said, there were certain people within the council at the time with a strong influence as to decision making on behalf of the Town Council.

The high pavement in the High Street just opposite Roebuck Street showing Beaumont's Laundry at Nos. 97.
Notice the sheer lack of railings then! This had nothing to do with the railings being removed during the last conflict for war weapons etc.

The High Street, and the old Customs House (on the left)
the Post Office is to it's right.
The old Customs house buildings were later demolished,
and replaced with Philip Cole Close.

The High Street opposite Swan Terrace.

The Swann Inn, High Street.

The 'Mitre Restaurant' that was taken out when the Swan Inn was bombed.

NEW
THE 8 h.p. AUSTIN VAN

BIGGER — FASTER — BETTER LOOKING!

Save time . . . Save money. Let this new Austin solve your transport problems. The van has a bulk capacity of 82 cubic feet—more space that means fewer journeys. 4-cylinder engine with aluminium head for speed, and fuel economy. 4-speed synchromesh gears and powerful Girling brakes. *Invest in an 8 h.p. Austin and have the smartest van in town!*

PRICE £120
(*at works, in priming colour*)

18 WESTERN ROAD
ST. LEONARDS.   TEL. 628
18 CAMBRIDGE ROAD
HASTINGS   TEL. 877

Skinners (Hastings) Ltd.
MOTOR ENGINEERS

OLD TOWNER'S MOVE OUT

AND THEY ARE ALL VERY PLEASED ABOUT IT!

FAREWELL TO SLUMS
January 1936

Eighteen families have left the Old Town this week----
The first of those who, in the course of the next year or two, will be moved to the 124 new houses now being built under the Hastings Corporation's slum clearance scheme. These 18 families have gone to Red Lake, where the first batch of houses has just been completed.

Those people that prophesied that heartbreak would follow the wake of the Councils slum clearance orders should have accompanied me (writes an Observer reporter) in a visit to these new houses, and seen the bright smiling faces and heard the joyful remarks. At nearly every house at which I called I was invited to go over the building, while the new owners extolled their virtues and compared them with their previous dwellings.

I called first on Mr. and Mrs Fountain, who had moved the previous day from Hope Cottages, where they have been living for the past eight years, and asked them what they thought about the change. Mr. Fountain took a deep breath, "After the other place it's like being in heaven" he declared. "Come in and see the house for yourself. We hardly know where we are, after living for so long in a house with no sanitary conveniences at all. Before there wasn't even a back door, so it was pretty draughty. In fact the only convenience we had was the water pouring through the roof. And now this" – and almost unbelievingly he turned on the hot water tap and held his fingers in the steaming jet.

TWO BEDROOMS FOR SEVEN

"At Hope Cottages," he continued "we had only one bedroom and one box room for my family of seven, and as for being damp—you ought to have seen the water run out of the mattress of my bed when it was taken out of the room. Here we have three bedrooms, so we are very comfortable."

"Do you think it will be more expensive to live up here?" I inquired.

"Well," he replied, "it's going to cost the wife a little more when she wants to go into town, but we are quite prepared to put up with that when it means such a difference in comfort."

"Yes, I am quite satisfied, and I think everybody else should be too.
They ought to settle down and look after the houses."
Mr. H. A. G. Upton, who had just moved from Tackleway, had much the same story to tell.
"There is even more room here than we expected," he said, "and I am perfectly satisfied with the change. It's certainly different from what we've been used to—in the other house there were more mice than the King had horses, and they actually frightened the cats away."

RACK AND RUIN

"And we would lie in bed and feel the water coming through the ceiling," added Mrs. Upton. "We had only one bedroom we could use, and even there the floor boards were rotten."
Next I called on Mrs. L. Chatfield, who had lived in Woods Row for the past 19 years.
"We are all very glad to get out of it, I can tell you," she declared. "When we took the house first it was very nice, and quite dry, but in recent years the place has gone to rack and ruin. Before we had no scullery or conveniences in the house—and now look at us! We have electric light, gas, and a bathroom!"
"And how do you like living up here compared with the Old Town?"
"Oh, I prefer it," she answered without hesitation.
Several other families told me the same thing. Mostly they explained that the change would enable them to keep the children fit, instead of having them continually suffering from the ill effects of dampness and so on.
"It's very nice to be out of the rabbit hutch," commented Mrs. J. Mitchell, "and the children will enjoy the recreation ground over the road."
The moving of the families was spread over three days—Wednesday, Thursday and Friday.
As early as seven o'clock each morning the removal men were busy.
Every piece of furniture that could be taken to pieces had to be taken to pieces, for it was no easy task persuading such things as beds and wardrobes through tiny windows and long narrow curving passages. In several cases doors and windows had to be taken off their hinges for the sake of the extra few inches of clearance that that yielded.
The loaded vans were then driven to Rock-a-Nore, where all goods taken from the condemned houses were fumigated. This process took about four hours, after which the vans were driven to Red Lake and unloaded.
The object of such an early start was to give the people an opportunity to get the furniture moved in before darkness fell.
On Thursday, before daylight, I was watching the preparations for moving
from houses the Ministry of Health inspector had decided must be the first to be emptied. Two of these were in passages off Ebenezer-road, and I peered into low ceilinged rooms, lit by one glittering candle, and shuddered as I saw

windows stuffed with paper to keep the draught out, and a hundred other details which scarcely add to comfort.

SEEING THROUGH THE WALL

A most anomalous feature about one of the houses, however, was despite its discomfort in practically every other direction; it was lit by electricity.

I spoke to a woman who has lived in Providence-row for 23 years. She is due to leave her house, which is built almost entirely of wood, in a month.

"Do you want to leave?" I asked.

She looked at me with a pained expression. "Follow me," she commanded, and led the way to the back of the house.

There she caught hold of one of the many planks which formed the side of the house and which were bright green with the damp. A slight pull, and a great piece of rotten wood broke away at once.

"You can see through the wall of the scullery outside," she explained. "Yes, we are certainly looking forward to moving. I have brought up a family in this house, and it has not been a pleasant job—the place is fairly running in water, and the mattress on which we have to sleep is white with mildew. You can't keep the children well—my daughter has bronchitis, and my son rheumatism."

"To get water you have to go out what ever the weather, and walk down the passage way for about fifty yards. And it's impossible to do any washing in the house, that has to be done in wooden tubs a hundred yards the other way."

THE REASON

I heard the same story from nearly every person to whom I spoke; everybody except a few people who have been included in the clearance scheme "unnecessarily," as they described it, because their houses are clean and comfortable, is anxious to move to one of the new houses at either Red Lake, Bembrook Farm, or Hollington. Sentiment makes many leave the district with regret, but they look forward to returning to the Old Town when demolition has been succeeded by new houses.

"The reason for all this talk about Old Town folk not wanting to move is because a few that don't because they are comfortable where they are, talk about it a dozen times as much as the people who do want to move," one woman told me, to sum up the position.

Old Town Rebuilding.
Blocks of Flats and Houses.
October, 1936.

Plans for the first instalment of rehousing in the Old Town slum clearance areas came before the Housing and Improvements Committee at their meeting this week, and will be presented at the next meeting of the Council for their approval. The plans prepared by the Borough Engineer Mr. S. Little, are for a block of dwellings to be erected in the East Street and John Street area.

The block comprises a total of 18 dwellings, and a novel idea has been introduced of having flats on the ground floor, and two storey houses above.

There will be six flats and twelve houses, each having one living room, and three bedrooms. Each flat will be self contained, and includes kitchen, bath and store for food. Accommodation is also provided on the ground floor for the occupants of each of the houses above to store a bicycle or pram.

The front elevation of the buildings is to be finished in special Accrington bricks, and there will be balconies at the front and back of the houses.

The total cost of the scheme is £9,972, to which £500 has to be added for roads and fences.

New Diesel Lorry

Above is a photograph of the New A.E.C. Diesel lorry, which the Hastings Corporation have just purchased, this replaces the old steam wagon that was previously in use for many years. This is powered by an oil engine, and with trailer is capable of transporting loads of up to 15 tons.
The complete lorry was supplied by Caffyns, Ltd. St Leonards.

This was the Roebuck Inn, Roebuck Street now enters through the archway today, and the Inn has been replaced with the
Roebuck Doctors Surgery.
The Breeds and Co public house as seen on the right hand side is now the Duke of Wellington public house.

The top end of High Street

This is the bottom of the High Street,
with a Policeman on point duty at the junction of George Streeet.

Shop on the corner of Courthouse Street.

215

Site to be acquired for 300 houses at Ore.
November, 1936.

Three hundred houses for people displaced from clearance areas are to be erected on a site at Ore, which Hastings Town Council decided to purchase at a special meeting held recently.

The Housing and Improvements Committee reported that they had considered the matter of the acquisition of suitable land for a housing site for the erection of dwelling accommodation for the rehousing of persons about to be displaced by the carrying out of clearance orders in areas declared by the Council to be clearance areas, and for accommodating persons to be displaced from houses, which are overcrowded, and they instructed the Borough Engineer to report upon suitable sites. The Committee had now been informed by the Borough Engineer that he considered the Corporation should purchase forthwith land situated at the junction of Rock Lane and Winchelsea Road, in close proximity to the Councils housing site at Red Lake, for the erection of further houses.

Having regard to the urgent necessity for proceeding with the clearance of the areas already defined by the Council, and the need for provision of houses to deal with the matters relating to overcrowding, the Committee recommended that the Council should therefore exercise their powers for the compulsory acquisition of the land; and that the Town Clerk be instructed to take steps for giving effect to the recommendation, and making effective the compulsory purchase order, and that application be made to the Ministry of Health for the confirmation of the said order, and for the sanction to the borrowing of the amount ultimately found to be payable by the Council in respect of the acquisition of the land. The land in question comprises: 4.972 acres of allotment gardens, enclosures, huts, grass margins, occupation roads, footpaths and pond (part of), situated off Rock Lane, in the rural district of Battle, the owner being, Major Alfred Carlisle Sayer.

4.09 acres of field and shed, situated off Rock Lane, in the rural district of Battle, the owner being, William Nye Wells.

74 acres of field and pond (part of), situated south of Brick Works, Rock Lane, Guestling in the rural district of Battle, the owner being, William Nye Wells.

.63 acres of garden enclosure, piggeries and pond (part of), situated south of Brick Works, Rock Lane, Guestling in the rural district of Battle, the owner being, William Nye Wells.

6.46 acres of field and pond (part of), situated off Winchelsea Road, Ore, in the rural district of Battle, the owner being, Thomas William Wells.

5.86 acres of field and pond (part of), situated off Winchelsea Road, Ore, in the rural district of Battle, the owner being, Thomas William Wells.

.91 acres of field, situated off Winchelsea Road, Ore, in the rural district of Battle, the owners being, Alfred Samuel Swanson, and Emma Swanson.

5.30 acres of field, pond and public footpath, situated off Winchelsea Road,

Ore, in the rural district of Battle, the owner being, Major Alfred Carlisle Sayer.

The Committee had a lot of work before them, and could not make a move until they could provide accommodation for the people displaced. The matter was also urgent in another sense, as they were running out of time when they could claim subsidy. In less than two years from now the subsidy would either be stopped or greatly reduced.

The Borough Engineer explained that if these sites were acquired now, this would provide accommodation for 300 houses, which was about the requirements for their immediate needs. And if a further 100 dwellings were erected at the same time, the Council would have no trouble in letting them out at once. Part of the land was designated and zoned as allotments, and part was being cultivated as such, if the necessity arose to provide alternative allotment space, they felt it their duty to alter the town planning map. There was suitable adjacent land that could be used for allotments, which could be purchased at a reasonable price.

A question was raised as it had been many times before, that tradesmen in the Old Town were suffering from the lack of work now, and many were closing their businesses due to this, and now the Council wants to move 300 people from the Old Town at least 2 miles away, the Council should be ashamed of themselves in even considering this as a solution to the rehousing problem, these people belong in the Old Town and that it to where they must stay, besides if they were to be rehoused there by no fault of their own, it would cost them 3 shillings a week in trolley bus money just to get to work.

There was no sympathy given for the distance from the Old Town by a few stray Councillors, all the overcrowding was not just in the Old Town, and no matter to where they put their housing estates, someone would complain and have to go a long way in which to get to it. Besides, Ore is one of the best areas in the town for public transport, as from Ore to the town centre there was a vehicle every 2½ minutes. As regard to the question raised about the smaller tradesmen going out of business, the Council should consider some form of compensation for these people, as they have lost everything they ever worked for and gone in a flash. The sheer state of the mess left in the Old Town is an utter disgrace, it's of no wonder no one can make a living any more, there's nothing there apart from piles of bricks and rubbish, why has all this stopped, and why isn't this mess being cleared up. As normal there was no direct answer to any of the questions raised, and the Council swiftly moved onto another subject before another interruption came about. There was a comment made in response to his question from another Councillor, and he said to the Chairman of the Committee, "the finest thing you can do for the whole Borough is to get the Old Town cleared up and in order, so that if His Majesty does happen to pay us a visit, we shall have something to show him with pride." again not a word in response!

More buildings proposed for demolition.
St Leonards and Old Town
January, 1937.

Further parts of the town likely to be included in the Town Councils slum clearance were toured by members of the Housing and Improvements Committee on Wednesday morning.

The party were accompanied by Dr G.R. Bruce (Medical Officer of Health) who indicated the properties he has recommended for demolition.

These areas comprise Crystal Square and Market Passage (St Leonards) and Zuriel Cottages and Waterloo Passage (Hastings).

The four areas contain 38 buildings classed as dwelling houses, of which three are derelict or unoccupied, and in four cases a shop or store forms a subsidiary portion of a dwelling house stated to be unfit for human habitation.

No business premises are included as independent buildings.

The number of families, including sub-tenants for the 38 houses, is 37 and the total population is 100.

Three of the four areas are definitely congested areas and therefore lacking in external air space – the Crystal Square area, 143 houses per acre; Market Passage area, 124 houses per acre; and Waterloo Passage area 103 houses per acre.

The areas as a whole, and individual houses throughout the area, are stated to fall seriously below many of the building by-laws in force.

Dr. Bruce's report summaries the main conditions of disrepair and sanitary defects as follows for the Old Town properties only:-

ZURIEL COTTAGES

Old London Road. Nos. 110,112,114 and cottage adjoining No.114. This is a small area, consisting of four small cottages of wooden structure, three occupied, one unoccupied for several years and derelict. The defects are both fundamental and due to the fact that the wooden fabric of the houses outside and inside is generally perished and worn out. For example:

(a) Wooden walls perishing and rotten in many places.

(b) Main roofs defective.

(c) Stairs narrow, dark and no handrails.

(d) Defective plaster woodwork and floors.

(e) Small, poky rooms, with low ceilings. Cubic capacity of bedrooms as low as 460 cubic feet.

(f) Lighting and ventilation defective. No chimney ventilation in small bedroom.

RADIOGRAMS

WE CAN SUPPLY FROM STOCK
(SUBJECT TO BEING UNSOLD)

PAMPHONIC BUREAU ... 65 gns. or £10-10-0 deposit
ULTRAGRAM ... ... 72 gns. or £11- 8-0 deposit
REGENTONE ARG77 ... ... 49 gns. or £ 7-15-0 deposit
FERGUSON 326 BUREAU 69 gns. or £10-18-0 deposit
FERGUSON 327 ... ... 49 gns. or £ 7-15-0 deposit
FERGUSON 391
TABLEGRAM 39 gns. or £ 6- 3-0 deposit

All above instruments 3-speed Auto Change

REDIFFUSION TELEVISION

will shortly be available for Clive Vale, Old Town and East
End of Town

ALL TELEVISION RECEIVERS STOCKED BY

Callow for Radio

ARE SUITABLE FOR CONVERSION

to work off Rediffusion Signal. We are at all times pleased
to demonstrate without obligation

41a **ROBERTSON STREET** • Phone 5863
325 **OLD LONDON ROAD** • Phone 3479

(g) Much dampness, both rising owing to sandstone foundations, also penetrating.

(h) W.C. outside and shared.

(i) Water supply outside and shared in wash-house.

(j) Sink outside and shared in wash-house.

(k) Defective cooking stoves.

(l) No ventilated food cupboards.

(m) Paving of yard defective in places.

These houses are, therefore, entirely unfit for human habitation.

The four houses contain three families. One house is empty and derelict.

WATERLOO PASSAGE.
PROPERTIES WITHIN THE AREA.

(a) High Street – Nos. 20, 20a, 20b, 20c, 21d.

(b) High Street – No. 16a. Workshop and dwelling house over at rear of Nos. 17 and 18, High Street. No. 44a, Bourne Walk.

(c) Bourne Walk – Nos. 40, 41 and 42. Waterloo Passage – Nos. 4, 5 & 6.

The dwelling houses within this area, although differing widely in type, give definite examples of the fundamental sanitary defects and conditions of disrepair as specified, e.g.:

(a) Lack of air space.

1. The whole area is congested – 103 houses to the acre.

2. The High Street group is jumbled up, both inside and outside, in and around a narrow passage between Nos. 20 and 21, High Street.

3. The high wall, about 9ft. high, on the north side of Waterloo Passage, about 4ft. wide, limits air, light and ventilation from houses opposite. At the back are small yards with outbuildings also restricting air space.

(b) Bad arrangement. The High Street group is typically bad, both inside and outside. So also are the backs of the Bourne Passage group (practically a narrow passage, with one house, No. 40, entered underneath) and the backs of the Waterloo Passage houses.

(c) Restriction of air space inside. Notably in the High Street group, but other examples of small, poky rooms are found in various houses in the area.

(d) **Defective ventilation.** Many cases are found, particularly in the High Street group; also in the Bourne Passage and Waterloo Passage groups, particularly the ground floors No.16a High Street, is in effect a back to back house.

(e) **Defective natural light.** For the same reasons, restriction of air space, outside and inside, numerous instances throughout the area are found. Several rooms are quite unfit for this reason.

(f) **Presence of dampness.** Rising dampness is present throughout; also various instances of penetrating dampness, through walls and by reason of defective roofs, gutters, spouts, etc.

(g) **Water supply.** In many cases this is a tap outside and in such cases there is no sink.

(h) **Water closet.** These are outside and in various cases shared. Defects in structure and condition are noted in the schedules.

(i) **Other conveniences.**

a. **Sinks**. Generally stone, untrapped, and defective; in certain cases none are available.

b. **Washing accommodation**. In a considerable proportion of the houses none are available.

c. No ventilated food cupboards provided.

(j) **Paving or drainage of courts and yards.** These are defective in various instances.

(k) **General disrepair.** All defects of the fabric, outside and inside, are recorded in the individual schedules, including walls, roofs, chimneys, stairs, woodwork.

Though in these areas, there is much evidence of disrepair, including perishing of brickwork and pointing, plaster, roofs, woodwork generally, including window frames. Typical examples of houses in such a state of disrepair as to warrant the term " generally worn out" are; No. 4, Waterloo Passage, No. 44a, Bourne Walk. The 14 houses contain 15 families including two sub-tenant families. One house is empty.

It is understood that members of the Housing and Improvements Committee concurred in all Dr.Bruce's recommendations.

ROAD THROUGH THE BOURNE.
Town Council Welcome Reconstruction Proposals
January,1937.
When the work will start.

Hastings Council in Committee adopted a scheme prepared by the Borough Engineer Mr. S. Little for dealing with the Old Town problem, embodying the construction of a road through the Bourne and new dwellings to replace to some extent those demolished under the Council's slum clearance scheme.

The scheme was greeted with enthusiastically by members of the council who warmly congratulated Mr. Little on his proposals.

The importance of preserving the character of the Old Town was emphasised and reference was also made to the traffic problem in High Street.

The Housing and Improvements committee reported that, they had considered the petition from residents and ratepayers upon the need for a complete and comprehensive reconstruction scheme in the Old Town.

The Committee had received a report from the Borough Engineer stating the he has given the matter very careful consideration and had come to certain definite conclusions as the result of some years' study of the problems; and that before any scheme could be finally settled and embarked upon, it was essential for the Committee and Council to decide whether the scheme should have as its main object the preservation of the Old Town or the provision of increased and ample traffic facilities as both could not be provided, and drawing attention to the following factors which could not be escaped:-

(1) The existing house and dwellings are much more dense and more closely packed than would be allowed under modern rules and conditions, and, therefore, any houses demolished cannot be replace by an equal number. This means that any scheme which necessitates further demolition must eventually result in further reduction of the population.

(2) The original Old Town consisted of properties facing High Street and All Saints Street, with building depths at the rear running down to the Bourne Stream. From this it follows that considering the area between High Street and All Saints Street, it is only the buildings facing the main streets that can have any historic value and the remainder are of comparatively recent construction.

(3) The width between All Saints Street and High Street varies between 360 feet and 400 feet.

Above 13 & 14 Bourne Walk
Below 1 Brewery Cottages

TWO ALTERNATIVES

The Borough Engineer pointed out that in considering the construction of the new main road, the obvious and natural location for such a thoroughfare to deal with the traffic was through the Old Town, and two alternatives are available:

(a) To widen High Street by rebuilding a new frontage behind the existing buildings, and then demolish the old properties; and,

(b) To form a new road between High Street and All Saints Street.

The following were the general effects of the two schemes regardless of their relative merits.

The Ministry of Transport Officials had expressed the view that if a main road were made through the Old Town there were no physical difficulties in providing a road 80 feet wide, and this was the minimum width which should be contemplated.

High Street is about 25 feet wide, and the new building line would be 55 feet back from the present one and the new buildings to be erected would have to conform to modern building requirements as regards air space, etc., and it would therefore entail wholesale demolition of the existing properties behind.

With regard to a roadway 80 feet wide between High Street and All Saints Street, the minimum width between the two streets was 360 feet and after allowing 80 feet for the roadway the 280 feet which would remain was totally inadequate to form buildings depths to High Street, All Saints Street, and one on either side of such a new road.

In either of the schemes a reduction in the number of houses and population would inevitably result.

FOSTERING TRADE

In the event of it being decided that the preservation of the Old Town was of paramount importance, it appeared that the population must not be depleted and every endeavour must be made to foster the trade and thus enable the owners and tradesmen to maintain the buildings in High Street and All Saints Street.

The Borough Engineer suggested in his report that a practical solution to the problem was to form a road 40 feet wide overall along the Bourne without attempting to provide a building frontage on such road and to utilise all the available space for rebuilding to give the maximum number of houses permissible under the by-laws and to lay out the land which was too small and irregular for building purposes as gardens, etc.

The Committee considered the report and instructed the Borough Engineer to prepare a scheme for a road 40 feet wide through the Bourne, such scheme to provide as much housing accommodation as possible and they now submitted the following report and plans received from the Borough Engineer:-

"I have pleasure in submitting a scheme for the reconstruction of the Old Town which conforms with the decisions made by the committee at their last meeting. "The completed scheme and has for its definite objects:-

(1) Reducing to a minimum further demolitions and providing the maximum number of dwellings on the area. The houses demolished cannot be replaced by an equal number.

(2) Retaining the character of the Old Town. This follows generally from: (a) the fact should not be overlooked that the trade of the Old Town must be maintained, otherwise the business premised in High Street and All Saints Street will die out, and therefore the number of inhabitants is of prime importance. (b) Designed so that it can be carried out in stages if so desired. (c) Provision for local traffic requirements.

THE NEW ROAD

Considerable care has been exercised in defining the line of the proposed new road. It has been laid out in relation to the various clearance areas so as to admit of the greatest number of houses being erected on those areas; where the depth is shallow it skirts it, and where deep passes through the centre so as to obtain a double building depth. Also it will be noticed in the majority of instances the backs of the old buildings are effectively cloaked.

The scheme is divided into five stages. These areas are to show the stage in which they would be dealt with.

Stage 1: This includes for work on existing clearance areas only and can be given effect immediately these areas are cleared . It consists of four houses on the west side of All Saints Street, two facing High Street, and a total of 18 dwellings in clearance areas near Bourne Passage, Bourne Walk and Waterloo Place. There is a total of 24 dwellings in this section, including one block of three storied dwellings. New increase 24 dwellings.

Stage 2: This deals with the clearance areas near the northern end of Bourne Walk near St Mary Star of the Sea Church, Stanford Cottages and Woods Row. To carry it into effect it is necessary to demolish 13 cottages, which will be replaced by 16, or a net addition of three for this stage. Net increase of Stages 1 and 2 is 27.

Stage 3: This provides for development on the brewery site and adjoining clearance areas. There are 16 additional houses, including 2 three-storied blocks. Two cottages would have to be demolished and net addition for this stage is therefore 14.

Stage 4: This consists of a final clearing up for the road. For this purpose it would be necessary to demolish 29 houses and there would then be sites for 4, or a net decrease for this stage of 25. Net increases of Stages 1, 2, 3, and 4 is 16.

With the scheme completed there would be 60 new dwellings and 44 old dwellings demolished, or a net increase of 16; to this number should be added 18 dwellings in the flats and 8 houses in All Saints Street.

I do not propose at this stage to give details of the houses to be erected, and will only remark that they will be designed with proper regard to the sites they are to occupy, in the same way as those at Bembrook Farm and the houses in the important site in All Saints Street, which have already been passed by the Committee and Council.

The Committee stated that they were not in a position at this stage to submit estimates of the cost of the work involved for reasons which were apparent, but they recommended that the scheme as submitted be approved and that the Borough Engineer be instructed to proceed with the preparation of details and estimates of cost for the purpose of an application to the Minister of Health for sanctions to the borrowing of the amount involved in the carrying out of the scheme.

BOROUGH ENGINEER EXPLAINS

Explaining the scheme the Borough Engineer said the great advantage of the scheme was that it could be carried out in various stages. In part one they had an area which was approximately that of one of the cleared areas. They could get on with stage one almost immediately, and having done that could proceed with stage two. The final stage was when they came to make their roadway.

Up to the end of stage three they had a net increase of 41 houses, but when they came to the final stage they would have taken down so many houses they would reduce that number to 16. That was the effect of making the road.

The Committee had to choose between a wide road that meant the demolition of a great number of buildings that could not be replaced and the present scheme, which provided for the building of as many houses as possible, thus keeping trade in the Old Town. Referral to the recent petition from 2,700 citizens, a very moderately worded petition, referred to chaos, but this present "chaos" was nothing like what it would be when the clearance was completed. They were up against a very difficult and urgent problem. The suggestion made for widening High Street did not help them, but added to their difficulties. There were almost as many tenancies on the east side of High Street as there were properties scheduled for demolition. The proposed road was only wide enough for local traffic, and it would avoid too many demolitions. The number of houses that were condemned north of Courthouse Street was about 98. The Borough Engineer would have to demolish for the purpose of the scheme 44 more houses. That would allow him to build 60 new houses. They had to consider the problem that they were putting back one sixth of the houses demolished for slum clearance. But he suggested this was not an unreasonable proportion, considering the congestion that previously existed. The total number of new houses was 60 in the Bourne, 18 new flats in

John Street and 8 new houses in All Saints Street. On stage one there was not a single house that had to be demolished, and in three months' time they could make a start. They would have to find houses for 15 more tenants, but by the time they were ready to go ahead he believed they would have them ready on sites in other parts of the town.

He hoped the Council would be satisfied with the type of houses that it was proposed to put up. The Borough Engineer was very anxious that they should be in keeping with the character of the Old Town. They would see the same red roofs between High Street and All Saints Street, but not so congested, and diversified by open spaces of green foliage. He thought the Old Town would look just as beautiful from the hills and it would have lost its slum character. He expressed the Housing Committee's gratitude and relief for the Borough Engineers proposal's and these were adopted.

It had been suggested that they should get in experts to advise them.

The Borough Engineer had lived with the problem for years. The expert came for a week and went away with £100 in his pocket.

Councillors thought the Borough Engineer's report was of the finest that had ever been brought to the Council. He wanted a start made as quickly as possible. They had heard nothing but praise for the scheme.

The scheme should include provisions for ample traffic facilities in High Street and to provide as far as possible for the erection of dwellings of Tudor appearance, and make the area completely novel as regards its appearance from the historic standpoint as they wanted the Old Town to be a great attraction to the visitors.

As to the traffic problem in High Street, there were parts of the high pavement that were unnecessarily wide. Was there going to be any provision for the diversion of the trolley bus system? They would always get congestion in High Street while they had the trolley buses running through the street.

The biggest part of the trouble in High Street was the opposition between different bus operators. The other aggravating factors in High Street had been lorries stopping to deliver goods and the desire to pass on the part of the buses. There was no reason to why the scheme should not start on stage one in three months time and follow on with the other stages. The scheme would be complete, and the mess cleared up in a reasonable limited time, and not go on for years and years.

The Town Clerk said the Committee has instructed him where necessary to serve 28 days notice on owners and occupiers under the 1926 Act. In view of the rehousing of the people in the Old Town, the Corporation would be entitled to serve 28 days notice on either the owner or occupier or both to obtain possession of premises and then proceed to agree as to the value and price. The 1926 Act, protected the individual and that the Corporation could not get possession until the tenants had been provided with alternative accommodation.

Purchase of Roebuck Yard by compulsory order.
October, 1937.

The Housing and Improvement Committee had been informed by the Town Clerk that after lengthy negotiations he had now agreed with the executors of the late Mr. F. W. Verrells, for the Corporation to purchase the stores and yard at Bourne Walk, also known as Roebuck Yard premises, and used for the purpose of the business of a marine store dealer, the agreed price was £1,000, and to include the vendor's solicitors' costs. The price was to include compensation in respect of the business, and vacant possession was to be given at March 31st, 1938., the Committee recommended that the terms agreed upon by the Town Clerk be approved.

The old stables block at the top of High Street. c1949

THE HOUSING QUESTION IN THE OLD TOWN.
1937

Sir:- When a Hastings resident was deprived of his house last year, certain Councillors pleaded that the Council could not help itself as it had to carry out the instructions of the Minister of Health.

The hypocrisy of this plea has now been made clear by the attitude of the Mayor a week or so back when; he appeared on the same platform with the Minister of Health here in Hastings.

Instead of seizing an excellent opportunity of tackling the Minister on the subject, the Mayor actually lauded the whole business to the skies. In a special reference to what he euphemistically termed "Slum Clearance." The Mayor quoted Blake's immortal lines about building "A New Jerusalem in England's Green and Pleasant Lands." If building a new Jerusalem means invoking the Housing Acts where the Council wants to make a clearance for a new road;

If it means the arbitrary selection of a few old houses for confiscation out of a town full of such buildings; If it means favouritism in the treatment of a minority of house owners in the clearance area; If it also means fat compensation to Tradesmen for small stores in back streets, while poor house owners are deprived of their property for a song- Then it strikes me that the new Jerusalem will be a Jerry-Built affair.

Property Concerned	Compensation Paid	
	£	S
House 6 Bourne Passage.	15	0
Store next to 18 Winding Street.	60	0
Houses 12, 13 & 14 Winding Street.	30	0
Houses 28 & 29 John Street, House next to 28 John Street & Store above.	200	0
Shop & House 17 John Street.	950	0
House & Shop Commercial road	80	0
House 10 East Street.	375	0
House 9 East Street.	500	0
House 11 East Street.	650	0
House 18 Winding Street.	12	10
House 3 Winding Street.	25	0
Store 22 John Street, next to 4 East Street.	700	0
House 16 John Street.	35	0
House 7 Winding Street.	20	0
House 10 Winding Street.	30	0
Houses 4 & 4a John Street.	40	0
House & Shop John Street.	50	0
Stores 4, 4a & 5 John Street.	475	0
Stores 20 John Street & 5 East Street.	600	0

Stores & Premises 1a Commercial Street.	675	0
Store next to 5 John Street & Store corner of Winding Street.	700	0
House 7 Bourne Street, House 1 Winding Street, 14 East Street & Store next to 20 Winding Street.	1300	0
House 3 East Street & House 23 John Street with Smithy & Warehouse.	130	0
House & Shop 8 John Street.	40	0
House 4 East Street & 21 John Street.	50	0
House & Restaurant.	1725	0
House & Shop John Street Tea Rooms.	80	0
Store & Office 24 John Street.	3000	0

H.W.Wright.
15, Wellington Square
Hastings

P.S. I am sending copies of this list to the highest quarters in the land.

Listed below are as many of the streets, alleyways and twittens that we could find that were mainly lost to the demolition, when the major new road was built through the heart of the Bourne. Some still exist today in part.

All Saints Place, Garden Cottages, Providence Row, Hope Cottages, Union Row, Stansford Row, Woods Row, Wellington Cottages, Henrys Terrace, Zion Cottages, Woods Passage, Bentinck Cottages, Strongs Passage, Belle Vue Cottages, East Hill Passage, Tressells Cottages, Trafalgar Cottages or Williams Row, The Creek, Oxford Terrace, Carpenters Passage, Starrs Cottages, Amphion Place, Crown Cottages, Albert Cottages or Row, Scrivens Buildings, East Hill Cottages, Tamarisk Steps, Bossom Square, Richardsons Cottages, Nelson Passage, Pleasant Row, Mercers Bank, Waterloo Passage, High Street Passage, Smiths Row, Fishers Cottages, Vines Passage, Bourne Passage, Roebuck Yard, Brewery Cottages, Croft Terrace, Gibbons Square, Sinnock Passage and Square, Wellington Court, Cavendish Cottages, Isabella Cottages, Gloucester Cottages or Place, Church Passage, Cavendish Place, Cobourg Place, Post Office Passage, West Hill Cottages, Oak Passage, Bruce Cottages, Light Steps, Hoppers Passage, Market Passage or Anchor Passage (1880), Bourne Street, Commercial Street, Ebineezer Road, Hill Street, Croft Road, The Croft, Exmouth Place, Swann Avenue, Swann Lane, Love Lane, Salters Lane, Courthouse Street, John Street, Winding Street, East Beach Street, East Street, East Bourne Street, Crown Lane, to name but a few!

All these were taken from ordinance survey plans of 1928 and earlier, but this gives you an idea to how large the area was before the axe fell.

Compulsory purchase Orders sent out!
October, 1937.

The Housing and Improvement Committee had received reports from the district Valuer on his negotiations for the acquisition of the under mentioned properties, which are situated in the areas in respect of which, the Council made compulsory purchase orders on March 28th, and May 11th, 1934, that had authorised settlements on the following terms, and recommended that their actions be confirmed:-

House, 3, East Street, and house, smithy, and warehouse, 23, John Street. Purchase price £130, and vendors solicitors' cost, and negotiations fee, and certain other conditions not material for the purpose of the report.

House and shop, 8, John Street, Purchase price £40, and vendors solicitors' cost, and negotiations fee, and certain other conditions not material for the purpose of the report.

House, 4, East Street, and 21, John Street, Purchase price £50, and vendors solicitors' cost, and negotiations fee, and certain other conditions not material for the purpose of the report.

House and shop, Parks Restaurant, Commercial Road, Purchase price £1,725, and vendors solicitors' cost, and negotiations fee, and certain other conditions not material for the purpose of the report.

Stores and premises, 1a, Commercial Road (Lessee's interest), Purchase price £450, and vendors solicitors' cost, and negotiations fee, and certain other conditions not material for the purpose of the report.

House, shop, passage, yard, and out buildings, the John Street Tea Rooms, 3, John Street, Purchase price £80, and vendors solicitors' cost, and negotiations fee, and certain other conditions not material for the purpose of the report.

Store and Office, 24, John Street, Purchase price £125, and vendors solicitors' cost, and negotiations fee, and certain other conditions not material for the purpose of the report.

House, yard and out buildings, 7, Bourne Street; House, 1, Winding Street; Deeze, No. 14, East Street; Stores next to 20, Winding Street, Purchase price £1,300, and surveyor's fee (£28) and vendor's solicitors costs.

Some Councillors protested against the amounts to be offered in compensation to these people as being grossly unfair.

It was also stated that some of the properties taken had been recently improved at the owners own cost, and were worth many hundreds more than given.

The Town Clerk said that, if this matter had been taken to arbitration, the amount paid would be little different from what they have got now and agreed upon.

Leslie Badham's, All Saints Street.
Bottom: Corner of East Bourne Street & Nelson's Passage from Bourne Street.

Leslie Badham's, Nelson's Passage from Winding Street.

Old Town Redevelopment Plan.
April, 1938.

The Housing and Improvements Committee reported that they had considered the reference to them by the Council at their last meeting on the subject of the submission to the Council of a complete plan of the redevelopment of the Old Town from the south end of Bourne Street to the top of High Street.

The Committee had discussed from time to time the criticisms which had been made in relation to the clearing of the sites in the areas dealt with under the Housing Acts, and as they felt that there had been a lack of knowledge of the real difficulties of their duties, they wished to take this opportunity of outlining the work which had been carried out under the compulsory purchase orders in respect of Areas Nos. 1 to 10, 12 and 14 to 17.

These orders were confirmed by the Ministry of Health on November 9th, 1934, and again on January 4th, 1935.

After confirmation, the notice of the orders had to be published in the local Press, and a further period of six weeks had to elapse before such orders became operative. It was then necessary to notify the owners of the properties and to serve them with notices to treat.

The claims, when received, were referred to the Valuation Department of H. M. Inland Revenue for negotiation, and the Committee emphasised that 85 per cent, of the properties to be acquired, under the provisions of the orders, were at site value only.

This apparent hardship, although strictly in accordance with the provisions of the Act, could not be obviated, but caused much criticism, irritation and delay.

It was then necessary for the Council to provide housing accommodation for the persons to be displaced, and the Council had erected 126 houses, all of which had been completed and occupied. Six hundred and fifty seven (657) persons had been rehoused to date.

The fundamental reason for the making of the orders was for the removal of persons from premises classified as unfit for human habitation, and not solely as a redevelopment of the area. In connection with the clearance areas, 170 properties had been acquired, and 163 had been demolished, although in several instances the owners, had not completed the transfer of the sites to the Corporation, after agreeing the terms, and, even at this stage, it be necessary to refer this matter of certain site values to arbitration, but this would not interfere with the redevelopment of the areas, although emphasising the difficulties and delays encountered.

At the present time only 13 houses remained to be acquired in the areas, other than those which might be referred to arbitration as mentioned, and it was believed that the whole of the sites would be cleared by the end of April.

The Committee drew attention also to the large proportion of business properties in Winding Street, peculiar to the Old Town, the greater number of which, were to be purchased at market value in accordance with the terms of the orders, and, in consequence, the negotiations by the Valuation Department of H. M. Inland Revenue were lengthy and intricate.

It entailed the engagement of a firm of Chartered Accountants to investigate the books of the various traders, and great difficulty was experienced in arriving at a satisfactory settlements for all concerned.

The Committee felt that it had not been appreciated, that these areas had been cleared by way of compulsory purchase, and not just a clearance procedure, and the Council were warned when this procedure was first adopted it would entail some years to carry out fully.

Owner offered just £15 for his house.
Judges strong comments to Corporation.
"I am treated like a sausage machine"
April, 1938.

"It is too much for me...I am a servant of the public, not just a rubber stamp...
I am treated like a sausage machine. I will not act in a case like this.
This man should have a fair and open hearing.
He feels he is being done, and that is not unnatural."

These were some of the outspoken comments made by his Honour Judge F. K. Archer, K.C., at Hastings County Court, when the Hastings Corporation claimed possession of 4, Winding Street, Hastings, a house occupied by Mr. Henry George Johnson.

"It is robbery with violence," said Johnson, who denied that the house was unfit for human habitation, and declared that he had been offered £300 for the house, of which he was the owner before that case came on, and now the Corporation wanted to take it for a mere £15.

"All my life savings are gone if they take this house," he added. "Everyone in the town is in sympathy with my case."

Mr. Ian R. Drummond, who appeared for the Corporation, said the Corporation was not the owners and were making the claim for possession under statutory powers. They had served notice to treat, and notice requiring Johnson to vacate the premises.

Interposing, Johnson said "the house was in perfect condition", and answering the Judge, said "he had not the slightest idea as to why the Corporation wanted to take his house". Mr. Drummond emphasised that Parliament had passed a Housing Act, which gave the Corporation statutory powers in the purchasing of houses deemed to be unfit for human habitation.

Judge Archer - "You are seeking to regard this house as valueless, and pay only for the land. Mr. Drummond - That is correct, Sir."

Judge Archer - "Where there is a perfectly worthless building that could not be inhabited at all, it is perfectly monstrous that local public funds should be depleted by payments of large values to a wicked property owner, this man, however, is living in his own house."

Mr. Drummond said that the Council had been given powers by the Ministry of Health to buy the house at site value only.

His Honour - "But this man is living in the house itself and it is of value to him, and yet this house must be compulsory taken without giving him a penny of its true value." "What is the reason as to why this man has got to give up the house?"

Mr. Drummond - "It is unfit for human habitation." Johnson strongly denied this. The general principle was, added Mr. Drummond, "that the site value should be paid for a house if it were unfit for human habitation, and this was fought out at the public enquiry."

"No Discretion"

His Honour observed that these powers were very great, and very high, and must be handled by the authorities concerned in a way that would commend itself to everyone.

That day was faced with a claim for possession, and defendant came into the witness box and said: "I am being turned out, although I am living in my house, on the ground that it is not fit for human habitation. But I am not being paid a single penny for it." he would like to know, went on his Honour, "whether the house was unfit for human habitation," and said "that as far as he could see he had no discretion to exercise in the case." "If a Judge has no discretion, the sooner the country knows it the better." "It is a farce to come before a Judge in a case like this when it can be done with a rubber stamp."

"If I have discretion, I will not turn this man out of his house on the grounds that it is unfit for human habitation, unless I know that it is."

"If I have no discretion, it makes a Judges position absolutely impossible. You must go to the High Court and get a ruling, and then tell me what I can do."

Mr. Drummond pointed out that there was an alternative method that was far more efficacious, by which an occupier of a house could be turned out of the house straightaway, but the Council preferred to let the man come to that Court and have a fair hearing. His Honour - "But where is the fair hearing?"

"I cannot believe that an Act of Parliament intends to submit a matter to a Judge, and his position is such, that the Judge has no power, and no authority to act upon. What is the object of your coming to the Court?"

Mr. Drummond replied that "they could enter by force, but they came to the Court to protect themselves."

"Too much for me"

His Honour - "I feel this is too much for me, and I really can't face it, I don't mind what the question is so long as I have something to try, but in a case like this, when there is nothing to try, and no question, and I am treated like a sausage machine, I begin to think that there is something wrong somewhere."

Mr. Drummond - "it is not our fault; it is the fault of the Act of Parliament."

His Honour asked Johnson whether he attended the public enquiry, when the question as to whether the house was unfit for human habitation was gone into. Johnson said "he had, and the only complaint was that the house was dark at the back." It was a six roomed house, and he had a family of six living there. "Everyone in the town is sympathetic to my case," added Johnson.

His Honour - "If you could have sold it, what would you have got for it?"

Johnson - "Just before this case came on I was offered £300 for it, and the Corporation offered me a miserly £15. It is robbery with violence," added Johnson. "I have seen no Valuer."

Mr. Drummond - "I am quite sure that the house is unfit for human habitation. The question of unfitness, however, cannot be gone into. This order is sufficient evidence in any Court of Law."

His Honour - "It is too much for me, I cannot sit here and pretend to be a Judge when I am not, without guidance of some sort, I will not act in a case like this. This man should have a fair and open hearing in a Court somewhere, with witnesses to say whether this house is fit to live in or not. He feels that he is being done , and it is not unnatural."

Mr. Drummond - "The Housing Act has given him his remedy."

"What your Council says," went on the Judge, "is we don't want to go and take the risk of entering, although we have got the right, without the order of the Judge.'"

"Pure Farce"

"It was a pure farce," continued his Honour, "to come into the Court, and just get the Judge to make an order, he supposed it looked better to have a Judge's order, well that is not going to be the case here, I don't see why the Corporation should not take the risk if they feel so sure of their case," he added.

Mr. Drummond said "their alternative method was to issue their warrant to the Sheriff."

Johnson - "My life savings are gone if they take this house. You fight for your country, and they give you £15 for your house. Yet the Corporation gave £3,000 for a shed with no living accommodation."

Mr. Drummond - "the Corporation cannot help themselves.!"

His Honour - "Mr. Drummond don't tell me that! This man says his life savings of £300 are in this house, and but for the Corporation he could sell the house, and now he is offered the sum of just £15."

"You cannot say the Corporation cannot help themselves; they need not do it at all. Parliament cannot possibly have meant to bring about a state of affairs where a Judge is to be used like a machine. I am a servant of the public, not just a rubber stamp."

"If it is true," went on Judge Archer, "That you can get a Sheriff's warrant without application to me, then this application should not have been made. These applications are misleading. It looks as if the Judge is blessing the whole thing from beginning to end." "You had better get your Sheriff's warrant, but I think that sooner or later, if the Corporation do things that way there will be a disturbance and row. Why not pay this man the market value of his house." Replying to the question, Mr. Drummond said "it was a legal reason, due to the fact that the house was unfit for human habitation."

Johnson interposed and said that "this was all bluff, and wished that his Honour could visit the house. I can see the West Hill and right over the sea," added Johnson. Summing up, Judge Archer said "the case involved a very serious question of principle that needed to be carefully considered." He was not satisfied that the application was rightly made. To apply to the Judge for possession in a case where he was supposed to have discretion, then to say that under the Housing Acts there was no discretion, made a rubber stamp of the Judge. He would take a lot of persuading that the law meant that.

Adjourning the case for a month, his Honour, in addressing Mr. Drummond, said, "I think that you should have the instructions from the full Council, and I will consider it in the meantime."

His Honour expressed his full appreciation of Mr. Drummond's position, and the assistance he gave in those cases.

Insult compensation offered.

June, 1938.

A situation had arisen over the compensation that was offered for the purchase of 4, Winding Street, the owner-occupier of which, Mr. H. G. Johnson, is at variance with the Corporation owing to the fact that they are seeking possession under the Old Town Clearance Scheme at only £15 site value.

We had learned that a local resident has come forward with an offer to purchase the house from Mr. Johnson for £200, and to then hand it over to the Council, the local Samaritan wished to remain anonymous and had no connection with the Council. The money had been entrusted to Alderman F. W. Morgan, who had interested himself in the case in the Council, and would make himself immediately available if Mr. Johnson cares to take advantage of this offer, instead of facing the prospects of receiving only the site value of £15. Should Mr. Johnson take up this offer, this will not then allow him to be in any severe financial loss over the property.

The Press did somehow or other find out to whom the good Samaritan was, the kind person was Major H. C. Holman, of St Leonards.

Winding Street
June, 1938.

Please excuse the poor quality of these pictures, as they were taken from a newspaper of the time, and the clarity was far from good, even a computer found it difficult to enhance the pictures to an acceptable viewable status.

Winding Street Owner-Occupier Refuses £200 Offer.
July, 1938.

Mr. H. G. Johnson, owner-occupier of No. 4, Winding Street, which the Hastings Corporation are seeking to acquire at just £15 site value, under the Old Town Slum Clearance Scheme, has announced his definite decision not to accept the offer of £200, which Major H. C. Holman, of St Leonards, has made him for the property.

As reported in last weeks Press, Major Holman has offered to purchase the house from Mr. Johnson for this sum, and when all transactions were completed to Mr. Johnson's satisfaction, the property would then be handed over to the Corporation.

In a recent interview with the editor, Mr. Johnson said it was his definite decision not to accept the offer of £200. the editor tried to show Mr. Johnson that he was making a grave mistake, and would be a considerable loser by declining to accept the offer, but Mr. Johnson remained firm in his decision, and asked the editor to publish the following letter:-

Sir, I wish to publish in your paper the reason I refuse the offer of £200.

It is because I do not feel justified in accepting money from a strange person.

What I am asking the Corporation for is a house in exchange for the one I am still living in. I understand my house is not on the map, therefore it is for their own interest that they need it.

I do not intend giving up my house until I get proper justice.

H. G. Johnson

4, Winding Street

Hastings.

We have also received a letter from Major Holman, a copy of the following letter which he sent to Mr. Johnson this week:-

Dear Mr. Johnson, I confirm in writing the offer I made to you of £200, for No. 4, Winding Street.

Please understand, that I am in no way connected with the Town Council, and that I have not discussed the matter with any member or official.

It was only by reading the reports in the Press that I knew of your case, and being aware of the close interests of Alderman Morgan has always had in the Old Town, I asked him to make my offer to you, hoping to save you hardship and discomfort owing to your disturbance by the Corporation. If you accept my offer I shall give the property to the town, and you will receive the £200 clear of any expenses, but, of course, should the Corporation be obliged to take possession under their powers, then my offer is immediately withdrawn.

Can I help you further?

Major H. C. Holman.

January, 1939.

March, 1939.

July, 1939.

THE HOUSING QUESTION IN THE OLD TOWN
1939

Final decisions had been fought over and over in the Council chambers; Compensation payments were agreed upon and paid to many in 1937 but, it wasn't before 1939 when the scale of compensation paid to the property owners was first published for public viewing.

The Hastings Observer published the article under the heading of COMPENSATION PAID this was to show examples of what was offered to the home owners, headed by what one can only describe as a very controversial letter.

The question will still remain open even up to today; Was it really slum clearance, or was it strictly compulsory purchase for the want of a road by a few Councillors that were determined to split the Old Town apart for the sake of the motor car?

The only reason to why "Sidney Little's" super road scheme never took off was, that the war intervened, and was never given a second thought after.

Home owners get only site value!
Slum Clearance   Was it?

Under the 1925 Housing Act only the site value was paid to the home owners whose house was demolished. The details of the compensation paid are given in the letter below, which was taken from the H. & St L, Observer 1939.

Many people voted that the only houses in the Old Town to be cleared stood in the way of the new road, were these the only "Slums"? Had the property been bought under compulsory purchase orders to build a road, prices could well of been much higher.

THE ONLY WAY TO OBTAIN PERFECT, CLEAN COOKING WITHOUT DIRT, DUST OR FUMES

is to use

ELECTRICITY

De Luxe Model Electric Cookers on Hire at low charges which include free maintenance

---

MULTI-PART TARIFF (Hastings Area) $\frac{1}{2}$d. per unit (plus fixed charge)

Electric Cookery Demonstrations at "Electric House"
at 3 p.m. on Tuesdays and Thursdays

THE COUNTY BOROUGH OF HASTINGS ELECTRICITY DEPARTMENT, "Electric House,"
12 & 13, York Buildings, Hastings   'Phone: Hastings 3176 (day)   'Phone: Hastings 1298 (night)

Leslie Badham's, Winding Street.
Bottom: East Bourne Street drawn from Bourne Street.

Demolition of Old Town House.
Corporation win in appeal Court.
November 1941.

The Court of appeal on Friday of last week dealt with an appeal by Mr. H. G. Johnson of Croft Road, Hastings, from a judgement of Mr. Justice Humphreys at the Lewes Assizes in favour of the Hastings Corporation, in an action he brought against them in respect of the taking and the demolition of his house at 4, Winding Street, Old Town, Hastings.

Mr. T. Sophian appeared for the appellant, and Mr. G. Robertson for the Corporation.

Mr. Sophian said the appeal raised a number of questions relating to the acquisition and demolition of property. Mr. Justice Humphreys dismissed plaintiff's action, which arose out of the powers exercised by the Corporation under the Housing Acts. The Corporation had declared the site in question a clearance area, and this has been confirmed by the Minister in London.

Subsequently they served notice to acquire the property, and a notice of entry.

The appellant refused to go out or treat at all with the Corporation.

The Corporation then claimed possession and brought a claim for possession in the County Court, but the Judge held that he had no jurisdiction to deal with the matter. After three years had expired, Counsel said, they served the appellant with a second notice of entry, and eventually the Corporation went into possession of the building, and ejected the appellant from his property.

On this part of the case Counsel submitted that the Corporation had acted unlawfully, as the three years from the serving of the first notice had then expired, and their rights had ceased with the expiry of that period.

In Counsel's opinion the Corporation were barred from doing anything in the matter. The Corporation had served the appellant with a notice to treat, but this the appellant ignored as he considered the whole matter ended at the end of the three years. Ultimately the Corporation issued a warrant to the Sheriff, and he took possession and ejected the appellant, and put his goods in another house. They were then removed to a storage, they then proceeded to demolish the building, and Counsel then argued that the Corporation had no power at all to do this until they had acquired it. They had trespassed on the property, and committed unlawful acts.

Under these circumstances the appellant brought an action against the Corporation at the Lewes Assizes, and claimed damages for wrongfully taking possession of the building, and removing his goods and chattels. Damages were also claimed for ejection, and the wrongful demolition of the building.

The appellant also claimed certain declarations that the Corporation were not entitled to act as they did under the powers they had. The action was tried by Mr. Justice Humphreys, and it was dismissed.

Counsel said it was in March, 1935, that the Corporation served a notice to treat on the appellant. He refused to accept the amount offered. He also refused to go to arbitration. In 1939 the Corporation demolished the premises. Lord Justice Goddard pointed out that the appellant refused to be a party in ascertaining the compensation to be fixed, and by so doing he held the matter up. Mr. Sophian said his client considered that the matter had not been properly dealt with by the Corporation. Lord Justice Goddard pointed out that the Corporation could not be held by an owner who refused to treat for his property. Mr. Robertson said the Corporation had only acted in accordance with the powers vested in them.

The Court dismissed the appeal with such costs as were appropriate to a poor persons appeal.

Lord Justice MacKinnon, in giving judgement, said he was satisfied that the Corporation exercised their powers well within the period of three years, the notice to the appellant being served in April, 1936. The fact that they did not complete the demolition within the three years was not to the point. There was no limit until they had carried out the demolition, and they had exercised their powers of taking the land within the three year time period.

He agreed with the judgement of Mr. Justice Humphreys. The appeal failed, and would be dismissed.

Lord Justice Goddard, and Mr. Justice Hallett concurred.

This concludes the saga of No. 4, Winding Street, unfortunately, Mr Johnson was moved to Croft Road, but lost out on any money other than the £15 the Council offered him in the beginning for site value only. It is a shame that he didn't or wouldn't take up the offer of the £200 when Major Holman made a one time offer to help him out rather than see him lose everything in life.

How many other people within the Old Town probably would have gone through this same procedure of taking the Corporation to High Court if they knew how to, with regard to the poor compensation values on their property?

Now owing to the intervention of the Second World War, everything more or less came to a grinding halt for the duration, especially within the so called slum clearance areas of the Old Town. The Borough Engineer (Mr. Sidney Little) was seconded to the Admiralty to oversee the construction of the Mulberry Docks between the years 1940 -1944, and in his absence nothing really got done until his return, and even then, War damage took priority over everything else. The town was in a mess, not to mention what was just left in the Old Town, this was now placed on the so called back burner for a while.

Ministry Ban The Demolition of the Steel Houses.
"Modernisation" Move at Broomgrove site.

February, 1944.

As some of the Old Town's people that were made homeless by the compulsory purchase orders, when the slum clearance was started under the Parliamentary Act., as a slum clearance programme, a few were put into these steel houses on the Broomgrove site, and we thought it apt to include this report from the Council when they wanted to have them demolished, but the Ministry of Health opposed the move from every direction, even after the war, when several had to be demolished by the effects of severe damage caused by bombing raids over the town, and these few were caught in the bomb blasts, rendering a few completely worthless in the trying to effect a repair. Yes, the report might be long, but quite interesting, when you read it, you will wonder to whom was right, the Government, or our Council?

Housing Committee disagree with Ministry's decision.

The Committee related their unsuccessful efforts to get the Ministry of Health to agree to the demolition of the remaining 40 of the original 54 houses, and the use of the steel for war production. They stated that the Ministry desired an experimental modernisation of two houses to be undertaken, and protective work carried out on the others. The Council, adopting a recommendation of the Finance Committee, decided by a majority to agree only to the reconditioning experiment, which is to be carried out at cost of the Ministry, and to defer consideration of the protective work for the present.

In their report, the Housing and Improvements Committee stated that in consequence of the past enemy action, the Broomgrove site had suffered serious damage. It had been necessary to demolish 14 of the 54 houses, and repairs to make good the other damaged houses had cost the Council £962.

In view of the general dislike for steel houses and the difficulties which had been experienced with them for a period of years, the Committee made representation to the Ministry of Health upon the advisability of demolishing the whole of the houses, and making available the steel contained therein for war production, and a deputation interviewed Officers of the Ministry of Health back in September of 1942, and presented a case in favour of demolition. The Ministry Officers were very loath to agree to the demolition of any habitable houses, and as a result is was arranged that the Ministry would send down a technical officer with a knowledge of steel houses to prepare a specification of the work, which should be carried out to make the houses habitable and more attractive. In March of 1943, at the request of the Ministry, the deputation attended at the Ministry, when the proposals were discussed further in the light of the report of the Ministry's technical advisor upon his inspection of the existing structures, and the deputation took another opportunity of again presenting a strong case on behalf of the Council for the demolition of the houses, but without success, particularly in view of the anticipated high cost for the provision of houses after the war, and the present outstanding debt upon the existing houses.

Proposals submitted by Officers of the Ministry of the works which should be carried out to the existing 40 houses, not only to put them into a state fit for human habitation, but also to modernise them as far as possible, had been considered, and it had been suggested by the Ministry that the work should be carried out to one pair of the houses forthwith, and that they should be inhabited, preferable by tenants who had previously occupied steel houses, for the purpose of ascertaining whether such works had eliminated the objections which have hitherto been made against steel houses, and in addition protective works to prevent the existing structures for deteriorating further should be carried out by the Acting Borough Engineer at an estimated cost of £90 per pair of houses. The cost to carry out the works, excluding the protective works, £610 per pair of houses, without steel roofs and £671. 18s. per pair for the four houses with steel roofs, thus making a total cost for the whole of the works (including the protective works) of £13,424. The Committee said that they were advised that the outstanding debt upon the 40 steel houses, apart from the capitol remaining unpaid in respect of roads and sewers, was £12,852, and having regard to the total sum necessary to undertake the whole of the work, representation had again been made upon the availability of pursuing the course proposed. The Ministry having considered the matter further, together with the estimate of cost, had intimated that they were still of the opinion that the experiment should be undertaken, and that one pair of the houses should be made habitable and modernised in accordance with the proposals submitted at an estimated cost of £610, and that the protective works to the remaining 38 structures should be undertaken, the advisability or otherwise of reconditioning the remaining 38 houses at the termination of the war to be determined by the Council after consultation with the Ministry in the light of experience gained from the two houses reconditioned and occupied. The cost of the protective works (£1,710) was to be provided in the rate estimates in so far as it could not be met out of the housing repairs fund account, and the £610 for the reconditioning of the pair of houses was also to be provided in the rate estimates.

The Finance Committee reported that they had considered the financial proposal contained in the Housing Committee's report, and in view of the request of the Ministry, they recommended that the financial proposal so far as it related to the reconditioning of the two houses be approved, and that the consideration of the matter of the incurring expenditure upon the protective works to the remaining 38 structures be deferred for the present.

Councillor Mrs. Alexander, Chairman of the Committee, said that the steel houses on the Broomgrove site had always been very unpopular, "One does not know quite why?" The two steel houses in Beaufort Road St Leonards had always had satisfied tenants, but there has been a prejudice against those at Broomgrove. The modernisation of the two houses proposed in the report as an experiment was very good in our opinion, and almost entirely incorporated recommendations made to the Reconstruction Committee as to what was wanted, or needed in new houses after the war. "They will be very nice indeed, and I think that the housewife will be very pleased with them."

Houses after the war would probably cost £1,000 to £1,200 each to build, and by carrying out that experimental work, they would practically get two new houses at a cost of approximately £600, if they wanted to preserve the others for possible use, some protective work must be done at once.

If they could get those steel houses modernised it would at least help to carry them over the period of the most acute demand for houses when the men and women return home after the war, and would be wanting houses in far greater numbers than the Council could hope to build for some time.

Councillor Honnor, said that the L.C.C. were proposing to build steel houses on their Watling Estate at Hendon. "I don't say that these houses are all that could be expected, But I do say that we have not had the best tenants in them". The greatest fault was condensation of moisture inside the houses, and if the occupants would help by opening their windows when the rooms were warm, there would be considerable improvement." Some years ago, with two other Councillors, he inspected 17 of those houses and found the tenants perfectly satisfied. Councillor Rymill responded by saying that, on the result of that experiment they were proposing to spend £13,000. They were still losing money by keeping those houses going. Even bombed out people would not go into them. Nothing would do away with the condensation. We don't care the L.C.C. are doing. We know that steel houses are a flop. If the Ministry were prepared to pay for that work the responsibility for doing it should be thrown back to them. He supported the Finance Committee's recommendation.

There were many more criticisms from Councillors, but one did mention that it was wrong of the ministry to place people in these steel house after the conversion had been completed, whereby, they were going to be used as guinea pigs at the their own expense.

The steel houses built at the Beaufort Road site were of a different type, and consequently did not suffer the same fate as the ones built at Broomgrove, where they heavily laid in pools of condensation. There was no substitute for brick built houses, with a proper tiled roof, these would not suffer any effects of condensation at any time of the year. Despite the manufacturers claiming that the steel structure would last for decades, whereby the rust could be kept at bay by the prevention cures during building, this was a false claim, as many of the base lines started to rust heavily within a short period of time, and really there was no cure for it once started. To cure the rust problems alone would have meant that the entire structure would have had to of been taken down and treated from the underside, by which time, it would have been much cheaper to demolish the houses then, but the Ministry were adamant that these steel houses were here to stay. A wonderful comment was made that, "Those people who say we ought to keep these steel houses, ought to try and live in one - then they might not be so keen after that." No Englishman could be proud of living in his own "Castle" if it was one of these steel houses.

Hastings had produced housing schemes which had been admired as models, but Broomgrove was not one of them, and best kept in the dark.

In another report later on presented by the Borough Surveyor, it was stated that the steel houses were lined in the walls and the ceiling voids with a suitable fabric that was recommended to have great absorption qualities, this was then applied directly to the inside of the steel panels, which was said to have done the trick as regard the condensation problems. But this again after a short time failed, as the panels produced a smell in the hot weather where water had collected and fallen to the bottom and lay there as stagnant water.

Was there any remedy, yes.........Demolition!

Old buildings in The Bourne.

We now venture into the year 1946, and things never change!

This dilemma for a thoroughfare through the heart of the Bourne had been talked about since virtually the Vikings! We are of course talking the early 1920s. And, still apart from the spasmodic demolition of houses that littered the Bourne Valley from that date, no decision was ever been made final about a road through the Bourne. Many suggestions and alternatives were put before Council from previous and present Borough Engineers, even members of the general public took the time to produce scaled drawings of their own interpretation of what they thought the residents of the Old Town might have liked, should a roadway through the Bourne Valley was ever to become a reality.

Old Town Scheme is Stopped.
February, 1946.
Council alter their minds yet again as to whether the road through the Bourne should go ahead or be scrapped, yes, no ---- no, yes??

The area all over the Old Town looked like a permanent demolition site. There were areas to where houses once stood now left open and derelict, grass and weeds taking over the plots, all over the area were open spaces, some cleared completely, whilst others were strewn with large piles of bricks and old building materials, it looked a rubbish tip. There were also buildings that had been demolished when originally connected to others, but left without giving the attention needed to tidy up and weather the remaining standing buildings. Obviously, money had to be the biggest issue back in the early days, as the Council did not own sufficient land to build upon, nor own enough property of their own, then, to rehouse the number of people that was estimated in the region of 600 when it first started out (but rose considerably over the following years), whom, were going to be made homeless, and the capitol required would have broke the Council's finances completely.

Yes, there were Government grants available, but how was the Council to repay their debts in the 25 year lease term, let alone 50 years hence? The town rates would not have covered a fraction of the outlay, so the Council hadn't a chance in those times. But the question still remains in everybody's minds, that, if they hadn't got the money to rehouse these people in the first place that were being dispossessed of their houses through a "Slum Clearance Scheme," then why did they start such a large demolition programme in the first place, knowing that they couldn't complete? The question now arose as to when everyone would get the total satisfaction that someone one day would make that vital decision to finish the job and clean up the area? As war passed, there was still no movement, and the town was very slowly beginning to enter the race as a seaside town, what was here for people to view when they ventured into the Old Town area of Hastings. William the Conqueror was well known for making places untidy! But even he wouldn't of wanted to be made responsible for the mess that would have caught your eye when you entered the bottom end of the Old Town.

Hastings had to attract more visitors, in which to try and bring the borough into a more respectable place you could bring granny without shame, but all the time the area of the Old Town looked like it did, Hastings had to go a long way to not only clean up their act, but the Old Town as well.

The saga of the Old Town still rallied on as the stories continue:-

The Housing Outlook "Depressing and Discouraging"
October, 1946.

The hundreds of people on the waiting list for houses will gain small consolation from inquiries into the housing position in the borough made by a Press reporter this week.

They reveal the fact that despite all the efforts of the Housing Committee to get houses built little progress has been made.

Councillor Mrs. Boyd Alexander, Chairman of the Committee, frankly admits that she finds the situation "depressing and discouraging." She said "there had been so many setbacks in the past that she could not undertake to predict when any of the houses in the major schemes approved by the Town Council would be ready for occupation. No-one is more anxious to get on as quickly as possible with housing the towns people than the Housing Committee." Said Mrs Alexander, "and in this we have the support of the whole council, but at the moment I can see no point in acquiring more land because we have not yet put houses on the land we have already got."

On prefabricated houses, she said "that 30 aluminium houses had been promised for January and they could have 50 universal type houses as soon as the foundations were ready to receive them. Of these prefabricated houses, some 14 to 20 would be erected at Seaside Road, St Leonards, and the remainder would go on the housing site at Hollington."

"These temporary houses would have their disadvantages as they would delay the erection of permanent houses." Mrs Alexander said "the Council changed its attitude towards prefabricated houses in an endeavour to meet the emergency, but she still maintained that their original decision to have only permanent houses was a sound one. Work has actually started on preparing sites for temporary houses both at Seaside Road and Hollington."

"The aluminium houses have two bedrooms, suitable for mother, father, and two children, and perhaps a baby, a kitchen-dining room, which is well equipped with modern fittings, a good sitting room, bathroom and separate lavatory."

The hall is large enough to take a bicycle or perambulator, and there is an outside storehouse for coal.

The Universal type houses are almost identical, but are of asbestos construction. A great advantage is that they arrive on the site complete with fittings.

Under the apprenticeship scheme, two houses built in Old Church Road, Hollington, are already occupied and three more houses are nearly complete. The position on the other council housing sites is as follows:

Rock Lane. Plans for 200 houses have been passed and work has progressed so far that 50 houses have reached their early stages. Work is now held up, however, for lack of bricklayers.

Broomgrove. Fourteen houses are nearly completed. They are brick houses and will replace steel houses which were destroyed by enemy action. Work here is progressing.

Hollington. Here the Council planned to erect 300 houses, but no work at all has been started except preparations to receive the temporary houses.

Old Town. Twelve new houses are nearly completed under a scheme started before the war.

Councillor Mrs Alexander said that as soon as work at Broomgrove and the Old Town was completed, the men would be transferred to Rock Lane.

Requisitioning is still proceeding but the houses now being taken over are mostly big properties which will need a good deal of repairs and other work.

The Housing Committee in dealing with people on the waiting list for houses, has so ordered the points scheme that only local people are put on the list, with the exception of those who may have lived in the town before or are returning to take up jobs.

The committee is still appealing to people with spare rooms to take in other families, and also a scheme under which, people with houses, which are too large for them can exchange with a large family, which has only small premises.

Such people can be put in touch with one another through the W.V.S.

Years had passed as mentioned so many times before, but it wasn't now until the 1960s, for when we actually got the road through the Bourne, this time it was to cost 20 fold to what was originally estimated at when first planned back in the 1930s. Have we actually learnt something from these wasted years, and thousands of pounds spent unnecessarily of public money?

The simple answer to that is NO! The Councils not only here in Hastings, but most large towns throw away not thousands of pounds of our money, but millions on wasted and stupid ideas from people who think that they know better than most of us.

What the Bourne might have looked like in yet another scheme dating back to c1958
There would have been buildings crossing the main carriageway
in the form of a bridge

The Old Town problems still lingered on!

We are led back to the era of the 1920s, when life in the Old Town carried on the same as it ever did before, apart from the threat by the local council to compulsory purchase all the property that was deemed unfit for human habitation, if this threat was to be carried out to the full, half the inhabitants would be homeless; so what is the solution?

There were two problems set before the Council as long before this period also, and that was the sheer congestion of the area of tenements and narrow alleys between the High Street and All Saints Street, there was a need for a new wide thoroughfare to suit the ever growing needs of today's and of course tomorrows traffic.

With regard to the first problem, it was not that the Old Town was unhealthy, far from it, but the scores of dwellings, which did not satisfy the very elements of sanitation and decency could not be tolerated anymore by the public sanitary authority. The second problem seemed even more urgent. The two main streets are so narrow that at places two larger sized vehicles find it impossible to pass each other, indeed at one point in All Saints Street there is barely room for one. This latter problem might be met in two ways, either by widening one of the two streets, although High Street was suggested because of the benefit to all the local trades people who would have improved shop fronts to their premises (this was originally planned back in 1894 by Mr. H. Palmer then Borough Engineer, when it all came to nothing). The other solution was to cut a new wide thoroughfare up the line of the Bourne Stream, thereby, leaving the two streets either side untouched.

Without deciding on any outcome to the latter problem, the Town Council obtained powers under Part II (Improvement and Reconstruction Schemes) of the Housing Act of 1925 to deal with the former. Condemned areas were marked out, and blocks of flats, forty eight in all, were built for the dispossessed tenants on the former site of the residence of the late Mr. P. F. Robertson, formally M.P. for the Borough, on the Heights at Halton. These flats were virtually completed in 1926, and by late October of the same year twenty one tenants had been relocated into them. Meanwhile, negotiations were proceeding for the purchase of the tenements in the condemned area.

Under the Act, site value can only be given as compensation for condemned property. There was no doubt what so ever that some of the owners deserved nothing more than what was offered, but in other cases to where the tenants had invested their entire life savings in the purchase of their tenement, and in their cases there was human outcry against "robbery" seemed to be not unjustified. An amendment of the Act to provide for equitable compensation in such cases was clearly called for, but the Government had not yet introduced the necessary legislation, and meanwhile the complete clearance and rebuilding programme of the area with additional blocks of flats was now at a complete stand still, the scheme so far had proved nothing to alleviate the overcrowding in the area.

While this controversy was raging away, the Council received a deputation from the Society for the Preservation of Ancient Buildings, they along with the council surveyed the area of the Old Town affected by the proposals for a wider thoroughfare. The deputation presented to the council an important report. This report strongly apposed the widening of either the High Street or All Saints Street as destructive to the artistic charm of those streets and of numerous buildings of high architectural interest still remaining in them.

It suggested instead the adoption of a system of one - way traffic up the High Street and down All Saints Street; and only if this were found inadequate for the traffic did it consent to a new thoroughfare up the Bourne as a preferable to a widening of High Street and All Saints Street. The report also gave some important advice on the character of the tenements to be erected in the condemned area. It apposed anything in the way of a sham antique nature, and recommended buildings of two floors of simple design, built using the commonly used materials of the present period, roofed laid with common red tiles, which are generally used in the town today. Thus would its antique character be best preserved. It was stated that probably the problem of the wider thoroughfare will take several years to solve, and little did they realise that it wouldn't become a reality till the late 1950s early 1960s.

In the meantime, it should be possible to rebuild the condemned areas in such a way that, between the new blocks of tenements, space is ultimately left for a future new thoroughfare up the centre of the Bourne, if such an undertaking is again ultimately called for and decided upon.

The following years saw great changes in the Boroughs of Hastings and St Leonards, due to reduced incomes, and added to that the value of money depreciated enormously with the Great War in operation. The large houses in St Leonards became unlettable until they were sadly divided into flats.

Overcrowding among the poor was at its highest level ever. To meet the evil of overcrowding the Town Council embarked on schemes for building nearly 500 new tenements. The layout of the first two of these schemes, under Dr. Addison's regime, are admirable to say the least. The houses at All Saints sheltered by the trees that surround the church, render the approach to the Old Town, if possible, even more attractive than it was before. Those in Clive Vale, further up the Bourne Stream, are also in complete contrast to the haphazard building that has disfigured so many of our hills and valleys.

The four later schemes at Silverhill, Hollington, Broomgrove and Red Lake suffer from the economies imposed by the Government, but are at any rate are far in advance of the results of earlier private enterprise as seen at Halton, Bulverhythe and elsewhere. Among these later schemes was one of steel houses, the only serious defects of which so far are unsightliness, and probable high cost of upkeep. All the Council houses are let at about half the economic rent, the Government and the town sharing the loss. Even so, the rent is beyond the resources of most working people in the town, and overcrowding in poor tenements shows little amelioration. It is clear that the more houses the Council builds the more will be required, that as long as they go on building working class houses to let at uneconomic rents, none will be built by the private enterprise, and that the subsidies, which enable the houses to be let at an uneconomic rent to working people are partly paid for directly or indirectly by other working people, whose wages, low rentals tend to keep down at a low level. On the whole it is not to be regretted that no proposals for fresh housing schemes were made by the Council during the years of 1926/7, in spite of the continued overcrowding that still existed.

One of the difficulties to which overcrowding in the town leads is the difficulty of ejecting tenants from houses that have been condemned as unfit for human habitation, where no accommodation can be found for them elsewhere. Thus, although there were other properties in all parts of the town that ought to have been condemned, only seven closing orders were made during this period. A proposal was made in the Council for providing houses for the express purpose of housing families whilst their condemned tenements were put in a proper state of repair, but was not carried out, mainly because the owners of the tenements, with the odd one or two exceptions, either could not or would not undertake the expense of the work, and the property was not of a character that the Council as a sanitary authority could well purchase for the purpose. Instead, one block of the Hardwicke Road flats was alienated from its original purpose and let out to the tenants of condemned houses, which, of course did nothing permanently to increase the housing stock accommodation in the town. There were a few cases to where owners of condemned houses had them done up and then let them out at greatly enhanced rentals. Meetings had taken place between the Council and the local Social Services Centre in hoping that the Centre would form a Local Public Utility Society for the purpose of purchasing and reconditioning of such condemned property, whereby, keeping the rental down to a minimum that people could afford.

Private enterprise was a little more active with regard to a rather superior type of house, but was not really interested in the working class type of buildings.

Under the Housing Act of 1923, subsidies were granted by the Town Council for the erection of thirty three houses, and under the Small Dwellings Acquisition Act, twenty seven advances were made in the year under review.

A new Housing Act, which came into force in July of 1930 stated:-
Sixty five sections and six schedules. Repeals 50 sections of the principle Act (Housing Act of 1925), and some minor amendments. It is a great attack on slums. Provides for the clearance or improvement of unhealthy areas, the repair or demolition of insanitary houses, and the housing of the working classes, compels rehousing. Provides for differences in rents of houses to meet the poor and alters subsidy. A new system of unit grants was adopted.

The grant is based on the number of persons required to be displaced or rehoused. The grant is £2.5s.0d., per displaced person payable annually for forty years. The grant will be increased to £3.10s.0d., (1) if it is necessary to provide buildings of more than three storeys. (2) if building on another site which costs more than £3,000 per acre. The grant is available for rehousing not only from clearance areas, but also from the new "Improvement areas."

A further interesting point was pointed out in the Rehousing Act, that, whatever action the local authority may take as regards clearance areas or improvement areas or individual unfit houses, they must provide new houses for displaced persons. Section 9 of the Act states that they must satisfy the Minister on this point that they (the Council) have carried out the agreement to the full. Rehousing may be undertaken by Public Utility Societies (private housing associations as we know them today).

The standard of accommodation and size must be within the limits as prescribed by the Act of 1923.

The number of houses to be built will be dependant on size and type, and will be fixed by the Minister before displacement takes place. (The standard will vary for flats.) the normal standard of accommodation for certain types is:-

2 bedroomed houses = 4 persons.

3 bedroomed houses = 5 persons.

4 bedroomed houses = 7 persons.

The new houses must conform with the measurements under the Housing Act of 1923.

The Housing Act of 1925 did spread into many more pages with information we considered was not relevant to this book at this stage.

SOUTH COAST BEDDING Co.

(H. V. SIBUN).

PRICE LIST.

NEW MATTRESSES—	2ft. 6in.	3ft.	4ft.	4ft. 6in.
Wool	13/6	15/6	17/6	19/6
Wool and Hair	29/6	32/6	37/6	39/6
All Hair	39/6	42/6	47/6	49/6
RE-MAKING MATTRESSES—				
In your own ticks	5/-	5/6	6/6	7/6
In new ticks	11/6	12/6	13/6	14/6

61, HIGH STREET, HASTINGS

1,000 'Unfit' Houses in Hastings Still.
February 1961

There are about 1,000 unfit houses in Hastings to be dealt with in the next 12 years, 400 of which come into the Town Council's five year programme (1955-1959), it is stated in the Borough Medical Officers report for 1959. during that year 69 houses were demolished. 29 dwellings were represented as unfit, and as a result, 5 demolition orders, and 23 closing orders were made.

20 families were rehoused, 11 premises were restored by private owners to an approved standard, and to date 58 dwelling had been dealt with in this way.

There was still an appreciable time lag between the making of an order, and the rehousing of the tenants, provisions of alternative accommodation never appearing to catch up with what was really a modest rate of dealing with unfit housing conditions. At the present rate of progress, there appears to be no end to this problem, little impression being made on the overall problem of sub standard housing. A vigorous policy is urgently called for, not least important being a recommendation of routine house to house and street by street inspection, as carried before in 1939, proceeding parallel with the slum clearance programme. Unless large numbers of sub standard houses are saved and improved, the end of the current programme will be followed by yet another, as this had happened so many times in the past.

BRYANT & SONS
For Up-to-date REMOVALS & WAREHOUSING.
ESTIMATES FREE.   Telephone No. 119 Y
The Noted House for New & Second-hand Furniture.
Surplus Furniture Bought or Exchanged. . . . .
Offices & Showrooms—44 & 45, QUEEN'S RD., HASTINGS.

£180,000 New Housing Schemes.
April, 1961.

The Town Council is being asked by the Housing Committee to approve two new housing schemes, together costing £180,000. One is for 73 houses and 12 garages to replace the 40 steel houses at Broomgrove, and the other is for the construction of 22 dwellings and 14 garages for the Gate Farm extension at Hollington. At Broomgrove the development scheme requires special site works, retaining wall, steps, removing and diverting old drain, diverting the old water services, and electricity cables, the Borough Engineer Mr. Baxter told the Committee. Certain economies have been made at the Gate Farm scheme where a total saving of £1,154 could be achieved.

There was also a suggestion that the layout of the site should be reverted back to the original plans for old peoples dwellings, with a meeting hall, or, alternatively, that the house, flat and bungalow plans be completely redesigned on much reduced standards, bearing in mind the Ministry's latest requirements as to standards. If either of these suggestions were to be adopted, it would require a period of about six months to prepare new designs, and other matters, and the Borough Engineer has pointed out that costs on the scheme already approved have gone up by a further 2½ per cent., and any other further delay might result in the tender being withdrawn, which might prejudice other contractors in submitting tenders for future schemes.

Following completion of improvements to the first four flats at Willingdon Avenue, and Old Church Road, Hollington, the Committee have decided to increase the weekly rents to £2. 7s. 1d. inclusive, the weekly amount broken down (£1. 18s. 7d. rent, and 8s. 6d. rates).

Bourne Road Clearance Plan Attacked at Inquiry.
April, 1961.

Proposals for the redevelopment of a total area of about an acre of land in the Bourne Road area of Hastings Old Town was mentioned at an enquiry at the Town Hall recently, when the meeting was conducted by Mr. H. R. Parkin, an inspector of the Ministry of Housing and Local Government.

They were vigorously resisted on behalf of and by a number of Old Town residents, some of whom had been living there for many years.

The area concerned is between the backs of properties in High Street and All Saints Street. The Deputy Borough Engineer Mr. Cowling spoke of the building of two storey Council dwellings, probably in the form of a terrace, and the provision of car parking facilities, lock up garages, for which the demand was very serious, and possibly lay-bys.

A number of small areas are concerned, and the Corporation wish to clear them and redevelop.

The Deputy Town Clerk (Mr. Aston) before calling his evidence, said it had been represented by the Hastings Cottage Improvement Society, owners of one property, which was in Courthouse Street, and was almost entirely devoted to commercial purposes, much of it occupied by one commercial undertaking, a large secondhand furniture business, that the building should be allowed to remain up to be used for commercial purposes, as it did not cause congestion to any neighbouring properties.

He said the Corporation had agreed subject to the Minister's consent, to the arrangement. Mr. Aston said the only satisfactory way of dealing with the clearance areas involved, was that they should be acquired by the Corporation, and used for redevelopment by them.

Dr. Parkman, Medical Officer of Health, said 34 families were involved, and the building dates of the houses varied from pre 1780 to 1900. the standard of housing and the lack of essential conveniences and amenities was definitely below the average standard in the district, and the most satisfactory method of dealing with this was by the demolition of all the buildings.

He told Mr. Baldry, for the Sussex Mutual Property Society, that he could not say where people were likely to be rehoused. It was the Corporations policy to rehouse them as near to the site of their homes as possible, or wherever else they wished to go. Dr. Parkman, re-examined by Mr. Aston, said he was not influenced in his representations by any consideration of the Bourne Road proposal. Mr. Baldry told the inspector that the Society, which acquired property, improved it and let it at reasonable rents, and had made several worthwhile improvements in Hastings. He referred particularly, to 10 - 13, Brewery Cottages, where modernisation had been carried out, a grant of £600 was obtained from the Corporation, and said that the Society had been seeking permission also to modernise 8 - 14, Roebuck Street, a very similar block.

It is inconsistent and unkind to allow four houses to be improved and deny other tenants similar advantages, he said, some of the tenants have spent their whole lives living in the Old Town, and have no hope in getting other accommodation in that district if they are displaced.

Mrs. Vera Chantler, of 14, Roebuck Street, in a short, hard hitting speech, declared, "I have lived here for 45 years, my mother brought up a family of four, and I have a little one. We are all in good health. How you can talk about unfitness for that house I would like to know."

"We have lived in the Old Town all our lives. Why should we be suddenly be taken out of it?"

Mrs. Mable Violet Swain, of 2, Brewery Cottages, said vigorously, "I have three strapping children, the finest in the British Isles, they stand six feet tall and have never ailed, all the time they are shouting down our throats that it is unfit for human habitation. I have lived there 26 years, and if it is modernised I would live there for another 26 years." Giving evidence on behalf of the owner of 11, High Street, Mr. Dennis Simmons, Chartered Surveyor, said, "It is the policy of the Corporation to retain the old buildings in this area of architectural merit and it is, therefore, ridiculous to redevelop this part of the clearance area and replace with high density modern housing, which is not likely to be in keeping with the tone and tradition of the old properties, which the planning authority and local societies have expended so much money in renovating and maintaining."

Mr. Beckett, for the owner of 135b All Saints Street described by Mr. Godfrey West (Estate Agents) as an 18th century cottage of considerable charm, said "this was an application which ought never to have been made. His client had been led to believe that his property was to be kept out of a Clearance Order."

"Mr. Fullager had been deliberately encouraged to spend money on new construction, and they now have the temerity to come to you and say this property has always been in their minds for clearance."

"It was said to be unfit and a danger, by reason of its situation." Mr. Beckett continued; "It is wanted not because it is injurious to health, but for garages, and this is a good property to be got rid of, very conveniently for the new Bourne Road."

There were sharp exchanges during the course of the day, particularly between the Deputy Town Clerk and Mr. Beckett. At one time Mr. Aston accused Mr. Godfrey West, a witness of Mr. Beckett's of 'rummaging around for red herrings.' a little later the Inspector interjected, "Let us have less argument and get on with the inquiry." when there was altercation between Mr. Beckett and Mr. Aston.

When Mr. Aston interrupted Mr. Becket, the latter said, acidly, "I am making my submission." Mr. Beckett replied, "there is no need to be so offensive!"

Mr. Aston replied to the comment by saying, "you are making allegation after allegation." When he spoke, following Mr. Beckett, Mr. Aston told the

Inspector, "I apologise to you personally for having become a little aggressive and argumentative, you have been most patient. I want you to say that I have been labouring under extreme provocation by my friend, who has tried to cry 'stinking fish' all the time, and has avoided the real issue."

The Inspector said that he was unable to record Mr. Astons wishes, but said the whole enquiry had been a trying one on every ones part.

1962

An article appeared in the Hastings & St Leonards Observer relating to the demolition of the Bourne in 1962. 'I quote'; "The line of the Bourne Road of course, involves the demolition of the old Technical Institute which lies squarely in its path, also two cottage properties as well as adjustments to the [1]curtilages of various other properties.

As was stated in last weeks leading article, 'the new road through the Bourne should be a real value to Old Hastings for taking, as it will, the bulk of through traffic. It will leave the delightful old world streets – High Street and All Saints Street – very quiet, so that not only will an increasing number of good type residents, who are making their homes there, enjoy much more tranquillity. But visitors and others will be able to wander in safety through these picturesque and historic thoroughfares."

[1] The enclosed area of land adjacent to a dwelling house.

April 1963

The first stage of the new Bourne Road was started in 1961/2, although a road had been installed leading up from Bourne Street to just north of Roebuck Street, it wasn't until all the Elm trees at the top of High Street in the 'Wilderness' were felled, did the road get fully completed in the April of 1963.

The construction of the new road through the Bourne by Courthouse Street.

Bourne Road Site Purchase Appeal.
January 1962.
Inspector's Recommendations and Ministers Decision.

The decision of the Minister of Housing and local Government on an appeal against the Council's Compulsory Purchase Order in respect of about half an acre in the Bourne Road area has been announced. The Minister said that so far as unfitness and the bad arrangements were concerned, he accepted the views and recommendations of the Inspector.

In general he accepted the Council's needs to acquire the site to secure satisfactory use of the cleared area, now in a multiplicity of ownerships, but was satisfied that reasonable redevelopment would be practicable without 135b All Saints Street. Accordingly, although it wasn't a listed building, he had decided to accept the Inspectors recommendation on this property, which would be excluded from the Order, with the exception of the part of the garden required for the new construction of the new road between High Street and All Saints Street.

A letter from the Ministry said that the Council wished to acquire the lands on the grounds that none of the cleared sites would be adequate for residential development, because of the provisions in the Development Plan for the road running between High Street and All Saints Street. They intended to use the land for a parking area and for lock up garages, and possibly lay-bys for bus stops. A number of objectors had contended that only parts of their gardens would be needed for the construction of the new road, and it was not essential for the Council to acquire such properties as a whole.

The owner of 135b All Saints Street contended that the property was neither dangerous nor injurious to the health of the inhabitants, and that its inclusion was a breach of faith on the part of the Council, who, in 1956, had informed her father, the then owner, that the house was not in an area considered for declaration as a clearance area.

Moreover, the Council had approved a scheme for improvements and not demolition! The house in question had some architectural merit and should not be demolished merely to make way for garages.

The owner of 26 Bourne Walk stated that numerous improvements had been carried out since he bought the house in 1949. The house fulfilled his personal requirements and should not be destroyed, when there remained a great need of decent houses. Other objectors had also claimed that their property was not unfit for human habitation as claimed by the Council.

It was submitted that 137a All Saints Street was in keeping with its surroundings in All Saints Street and High Street, and helped to preserve the character of the Old Town. It was in a good state of preservation, and since it would be free standing when adjoining unfit properties were removed, should be excluded from the Order.

The Council submitted that to secure satisfactory redevelopment, they should acquire the whole of the land, which was now in a multiplicity of ownerships. As far as 135b All Saints Street was concerned, the property was strictly worn out. In the case of 26 Bourne Walk they contended that the property was grossly overcrowded and could not be reasonably left standing, having regards to the needs for redevelopment.

The Inspector found that with the exception of Adelina Cottage, 137a All Saints Street, all the houses included in Part 1 of the Schedule to the Order, were unfit and therefore should be demolished. With regard to 137a All Saints Street, he was not satisfied that the house was defective as to make it unfit for human habitation, and he concluded that it should be retained in the clearance area on account of bad arrangement.

All the remaining properties included in the Order were, the Inspector found, property represented, and apart from 135b All Saints Street, their acquisition and clearance was necessary. In the case of 135b All Saints Street, the Inspector took the view that the property was in itself, worth preserving, and that the clearance of adjacent buildings within the Order would remove much of the bad arrangement. Coupled with these facts, the owner had expressed willingness to carry out further improvements, and the Inspector had therefore decided to recommend that they be excluded from the Order with the exception of that part of the garden required for the new road.

Claims for well maintained payments were made, and the Minister directed the Council to make these in respect of Nos: 33, 28 and 29 Bourne Walk.

December 1962.

Plans submitted for a Petrol Filling Station on the Bourne.

An application was presented before the Town Planners for the erection of a petrol filling station to be sited north of the Catholic Church Hall, near the entrance to The Stables Little Theatre, between All Saints Street and the new Bourne Road.

The Council stated that all surplus land in the area, and especially that in question was already allocated for residential housing, this development would have caused a major traffic problem, especially if it had been passed, as it would have been situated very near the junctions of Harold Road and All Saints Street. Apart from the fact that the Local Development Plan for the area could or would not accommodate such a commercial development as a petrol filling station, this would have been totally out of character for the area, consequently, this application was thrown out on the grounds a traffic hazard, and not in keeping with the character of the surrounding area, and would detract from the special interests and visual amenities of the vicinity, which includes a number of note-worthy buildings.

Committee's 'No' to The Bourne.

The Old Hastings Preservation Society made a suggestion to the Highways and Works Committee that the new Bourne road should be renamed 'The Bourne' on the grounds that the new road now stands alone as a sign of the ancient Bourne Stream, and roughly traces the course of that stream.

That it would give more point to the names of the 'Twittens, such as 'The Creek' still leading from it, and the name The Bourne would acquire character and would not be 'just another road.'

The Committee are therefore recommending that the Town Council at their next meeting reconsider the suggested name given, although an overwhelming majority of the Highways and Works Committee wanted the name Bourne Road and not The Bourne. But after a long and heated argument between the Highways and Works Committee, and representatives from the Old Hastings Preservation Society, a decision was finally reached on a very tight majority that the name to be used now should read, The Bourne.

There were many requests from residents who wanted the area softening!

People wanted to see a whole host of trees planted to take away the stark impressions of a plain tarmacadam road laid through the middle of the Old Town, which would reach maturity in a few years, especially at the junctions where High Street, Harold Road, Old London Road and All Saints Street meet. The Council passed all their views over to Mr. Cassidy the Director of Parks and Gardens. It was felt that anyone viewing the top end of the Old Town from the advantage point of High Wickham, would only see the starkness of a road before them laid through the valley, trees and shrubs were now needed, the verges neatly grassed to disguise the fact that the Bourne was now cut in two by a large arterial road. Rockeries were also suggested planted between with a wonderful display of crocuses. Now of course, Old Hastings House and the Roman Catholic Church were now both fully exposed, whereby, before they were both heavily disguised with a surrounding of Elm trees, now the entire area has been cleared these wonderful buildings deserve to be noted, and the areas around each should be landscaped to bring out the full potential of their architecture. What you see today has changed very little from the time the gardens were first laid out. It is with somewhat sadness that no more thought was put into the landscaping then and even now. There could have been a major feature displayed as you entered the Old Town in the form of an Old Fishing Boat or even a replica Net Hut! After all, this was the heart of the fishing community and not a lot has changed today, the fishermen didn't even have a say to what they wanted in their community, the Council did what they thought would please everyone except the people that lived and worked in the Old Town, the Council spoke for everyone, including the fishermen!

Did they get it right?

Memories of the past.

I have included some personal memories of the Old Town before its total destruction from a couple that lived and worked there, they recalled what living in the Old Town was like when there was a living community present.

It must be noted that, these statements were from memory, and some might not be as accurate as you might interpretative yourself. But, these were purely taken from a couple that had experienced living there during the earlier days before the Bourne was separated by a thundering great big main road installed through the heart of the Old Town. Errors in stated facts cannot be the fault of anyone, remember these are memories going back some 6 to 7 decades, there are bound to be some minor misdates etc.

We start when Mr. & Mrs. Parsons lived in a cottage in Ebenezer road just off All Saints Street, they recalled that they remembered being told by an elderly neighbour of theirs that at 131 All Saints Street she believed that to have been a registry office for all births deaths and marriages within the Old Town, but no one could verify this story, but Mr. & Mrs. Parsons thought this to be true as the lady was very old and had no reason to doubt her word as she had lived in the Old Town all her life. Next door lived a Mr. Frank Dicker at 130 All Saints Street who was a jobbing builder, Mr. Parsons had done many a job for him when he was a plasterer. Mr. Dicker had mentioned that between Waterloo Passage, and nearing the bottom of All Saints Street was said to have been as many as 300 dwellings, some back to back others side by side, whilst others were crammed into such small spaces, little to no distance apart from each other, but many were in a state of total disrepair where no maintenance had been carried out over a period of many years. It had been mentioned before that many landlords were eager to take rent but were totally ignorant when it came to maintaining their property. Some were owned by the 'Hastings Cottage Improvement Society' and these were looked after to a reasonable standard by all accounts. Mr. Parsons remembered back to around 1945/6 when he was an apprentice plasterer (plastering went back over six generations in his family) said, that the car park in the Bourne (which is now), was used by the Technical School opposite as a practice area for plasterers and other likewise trades, who used the walls to practice on, and some of their work is still visible today. He did work on 'Fishers Cottages' and many other places that have since been demolished.

Coleman's Passage was mentioned as one of the many areas that were given reference to a shop that was in that street, this particular passage was named after Mr. Coleman who had a grocers shop at the top, so hence it was known as 'Coleman's Passage'. Another little quirk was, that in Waterloo Passage lived a little old lady who ran a sweet shop from her front room who kept a large parrot on the counter, and this bird made a racket every time someone came in, perhaps this was a deterrent not to come in a pinch a sweet or two before she came into the shop from a back room? Mr. Parsons also mentioned that having worked in the properties there, you could walk the whole length of the row through the roof spaces, meaning that you could enter the roof area from the first house and drop into the last one! Had there ever been a fire the whole row would have burnt down, as fire would have spread through the roofs with no walls to stop it!

It is so sad that today you couldn't begin to remember the area as it was as so much has gone, it would be nice to just go back in time and see the Old Town as it was before the demolition really started! Yes, we have to admit that there were many places that needed urgent attention by way of making not only the buildings safe, but more important was to improve the sanitation in most of the properties, this could in our minds of been carried out without the spasmodic mass demolition that had taken place over many years, this is one of the reasons to why we moved out of the Old Town into Clive Vale soon after demolition started, if we had the choice we would move back in, but the atmosphere and community spirit have been destroyed, and is no longer the same place to what we knew. Mr. Parsons went on to say, at the bottom of Waterloo Passage was what was known to everyone as the 'Monster shop,' theoretically I suppose it was really an 'Off Licence,' as for a penny you could get near enough a large bottle of beer, and if you were better off you could double the amount better known as a 'Monster' for 2d. Just by the side of this house was a small passage way with about three houses in it and one was occupied by a Mr. Apps, who would recharge your accumulators for a small charge, these were only really for those that could afford a wireless set, the accumulator (battery) would normally last for a period of about one week if used moderately. The accumulator was a glass jar filled with a nasty acid with metal plates inserted into the liquid (these plates deteriorated after a while and had to be replaced), wires were attached to the plates and the chemical reaction between the plates, and the acid generated a small electric voltage that powered the likes of wireless sets and electric door bells. A terrible explosive gas was omitted from these cells when being charged, you normally needed at least two of these cells connected together to operate any device properly.

Mr. & Mrs. Parsons searching their memories remembered the days when there were many little shops within the Old Town, and when the Council sent out letters stating that there were to be compulsory purchase orders of a lot of property, this was to be the first stage of upsetting a whole lot of people, especially when told that many were to be rehoused in new houses on the Bembrook Road Estate, and Hardwicke Road areas. Many families had been associated with the Old Town all their lives and the last thing they wanted was to be moved completely away from the area. Many ran successful businesses in the area whilst others were fisher folk and wholly relied on being close to the beach. Yes, we have to agree that there were many of what one might have called slums, a few could have been thinned out, but not to the extent that demolition went to clear such areas to build a main coastal road through the heart of the Old Town. We knew that there were alternative schemes placed before the Council, but all were turned down for one reason of another, mainly money I suppose! The new Borough Engineer Mr. Sidney Little who we remember took over where others had failed, he submitted some wonderful ideas to bypass running straight through the Old Town; but as we said these were turned down, he simply had to follow rules laid down by the Council.

The Old Town consisted of a whole load of what we called 'characters,' there was one person of which I remember well that lived in the old work house back of the 'King John' pub, she wore an old dirty long trench type coat tied around the waist with a piece of string, and to that was attached an old enamel tin mug, many people avoided her in the streets, but she was harmless. There were many people just like her that made the Old Town what it was, it was without doubt a community, and everyone living there knew everybody else, and sometimes knew their business as well, probably better than they knew it them selves! The blocks of flats in the Bourne were built originally to house the fishermen and their families, several blocks were built along with a few individual houses, these all belonged to the council at the time they were built. The only two last remaining original cottages to be left standing untouched are by what is now the Bourne car park, and Waterloo Passage, these are known as 'Gilbert Cottages,' a plaque mounted between the two shows that they dated from 1852, these we believe have been sympathetically restored by their present owners. We both remember a so called restaurant or eating rooms that had opened up in the Bourne more or less backing onto the school in All Saints Street, here you could have a good meal for a shilling, this could supplement the rations, whereby, you didn't get a lot for your coupons, so if you were able to afford a shilling you had a good meal followed by a mug of tea served in the hall attached to the eating room sitting in Lloyd loom chairs.

At one time there were a colossal amount of drinking houses (pubs) located in the Old Town, if you were thrown out of one for being unruly, you just went virtually next door and started again and so on!

At the onset of the last war, the AFS (Auxiliary Fire Service) had installed large water tanks, one behind the wall at the top end of High Street in what was called the 'Wilderness' and the other we are led to believe was situated at the foot of Waterloo Place opposite 'Gilbert Cottages'. These tanks contained copious amounts of water in them in case of serious fires in the area, but to our knowledge they were never used in anger; they were removed after the war.

In Waterloo Passage once lived a Mr. Martino who made and sold ice cream from a decorated cart that he pushed around the streets. The ice cream was made in a shed type of building placed on top of a flat roof of his outhouse, the water for the mix was drawn from a hand operated pump in the passage way, this was a good play area for many of the Old Town children too. The water was drawn up from an old well and probably wasn't the cleanest of all waters considering the amounts of fowl water seeping into the ground from ruptured sewer pipes, you can draw your own conclusion to the taste of the ice cream.......a cornet or a wafer Sir? There was quite a large Italian community living within the Old Town, the Martino's, Dimarco's to just mention a couple, they all traded in the food line of one sort or another.

The wash house at the bottom of Bourne Walk was always very busy, ladies would carry their washing down to there in great big baskets, and for a small sum of sixpence they washed all your laundry goods, but the noise as you passed the place was horrific with all the clatter of pulley's and the machinery running, how the attendants managed to survive the day with that noise no one knows, no wonder people used to shout at each other, this wasn't in any arguments but normal talk.

Three large houses that stood at the top of the Bourne, 'The Wilderness', Merryvale', and 'Ravenhurst', these were all owned by the Catholic Church. My granny lived in 'Merryvale', which to all intense and purposes looked as though it might have been an Edwardian build, but the back could have been even older, it looked as if it could have been built in the Elizabethan style!

Sadly after the war started an aerial mine blew up in Old Humphries Avenue taking a property or two out there, also 'Merryvale' was to suffer the same fate, the house was demolished completely and fell like a pack of cards. 'Ravenhust', and 'The Wilderness' were also badly damaged by the same explosion, consequently these were never restored after the war and left to become derelict, these were completely demolished after the war, the grounds to where they stood were left vacant till the new road was pushed through, the Catholic Church never did rebuild the houses there or anywhere else for that matter.

Finally, I asked them what they thought of the improvements in the Old Town since the road was pushed through, they made some nostalgic comments, they both wished it was as before any modernisation was done, there was a strong friendly community in those days, even today, talking to people that were pushed out of their homely abodes say, they still strongly resent to what the Council did to their area in parting a life long community for ever, and destroying the history of Hastings that took century's in the making, and only a few years of careless thought of a few to destroy it for ever. Yes, the Old Town was over crowded in some ways, and sanitation wasn't what one might call up to standard, but with some serious thought this could have been got around without the cruel results that took place back in the years from the very early 1900's. Hastings has nothing to show the faithful visitors that flock hear year after year what the Old Town was really like when it was alive, now it's dead! There is no way Hastings can ever rebuild or relive the past, it's all down to what we can all remember of the good old days. Thank you.

Leslie Badham's, A typical view of the backs of houses in the Old Town.

Leslie Badham's, Part of Bourne Walk.
Bottom: John Street looking west.

The final word.

There were many many cases to where people were more or less forced to live in squalid conditions, despite all their efforts to try and keep the homes clean and tidy, but in most cases it was a waste of time, as water sodden walls left clothes damp continuously. Roofs leaked when it rained mainly down to poor maintenance by the scruple less Land Lords, many of which would not maintain their properties despite endless moans from their tenants. The Land Lords many of which lived in London and alike were obviously eager to take the rents, but not so eager to carry out essential repairs to their properties.

I understand that there was a dense nature of property within the Old Town, and something had to be done to alleviate the problems of extremely poor sanitation conditions that existed in the areas. The space between properties was extremely narrow in many cases, but this was Hastings Old Town.

We are totally convinced, that if given a proper amount of money and the right ideas, demolition to this standard might just of been controlled a little better than it was, we do agree that some properties were beyond their sell by date! Some would of eventually fallen down on their own accord if essential repairs had not been carried out to the main fabric of the buildings almost immediately. Most of these tenants were grateful to have been moved out into newer dryer accommodation, but the demolition went further than anyone might have dreamed. The heart of the Old Town was certainly torn from its limbs and body from an early time. It is with regret that neither time nor any amount of money can restore the past again, no one, no matter to how clever they may seem, can ever replace history once raised to the ground, we can build new to look old, but the characteristics will never be there.

The story continued through the years, as an on off operation until the ultimate conclusion was seen when the Bourne was finally completed and left alone to wallow in its sorrow from what the Council had done over all those years before. Perhaps the pain might not have been so bad if the operations and threats were carried out when first thought about back in 1850, by now, we may have all got used to it?

It will still never seem right for a 32 ton juggernaut lorry to thunder down the Bourne Road, and driving through what would have been some ones living room, just think of that every time you travel through the Bourne, who's house am I driving through? I do every time I go through the Bourne, you cringe!

If only we could turn the clock backwards! Was this really the right thing to have been done?

Despite what was spoken about Sidney Little, and all the damage he caused to the Old Town, he really only completed what others had already started. Yes he took the full force of everyone's anger when he visited the area, but it must be remembered that this all started back in 1850 by the dreaded Cresy Report.

Mr. Philip Palmer may have made the situation even worse if he had got his plans through Council, by the complete demolition of the High Street (high pavement side) along with All Saints Street.

I fear this may have just been the complete wrong decision if approved by Council, but luckily enough there were insufficient funds to proceed with the scheme, hence this was shelved to never see the light of day again. Can you imagine what the High Street would have looked like with little to no property at all on the banked side, only the gardens of the properties in Croft Road would have been visible. This would have killed trade in the Old Town dead from the very start, there would have been NO Old Town so to speak, don't forget All Saints Street was involved as well, and part of the bourne, this was a far bigger scheme than what you might have imagined!

Mr Philip Palmer then turned his eye completely on the destruction of the Bourne after his plans of 1894 were turned down. He would have made a bigger clearance than what we see today, but again the same old story comes up 'the lack of money.' Yes, there was money to be borrowed from Government, but at a price! There were strict regulations set down by the Ministry in pay back times. Hastings was at that time completely cash strapped, as little money was coming in through the rates, obviously insufficient to pay off a substantial loan, there were penalties imposed by Ministry if the monies weren't paid on time. There was other work to be carried out in the town beside a major scheme as the Bourne.

One of the main tasks Mr. Palmer had to do during his appointment as Borough Engineer was to sort out the drainage in the borough, this alone caused severe headaches to all associated with that scheme, as the drainage was early Victorian and was failing in many places. Even though some drainage was installed, provisions for the future were never really thought about, only just for the present day needs, this was to be found out in later years. Roads, although many were just cinder ash or cold tarmac tops laid on a soggy soil foundation, these were failing everywhere, consequently the horse drawn carts over a period of time left enormous ruts in the surfaces, and when it rained they just disappeared! Ok, unless you fell in one. This again was to sink the Councils capitol funding to an absolute minimum, of course at that time they were totally unable to take on any major schemes. But having said that Mr. Palmer did get his way to a certain degree by demolishing some properties in the Old Town along with a few more in St Leonards.

Records were quite sparse back in the 1800's, whereby, some are missing when researched today, so we are unaware as to where the people that were displaced then were rehoused. At that time the Council did not have any property of their own, nor did they have own any land to build on.

Yes, there are records available of certain aspects of the Council, but many financial ones have been mislaid!

As a small boy I lived and went to school in the Old Town (All Saints Street) but still remember quite well the mess that people had to live with day by day even then. As you walked to school there were great big caverns to where presumably buildings once stood, only to be replaced by piles of brick rubble and alike.

After school most days we played in what was the Wilderness on our way home, unless it rained of course! yes, what water was there was reduced to a small trickle and of course very muddy, but we all had a great time, it certainly wasn't the most hygienic places to play in, but we all survived. What is now the Stables Theatre was in our time a car repair workshop, and outside was a pile of old car parts, many a time we salvaged some of these parts and took them down to the stream and built up the weirdest of objects, probably might have even won a major prize today in modern art; who knows? The Old Town thrived as it had done for years previous. The High Street as like Courthouse Street and All Saints Street was adorned with a multitude of shops, there was no need to venture further than the Old Town as we were sure all your needs were there; the butcher, baker and candle stick maker! My mother rarely went into town as all her needs were sought out by all the banks and shops locally. Workmen still operated from the area going about their businesses. My father worked out of the High Street, he was a carpenter and joiner, and pushed a heavy old hand cart around the Old Town with all their tools and materials on it, quite a push up the Croft, and especially Crown Lane fully laden, quite often in the winter time, when there was frost and ice on the roads they lost control of their cart and it took off down the hills on its own, swiftly followed by the men on their bums! The carts were built so good that even by hitting a wall at the bottom of the hill it more or less only scratched the paint, there was more damage to the wall than the cart. Those were certainly the days I remember, and always will. The Old Town was a good community, but today its not quite the same, all the old businesses have gone, and so have most of the people with it.

If only we could look back into the past, perhaps we could take a few old Councillors with us and show them the errors of their ways, and to what they did for Hastings Old Town. With a little more thought, time they certainly achieved! They might have looked ahead of themselves, and preserved a major part of the Old Town as so many other older towns have done today, by turning the area into a very profitable living history museum, this would have preserved the majority of the older buildings whereby people could have walked the streets and twittens and even paying to enter certain preserved areas; but this was never thought of going back to when the big hammer started to fall.

Were the planners right in what they did to Hastings Old Town?

I have made up my mind as to what I think of the alterations.

what do you think??

These 2 pictures depict the Bourne before mass demolition started, but the blocks of flats were built, as can been seen in the lower picture.

A view up Bourne Street as demolition had already started,
some of the flats had been built and occupied.
Below is again Bourne Street, when demolition had started on a small scale.

These pictures show the new road layout at what was commonly know as 'The Top of the Town', shortly after it completion. In 1963.

The new road layout at the top of The Bourne,
again shortly after it was officially opened.

The new road layout at the junctions of Harold Road and All Saints Street.

The top photograph was taken off the scaffolding in the High Street
when Torfield Close was under construction.
Below, is 'Old Hastings House' now fully exposed from behind the trees
of what was the 'Wilderness!
All the pictures depicting the new road layout are credited to my late father,
Philip Pollard.

Leslie Badham's, A glimpse of Bourne Passage

Leslie Badham's, Courthouse Street looking towards the High Street.
Bottom: John Street looking eastwards.

Leslie Badham's, Wellington Court looking towards All Saints Street.

Leslie Badham's Waterloo Passage looking towards All Saints Street.
Bottom: Corner of Crown Lane, locally known as 'Punch & Judy Passage'.

Bottom end of All Saints Street.